Sexuality
Spirituality

By the same author

TEARS OF THE SUN GOD
MAKE BELIEVE
THE OF.TEN TALE
THE W.HOLE TALE

with co-author

THE ONCE AND FOREVER CHRISTMAS
THE QUESTION OF RELIGION
THE CHRIST STORY
THE HINDU SOUND
THE JUDAIC LAW
THE BUDDHA WAY
THE ISLAMIC SPACE

John Moore

Sexuality Spirituality

A Study of Feminine/Masculine Relationship

Element Books

ACKNOWLEDGEMENTS

Acknowledgement is made by the author of the following sources of quotations used in the text: page 22, *Hemisphere Function in the Human Brain,* edited by E. J. Dimond and J. G. Beaumont, published by Elek Books (by permission of Granada Publishing Ltd.); page 24, 'The Two Hemispheres' by W. A. Lishman (by permission of The Dartington Society, Totnes, Devon); page 27, *The Tao of Physics* by Fritzjof Capra, published in England by Wildwood House and Fontana (by permission of Murray Pollinger); pages 50, 192, *The Dragons of Eden* by Carl Sagan (by permission of the publishers, Hodder and Stoughton Ltd., copyright © 1977 by Carl Sagan); pages 54, 55, *Zen in the Art of the Tea Ceremony* by Horst Hammitzsch (by permission of the publishers, Element Books Ltd., Tisbury, Wiltshire); pages 168, 172, 173, *The New Sex Therapy* by H. S. Kaplan, published in England by Ballière Tindall.

© John Moore, 1980
First published in Great Britain by
Element Books Limited, The Old Brewery
Tisbury, Wiltshire

Printed in Great Britain by
The Pitman Press, Bath, Avon

Cover design by Humphrey Stone

ISBN 0 906540 10 0

Contents

1	Introduction	1
2	Definitions	11
3	Physiological evidence and scientific proof	22
4	Feminine-left and masculine-right characteristics	29
5	Conception to infancy	34
6	Childhood and self-consciousness	42
7	Brain development	56
8	Puberty and education; success and failure	64
9	The ideal and the perfect; romance and love	75
10	Transition from sexuality to spirituality	87
11	The age of majority	97
12	Marriage	103
13	Celibacy	112
14	Family relationships and private life	116
15	Beliefs; actuality, reality, illusion	128
16	Adulthood and the spiritual quest	136
17	Meditation; consciousness and sexual 'normality'	144
18	Illumination; mid-life	152
19	Reflections	160
20	Change of life	168
21	Love	176
22	Purpose in life	182
23	Retirement and reconciliation	188
24	Evolution of religion in the West	195
25	Parallels in individual psychology	209
26	Evolution of religion in the East	216
27	The possibility of spiritual revival	225
28	The masculine and feminine absolutes	230
29	Conclusion	236

This is as strange a maze as e'er man trod
And there is in this business more than nature
Was ever conduct of; some oracle
Must rectify our knowledge.

The Tempest

1 Introduction

The quotation from *The Tempest* on the opposite page is not intended to imply that what follows in this book is indeed the desired oracle. Far from it. It struck me however as being appropriate comment as preface because, of all enigmas encountered by Man during his earthly existence, the relationship between sexuality and spirituality is surely one of the strangest of all mazes.

Over the ages, men have held widely differing views as to how the problems generated by these two concepts so fundamental to human purpose may be resolved. At one extreme, opinion has held that they are virtually synonymous; at the other, it has asserted that they are incompatible and that spirituality requires denial of sexuality.

The history of beliefs on the subject indicates that religious doctrines in particular have been responsible for the modification of social attitudes towards sexual conduct. 'In this business' of spiritual aspiration, it might well be claimed—since the religious aspect of it has frequently called for sexual discipline, even abstention—that 'nature' was indeed 'not conduct of' it.

In my view, and in the terms through which I have approached the subject in this book, I consider religious influence, in the West especially, responsible for establishing the assumption that sexuality and spirituality are antipathetic. Many would not, I feel sure, disagree with that view. Rather more contentiously, I would go further in suggesting that the divorce has on occasions been taken to such misguided extreme that, as a direct consequence, common understanding of the nature of their relationship has suffered to the point of being almost extinguished.

This has resulted in a general discounting of the relevance of spirituality. Due to the decline and failure to understand its nature, and the responsibility it demands, a distinct imbalance has emerged in society. The present bias towards sexuality is creating a considerable degree of confusion, frustration and anxiety; this in turn begets violence, in the form of both violence to others and self-violation.

I accept that the above statements are sweeping generalisations but, once I have established the full implications of the terms 'sexuality' and 'spirituality', and have defined the full sense in which I am using them, I hope these observations will be to an extent substantiated.

Whether that will be judged to have been accomplished or not, the book will serve its purpose if it at least makes useful contribution to the current debate concerning masculine-feminine relationship—in the usual sense of relationship between man and woman but, more significantly, in the particular sense examined in this theme, that of the relationship between the masculine and feminine elements within the individual.

Perhaps as never before in human history, we now badly need 'an oracle to rectify our knowledge'.

The genesis of my interest in the problem of human purpose could no doubt in vague and general terms be traced a long way back through my life—certainly to hours of debate during adolescence. The questioning as to the relationship between human sexual and spiritual motivation I recall as being particularly vivid however on an occasion some years ago when I stayed as a guest at a monastery in Scotland.

I do not recall to what order the monks there belonged but they had taken vows of silence and lived an enclosed, withdrawn and contemplative life.

The only monk with whom it was permitted to converse was the guest-master. He did not seem disposed however to discuss matters any more profound than how much it would be appropriate to pay for the days of my visit, what was grown in the kitchen garden and whether I would be agreeable to delivering a parcel to his niece in London. He no doubt sensed that my wish to 'retreat' did not preclude my being curious about the monks' way of life and what they hoped to gain by it. And, understandably, that curiosity he did not wish to satisfy.

Since it was still winter and there were no other guests apart from the friend I was with, we were invited to take meals with the monks in their refectory. We also made a point of attending all services in the chapel, day and night. Denied verbal communication, it was therefore a case of silent watching and wondering, an experience I remember as being particularly vivid in the chill, candle-lit gloom of the office before dawn.

Such a disciplined and circumscribed mode of living was intriguing to a young man. What moved them to pursue it? Could I adopt it? Apart from not being able to grasp a valid and attractive reason or doing so, life outside was much too exciting and promising.

Had any of these monks ever had sexual relationship with women or had they taken their vows before the desires for sexual relationship had arisen? Presumably the latter. If so, it would perhaps not be too difficult to abstain from something never experienced? Yet these men must surely have had some experience of sensual pleasure? They must have had erections and emissions in their youth; they must surely have felt the desire for the gentle touch, the warmth of affection, the magic of being in love? What was the physiological and psychological effect of denying that human yearning year in and year out? What was it that could compensate for such denial? Was it that they thereby experienced some greater ecstasy or were they hoping through abstention in this world to gain something more rewarding 'in the next world'? How could one envisage such 'after-life' reward without a body to experience it? Because I am not moved to make such sacrifice, am I in any real, comprehensible way an inferior person? And so on, and so on . . . Many questions, and a total inability to answer them.

Left with the doubtful evidence of observation, it seemed to me at the time that those monks, all fairly elderly, showed no sign of enjoying their earthly existence. The silent and slowly-gliding figures in their dull habits, the monotonous and mumbled chanting, the pallid faces and dim, 'unlooking' eyes did not outwardly betray any vitality of spirit. If they had inward hope and conviction, then it was well concealed beneath the ordered and unremitting repetition of their daily ritual.

Long after the episode at the monastery, a distillation of the questions remained with me. In what terms appropriate to the twentieth century could there be said to be a connection between leading a natural, sexual life and leading what is thoroughly understood by the individual to be a spiritual life? Is it impossible to fulfil both—which is to suggest that one must be at the expense of the other? Is there any difference between men and women in this respect?

In this scientific and sophisticated age, is it possible to determine a sensible and logical explanation for the common assumption that the life of a monk is 'better' than the life of, say, a prostitute? In what readily acceptable terms (which is to say in terms other than those conditioned by centuries of religious doctrine) could one describe the 'higher aspirations' of the former as being preferable to the 'lower proclivities' of the latter?

Given that both people concerned are simply human beings conditioned to considerable degree by the governing circumstances they happened to encounter in existence, how can one be judged in concrete terms to have advantage or disadvantage in comparison with the other? If they were both born with inherited characteristics and dispositions, and neither had any say in what influences affected them when young, how could one be said to have 'chosen' a more purposeful and meaningful life than the other?

Whatever happen to be the governing circumstances in twentieth-century societies, each individual has to cope with them as best he or she may. But how did it become so complicated and confusing? Where did the spiritual influence come from and how did it arise? Above all, in what terms may we understand and express it today?

A society's attitudes to the sexual behaviour of its members changes as a compound of various relevant influences changes. The degree of licence permitted or the strictures imposed derive from a complicated interaction of ideological and pragmatic factors. It is usually a case of imposing restraint due either to economic considerations or to fashionable moral and religious beliefs and attitudes. No doubt other subtle environmental influences play their part also. In earlier days of human history, when life was less sophisticated, it would seem that psychological pressures were not nearly so complicated and confusing.

Some time after the monastery episode, I was fortunate to be a member of an anthropological and botanical expedition to South America, an undertaking which at one stage took four of us into the Xingu area of the Mato Grosso of Brazil.

We stayed there for a period with a tribe of Indians who had had very little contact with the civilised world. It was said that their mode of living was about equivalent to that of the Stone Age. The implications of that I found totally impossible to comprehend at the time. To me they were fellow human beings—and very friendly and handsome ones at that—who happened to live in a very different way from the culture to which I was accustomed in Europe.

On the other hand, I could appreciate—since their ancient, natural and traditional way of life, and their relationship with the environment, was so different from mine—that their mental processes of assessment and reaction must be utterly at variance with those I was accustomed to expect. There was no possible way of bridging that difference to any significant effect; but that did not preclude our ability as human beings to live together in harmony, demonstrating through conduct our respect for each other. We could not converse but we could communicate simple messages through exchanging signs. There was very little we could offer them materially but they gave to us generously, especially food. They allowed us space in one of their large huts, where we slept in hammocks adjacent to one of their families. They welcomed us to accompany them about their daily occupations.

They had no clothing to cover their healthy, lithe, well-proportioned and, in the case of the men, muscular bodies. By the second day of our stay, our own clothing seemed an absurd encumbrance and we happily abandoned it. I felt self-conscious only for a short while—not at being naked in public, but due to my pale tenderness compared with their glowing bronze, a contrast I felt to be between my superficial sophistication and their naturalness. This abandonment of clothing not only provided a physical sense of freedom but a psychological one also. Of course, we all undress frequently, but either in private for specific purposes or, if in public, still retaining covering for the sexually-associated parts of the anatomy. Few people in the temperate, civilised areas of the world have the opportunity to remain naked and carry out all manner of daily occupations from dawn to dusk. In discarding our clothing in that situation, it was as if one had also discarded a habit (so that I am sure the double meaning of that word is not simply coincidence).

The action was not just the abandonment of a physical protection and defence but was effectively the abandonment of a psychological one also. This immediately removed a barrier of pretension (erected by us) from between ourselves and these so-called 'primitive' people. This in turn promoted a natural empathy; we had, as it were, nothing to hide from each other.

I had also not realised until that experience the extent to which clothing creates a false sense of modesty. As a man from a culture where women are seen continually clothed in public, it was at first novel to encounter them naked at all times. However, it was not in the slightest erotic; and that in itself furthered the sense of relief and feedom.

No doubt subtle factors unconsciously influenced the sense of its being inappropriate to become sexually aroused in their company but, at the time, it simply seemed that the nudity of those women did not invite it. It was as if mentally or physically they were not radiating or projecting sexual desire, thus being 'naturally modest' (or, rather, in that context it seemed that the concept 'modesty' was quite irrelevant).

To what extent the Indians modified their behaviour due to our presence I do not know. All I can affirm is that the whole time we were there, I did not observe a single overtly sexual gesture. Undoubtedly the tribe observed certain practices and disciplines with regard to sexual behaviour; and that implies a socially imposed code of conduct. However, to the extent that we were able to observe their daily lives, their obedience to that code did not seem to be artificially restrictive or to be followed for appearance's sake only. The impression gained was that of their *modus vivendi* being one that any unaffected, natural group would adopt in unthreatened conditions.

Certainly the experience proved to me that the covering with clothing of the genitals and breasts in the interests of modesty is an absurd pretence. One of its main effects is to generate a frustration and tension in members of the opposite sex which, in turn, can then cause detrimental repercussions in society. In modern societies, particularly in the case of women's clothing, the token covering of sexually-associated parts of the body in the name of modesty is actually exploited to arouse the opposite effect.

To what degree it could be said that the sexual behaviour of the Indians was influenced by a 'religious' factor is hard to determine. We witnessed an elaborate ritual for girls at the age of puberty, dances suggesting acknowledgement of metaphysical influence and communication, and evidence of respect for the dead. It is hard for us, accustomed to the consigning of features of our lives into separate categories, to comprehend an ethos where it seems no such categorisation exists. I surmise that to analyse the behaviour of those people and to try to understand it in divisive, departmentalised terms—for example, its economic, political, social or religious aspects—would be to ignore, and probably destroy, the simple integrity of purely natural response to environment. It seems to me in retrospect that the conduct of their lives could most sensibly be comprehended as total attunement and obedience to the cycles and seasons they observed and experienced around them. For them it would simply be a time to be born and a time to die, a time to hunt and a time to fish, a time of fertility and a time for a woman to bear a child.

In such primitive societies, assuming they had no knowledge or means of contraception, could it be said that they only entered into the mystery of intercourse for the sacred purposes of procreating the species and of ensuring the tribe's survival? And that therefore the fulfilment of those purposes constituted in themselves the 'religion' of their lives?

Whatever interpretation I care to make of that South American experience, it is bound to remain speculative. Its relevance to me at the time was whether it helped me to understand the relationship between sexuality and spirituality; and that it did not do. If anything it increased the confusion.

The group-life of the naked Indian in his natural environment was in utter contrast with the solitary, celibate and withdrawn life of the monk. Thousands of years of human progress could be said to have separated them. In what manner though did the monk comprehend his life more intelligently (or less superstitiously) than the Indian?

The monk had chosen to suppress the sexual urges within him in the interests, as he understood it, of spiritual fulfilment; the Indian appeared not to be even aware of such a dichotomy in his life. What then has been accomplished by religious influence, especially in the West, through emphasising the dichotomy? On what grounds has it had the authority to persuade men that obedience to imposed codes of morality is beneficial to individual spiritual well-being?

It was not until about two years ago that I began to realise that my confusion over this issue was due to certain illusions acquired during the early days of my education.

Christmas season, 1978. Late one afternoon I was standing inside the doorway of a clothing store in Oxford Street, London.

There suddenly arose without deliberate effort one of those out-of-time experiences when the mind clears of personal involvement in, and concern for, the immediate situation. I was relieved of my relationship, as a separate entity, with it, and attention spread from the close activity to take in the whole scene. It was as a detached onlooker that I first appreciated paradoxical features of the scene, and then a means of understanding that paradox.

The store was brightly, even glaringly, lit; glittering and colourful metallic decorations festooned the walls and hung from overhead; ranks of counters were piled high with thousands of items of clothing. Shoppers of numerous nationalities—including a considerable number of Arabs in a style of dress alien to that of the articles on display—packed and jostled in the gangways. Eyes darted here and there, searching and scrutinizing; hands reached out, grasping, feeling, retaining or rejecting. Money poured into the numerous tills.

Not, on the face of it, a scene which one would think exceptional; it is common enough to witness such trade any day in the main shopping streets of modern cities. But . . .

This was England, a nation of Christians for some fourteen hundred years since missionaries from Rome had introduced and converted (or usurped) the power and lore of the Celtic religion. And now, at this time of the year, the nation was about to celebrate the birth of Jesus of Nazareth, the 'founder' of Christianity. The custom of giving presents to others on this occasion was responsible for this particular spate of trading; in fact, this religious festival is one of the peaks of commercial opportunity during the year.

It so happened, however, that this particular store was in business to profit Jewish financial interests. And there, conspicuous among the shoppers, were Arabs become wealthy due to fortuitous deposits of oil beneath their Middle Eastern lands, acquiring by the armful articles of clothing utterly alien to their traditional garb, and certainly in some cases alien to the ethics of strict Muslim-based cultures.

History records centuries of rivalry, discord and hostility between Christian, Jew and Muslim; creating deeply-embedded antipathies which erupt into violence to the present day. And yet in that store representatives of all three denominations were busily exchanging money for clothing. How was it that they could quite happily do this when, in another context, supposedly because of religious affiliation, they could be expected to harm or kill each other?

That question prompted me to reflect that unthreatened individuals behave towards each other in private, personal and natural situations quite differently from those situations where they encounter each other as representatives of group-ideologies, theologies, systems or other factions with which they happen to have become identified.

Apart from the question as to why people become so identified (which, of course, has bearing on this theme and will be considered later), I found myself drawn to the possibility that, if unthreatened, the individual is innately charitable towards his fellow human beings, and that hostility towards another is generated by the adoption of certain group-beliefs which are inculcated through social education. Some may be harmless and benign enough and there may be a minority of individuals who grow up to affect anti-social behaviour which needs to be contained by the discipline of the group. But there are other group-beliefs, some of religious origin, which encourage exclusivity and it is these which breed hostility.

Hostility arises through fear. In particular it arises through threat to survivial. The individual is called upon to defend the group with which he or she is identified and is continually required to reconcile his or her own individual understanding and disposition with the persuasion and demand of the group. If the two aspects are sympathetic and coincide, the individual lends his or her power to the group effort; if they are not, the individual will have to compromise or be alienated, both of which cause suffering and anxiety.

Whether or not these reflections are recognised as valid, as I stood in that clothing store contemplating the Christmas scene, certain concepts I had learned to interpret in a certain way suddenly rearranged themselves and presented to me a different structure of relationship. It was rather like shaking a kaleidoscope where the same pieces instantly fall into a totally new pattern.

I realised first of all that I had held a much too restrictive assumption as to what I understood by 'sexuality' and 'spirituality'. Sexuality really encompassed everything to do with *physical group-survival* and, beyond that, physical survival of the species itself; spirituality encompassed everything to do with *individual self-preservation*—all the way through from the searching for and preserving of worldly identity to the possibility of individual immortality.

Having understood that, I then realised that, between them, these two concepts accounted for the whole spectrum of human motivation. Everything anybody did was in the interest of one or the other; and, of course, those interests could be incompatible.

Finally, I realised that the group, sexual motivation was feminine in essence and the individual, spiritual motivation masculine.

The chapters which follow attempt to explain and substantiate those realisations, and the first step must be to define the sense and scale in which I am using the key words—feminine, masculine, sexuality and spirituality.

2 Definitions

The specific manner in which I shall be using the words male, masculine, female and feminine is easy enough to state and comprehend, but not so easy to hold continuously in mind.

Male and female will be used exclusively to designate and represent *physical entities*—which we recognise in human form, for example, as man and woman.

The words masculine and feminine will be reserved solely for differentiating between the dual aspects of non-material phenomena *which are common to both sexes*. These phenomena include, for example, principles, functions, qualities, properties, powers and forces.

Although what we call emotions and feelings are often manifested physically and have physiological effects, they are mentally precipitated and are common to both male and female. I shall therefore be referring to the masculine and feminine aspects of emotions and feelings, not implying thereby that they are exclusive to male or female. The same will apply when referring to the masculine and feminine nature of other mental phenomena—such as visualising, imagining, ideas, beliefs, logic, reason, intuition and so on.

It is very important therefore to hold constantly in mind that *masculine* and *feminine* when used in the following text have far wider applications, connotations and ramifications than simple association with physiological, male-female sex-differentiation.

To suggest that both men and women have both masculine and feminine non-material nature and characteristic is not, of course, an innovation. But it is crucial to state and emphasise the discipline being observed in this theme because it is very easy (as I found when writing it!) to slip into the conditioned habit of associating masculine with the male sex only and feminine with the female sex only.

When therefore I said at the end of the previous chapter that I discerned group, sexual motivation to be feminine, and individual, spiritual motivation to be masculine, this indicates that *both* motivations are present in *both* male and female.

Sexuality, as the human being experiences it, derives from the recognition in principle that throughout the higher forms of nature there are two physically-differentiated sexes. In particular and in personal experience, the individual becomes aware that he or she is physically identified as being one sex and not the other. It is then further understood that it requires one of each sex in specific physical relationship in order to reproduce further members of the species. The implications of sexuality thus tend to focus on the act of copulation and the consequent procreation of offspring.

The full ramifications of sexuality, of course, reach out far beyond those straightforward facts.

In general, apart from learning about the reproductive implications of sexuality, the individual first experiences the effect of his or her sexuality as erotic pleasure. This pleasure does not necessarily require the presence of a member of the opposite sex. It would, I think, be valid to say that, in civilised societies especially, the individual experiences and values the pleasure aspect well before the procreative aspect becomes of importance.

The point to be drawn from this is that the pleasure aspect of sexuality can be independent of its procreative purpose. This may be obvious but it is an important point to establish for later consideration of the relationship of sexuality to spirituality, and that of feminine to masculine.

It is also important to note a certain, inherent bias between the sexes in this dual aspect of sexuality—that of the female towards the procreative aspect and the male towards the pleasure. This is indicated physiologically by the fact that the male experiences his first involuntary orgasmic emission as highly pleasurable whilst he does not, of course, have the capacity to conceive and nurture offspring within himself. In the female, on the other hand, her equivalent, first, involuntary emission is of menstrual blood which is not an orgasmic pleasure. She is not only made forcibly aware of her procreative role by this experience but her orgasmic pleasure has to be deliberately induced.

This differentiation leads to a key principle for this theme. Psychologically, it is the *masculine* in the male and the female (predominantly in the former) which is motivated by the pleasure aspect of sexuality; and it is the *feminine* in the female and the male (predominantly in the former) which is motivated by the procreative aspect.

The ability to divide the sexual pleasure aspect from the

procreative, and to find differentiated masculine and feminine dispositions within that dichotomy, is important in itself; it is also important for consideration of spirituality. But for the moment, as far as defining the fulfilment of the sexual purpose is concerned, it could be said to have been achieved when a copulating man and woman reach simultaneous orgasm in the conscious and shared intent that the act should result in the conception of a child. In this ideal situation, the procreative and the pleasure aspects are in harmony and complement each other. Anything less infers a situation wherein the masculine and feminine aspects of both male and female are not fully engaged.

It should also be noted that, even in the ideal situation, there is no certainty that a child will in fact be conceived. This has its reciprocal in the spiritual purpose where there is no guarantee that communion with supramundane power will bring about the desired result.

Born into this world, the first years are, it could be said, sexually neutral. We are not aware, to begin with, of our existence as sexually-differentiated individuals. We simply react to pleasure and pain (which is not to say that our experience in that respect will not affect our later sexual and spiritual life).

Our early mentors, usually our parents and close family, provide for our well-being and, by example and instruction, inculcate the codes of behaviour appropriate to the society into which we have been born.

Sooner or later, we learn of the physical differentiation of the sexes and, as we become self-conscious, identify ourselves as being one or the other. Regardless of conducive or repressive factors—and malformations apart—each heads inexorably for that first male emission of sperm or female menstruation period. It does not matter for the purpose of this theme that a particular society may emphasise or demote factors in that maturing process. Whatever the practices and attitudes of the society, it will then through a process of education attempt to prepare the person to play his or her part in that society. Education will primarily be directed to the conveyance of information which will enable the adult to fulfil a function contributory to the wealth and welfare of the group. That is to say, it will be designed with the immediate intent of contributing to the particular, local group or society to which the child belongs; but, ultimately, this conditioning is in the interests of the overall purpose of sexuality—survival of the species as a whole.

Here we see the force of sexuality being in the interests of humanity *en masse*; continuation of society is more important than the fate of individuals within it. For example, I suggest that the laws and moral conditioning of a society—no matter how much it may justifiably be claimed that they are basically for the benefit of the individual—are *primarily* devised for the health and stability of the community as a whole. The individual may have certain rights and privileges and be allowed a certain degree of freedom to behave with autonomy; but let that member behave in a manner deemed to be detrimental to the group and that freedom is rapidly and forcibly curtailed. However liberal or repressive the regime, the dominant interest of the group is in its own continuation—not in the individual's aspirations, unless they conspicuously enhance the wealth, welfare and reputation of the group.

The dominant motive force of sexuality then is survival of the group or species which, in the terms of this theme, signifies the prevalence in sexuality of the *feminine,* procreative motive. Given the availability of healthy male and female members, protected and nurtured by the efforts of the society as a whole, new generations of offspring will ensure the maintenance and continuity of that society—its 'immortality'. In this aspect, the feminine in the female and the male subscribes to the belief that it is appropriate for the masculine in the male and the female to sacrifice its individuality— through work and, if necessary, in war—to ensure continuity and survival of the group, society, nation, race, species—or whatever scale of congregation is involved.

Physical survival inevitably introduces a basic concern for the availability of economic resources, especially territory both for living space and for the provision of material requirements. Land is required for the direct provision of food, fuel and other resources, or as work space for the manufacture of goods for home use and consumption, or for trading with other societies. Availability of territory, natural resources, human intelligence and skill thus dictate the wealth and power of the society and its capacity to maintain and increase its membership. At all times, the masculine, individual aspect has to compete and combat threat, either internal or external, to the group's survival, whilst the feminine, sexual, procreative aspect continues to produce and nurture new generations.

If we then take into account that the token of the society's wealth is money, we can then begin to appreciate the scale and implications of sexuality—the extent to which its influence motivates an enormous expenditure of energy to provide for the procreation of the species and the maintenance of an environment in which human society may survive.

Consider just a selection of human occupations concerned with this physical, sexual fulfilment—all those concerned with the growth, processing and supply of food, the provision of adequate water, the retrieval of fuel and the transformation of energy, the procurement of building materials and the construction of buildings for domestic, administrative and commercial use, the maintenance of health and social welfare, the means and methods of distribution and communication by land, sea and air, the manufacture of furniture, utensils and clothing, the valuation, banking and accounting of money, the administration, deployment and taxation of wealth, the maintenance of armed services, the conduct and effectiveness of government, law and order, the research into discovering new and more efficient materials and methods . . . all this and a legion of other occupations constitute the vast support mechanism required for procreation and survival. (I am not suggesting that these are the *only* purposes of all this endeavour; but I am proposing that they are the dominant purposes, upon which any further purposes depend.)

Factors of race, creed, culture and language notwithstanding—factors which tend to confuse, complicate and generate competition and conflict—the ultimate feminine motive in sexuality is the survival of the largest possible number of human beings on this planet.

But what happens when the masculine, pleasure-seeking aspect of sexuality gains strength, becoming divorced from the feminine, procreative motive? Confusion, frustration and distress. The devising of techniques of contraception and abortion are symptomatic of a trend which is causing uncomfortable and distorting psychological and physical consequences. This I will pursue much further later but, in principle, it could be said that the masculine, drawn into seeking *excessive* pleasure in the feminine, begins to fail in its procreative responsibility. The masculine is lured into this pleasure-seeking temptation due to its ignoring or being unaware of its spiritual purpose. To establish this proposition, it is necessary to explore further the meaning of spirituality.

I have sketched sexuality as being in its fullest sense a concept which embraces all mundane activity directed towards procreation and survival of the group. It has further been suggested that in its masculine and feminine dual aspect, it is the feminine which dominates and the masculine which serves. In other words, the sexual, procreative purpose is actively feminine and passively masculine. I emphasise that this does not mean that the male is inactive; on the contrary. It means that through social conditioning, individuality (the masculine in both male and female) becomes subservient or passive in relation to the active, group, procreative purpose (the feminine in both female and male).

In the spiritual aspect of human life—a phenomenon which appears to be exclusive to the human species on this planet—the masculine-feminine polarity reverses. The spiritual is again twin-aspected but the spiritual purpose is actively masculine and passively feminine. This means that the essential key to spirituality is the realisation of its being of concern to the individual, not to the group.

The reversal of polarity, or change of direction, required by the spiritual purpose has been the cause of great confusion and misconception in human history. In particular, it has played havoc with sexuality, usually therefore at the expense of the feminine. The main reason would seem to have been a failure to understand the nature of the reversal or change of direction.

It is one of the objects of this theme to provide evidence to demonstrate that spirituality is not in opposition or antipathetic to sexuality—nor, indeed, *vice versa*. Rather, it is more appropriate to regard the 'changeover' as a gradual transformation throughout the complete human life.

This is not to say that the transformation will be without difficulty or discomfort; in a wise and balanced society it perhaps could be. We live, however, in an era of masculine/spiritual weakness which means that the reciprocal feminine/sexual ethos is disproportionately strong. In this case, the individual is under threat and the spiritual effort seems arduous.

Nevertheless, spirituality evolves out of sexuality, just as the individual evolves out of the group (just as 'man is born out of woman'). The process of evolution or transition should not however countenance rejection of the sexual by the spiritual, nor rejection of the group by the individual, nor rejection of the feminine by the masculine. As suggested above, it must surely be possible for the human being to fulfil his or her sexual, group, procreative purpose *and* fulfil his or her individual, spiritual purpose also. It is a matter of understanding the nature of the gradual transformation from the former to the latter over a lifetime.

Consulting *The Concise Oxford Dictionary,* spirituality is described simply as 'spiritual quality'. Spiritual is then defined as: 'Of spirit as opposed to matter; of the soul especially as acted on by God, a spiritual life; of, proceeding from, God, holy, divine, inspired; the spiritual man, inner nature of man (also, especially in the New Testament), regenerate man (opposed to natural, carnal); concerned with sacred or religious things; having the higher qualities of the mind.'

In my view, this definition hardly helps at all. It is slanted towards the Christian religious context, presupposing familiarity with terms or concepts such as 'God' and 'soul', and implying the opposition of spirit to matter and regenerate to the natural or carnal. Depending on personal conditioning and interpretation, these terms and concepts may be vaguely and temporarily valid but I think they are now too restrictive, have become too familiar and too much abused, and have given rise to deeply entrenched misconceptions. Apart from begging such questions as 'Who is God?' and 'What is the soul?', they appear, due to the divisive propensity of intellect, to separate and set in opposition. For example, in the Christian context, it is not uncommon to find the persuasion that spiritual life requires rejection or suppression of carnal desire—which is all too readily associated with sin.

The emphasis of 'opposed to' in current usage has been to consider it as meaning antagonistic opposition rather than simply 'as distinct from'. The misconception resulting from this emphasis is to consider God, soul, spirit, and so on, as commensurate and on a level with that which is perceivable by the senses—matter, form, carnal man, 'religious things' and so forth. Appropriately, the spiritual should be perceived as simply not being in the same realm as the mundane. The former is inconceivable (though its presence and effect may be experienced); the mundane is conceivable and its nature is describable in quite distinct and sensible terms.

Thus, it will help to redress the balance and remove false assumption if 'opposed to' is held in its neutral meaning of 'distinct from'. In doing this, the excessive activity of intellect—its tendency to divide and set in opposition—is balanced by its passive capacity to reflect upon and distinguish between.

It is then easier to contemplate the meaning and purpose of spirituality for my contention would be that it is not possible to define, analyse and describe the spiritual in the same manner as it has been possible to consider the sexual. The spiritual cannot be 'brought down' to the level of observable form and provable fact. It does not take created form though it is 'the creative'. Thus the spirit is not 'a thing' but the essence of being of everything, in particular of each human being.

Perhaps the most restrictive and misleading practice with respect to the use of the word 'spirit'—and its derivatives 'spiritual' and 'spirituality'—has been the close associating of it with formal, establishment religion. 'Spirit' is a vital word which needs to be reinstated as the motivating essence of all individual purpose. In the context of human endeavour, the spiritual should be prised out of its constrictive connection with formal religious practice and be recognised in its broad perspective as the inner nature or knowledge which should guide and carry the man or woman to his or her fulfilment in life in his or her own terms. This individual realisation may or may not be judged significant in conventional religious or social terms. (In the perceptive and powerful words of the Qur'an, Surah 14: 'But Allah leaves in error whom He will and guides whom He pleases. . . .') Thus, a holy or spiritual life does not necessarily mean looking pious, praying regularly to the deity, being conventionally well-behaved and law-abiding; such habits may be contributory, but all too often they are but an outward, public show; and, all too often, they are but cover or substitute for an unfulfilled, inner development. Evolving the spiritual life is essentially becoming and being fully conscious that the individual destiny is being fulfilled in the manner specific to that individual.

Certain features of spirituality in its broadest perspective begin to emerge as misconceptions about it are discarded. These features are discerned as being distinct in nature from those of sexuality. They are difficult to describe because they are experienced as inner, private, abstract convictions and realisations. Their direction and purpose are quite other than the procreative and group-survival motivations of physical sexuality.

Definitions

Due to the educational process I experienced when young, I entered adulthood with certain assumptions which I now realise to have been deluding.

As the result of religious education in particular, I think I would once have defined spirituality as 'something to do with religion and with man believing in and trying to relate to an almighty deity or invisible power'.

Also, due to the Western system of 'departmentalisation', I had learned to divide concepts and information into categories and subjects. Religion (and spirituality) was therefore assumed to be just one among many human concerns in which one might or might not be interested.

Since my instruction took place in a Christian ethos, I further gathered that religion (and spirituality) was a quite separate concern from sexuality and that they had little connection with each other— except that involvement in the former seemed to require discipline, or even denial, of the latter.

However, as already described, some two years ago I saw that this view was ignorant and fallacious. Spirituality did not necessarily have anything to do with formal religion; it was essentially to do with individual fulfilment and destiny. This meant that the spiritual life of each person (which *every* person was involved in day in and day out whether or not they would recognise it as such by that name) was an inner, private challenge and exploration in which each was trying to understand for himself or herself the meaning and purpose of his or her life in his or her own terms. Inevitably, the fulfilling of this purpose did not exclude participation in the sexual life; on the contrary, sexuality and spirituality became increasingly recognised as inter-dependent and complementary.

Having seen that the spiritual purpose evolves naturally out of the sexual, it then became evident that they are simply two words denoting two aspects of 'the same thing'. In other words, since between them they account for all human motivation, they represent the essence and expression of every action. Furthermore, they are both always present; whatever is said to be sexual will always contain an obverse, spiritual element or aspect, and *vice versa*. This can be appreciated, for example, in a fundamental concept such as 'love'.

It is not easy to conceptualize what 'the same thing', of which sexuality and spirituality are the two aspects, might be but I have found 'energy' to be a useful analogue. The word 'energy'—and the concepts associated with it—is neutral and non-emotive. It has the appropriate property of implying movement and flow. It is also not limited, especially since science has now introduced the view that energy cannot be differentiated from matter; there is really only energy in various forms. The whole universe may be considered as one unlimited pattern of energy flow and exchange.

Spirituality then, as far as this theme is concerned, is not to be understood as a word representing an isolated human concern vaguely associated with religious practice and of interest only to a minority; nor is sexuality to be understood simply as a separate phenomenon of intimate concern in certain circumstances to the vast majority of creatures through most phases of their lives. Rather, I am proposing that the two words represent two aspects of the total energy-flow experienced by the human being. And, further, that it appears to the human mind that in one aspect the energy flows in one direction and, in the other aspect, in the reverse direction. That is *not* to say that they are in opposition to each other. It is one energy and the flow in one direction is complementary to, and dependent upon, the flow in the reverse direction.

Perhaps an analogy would help here, although it should be stressed that using physical, scientific models in what is essentially a psychological appreciation can be limiting and misleading if taken too literally and pursued too far. Such an analogy would be that of the electric-lighting circuit. There is the source of the electricity (equivalent to the 'creative power'), a 'live' or active wire through which the electrical energy is transferred to a bulb where it heats an element to give light (equivalent to the sexual purpose) and a negative or passive wire which completes the circuit back to source (equivalent to the spiritual purpose). There are, we say, two wires (aspects) but they may be considered as two inter-dependent features of one circuit of energy.

The limitation of this analogy lies in the fact that in the electric-lighting circuit one wire is always positive or 'active' and the other always negative or 'passive'. In the psychology of sexuality-spirituality, either aspect may be active or passive. In other words, the mind can actively give attention to the sexual flow (in which case the spiritual is passive); or it can actively give attention to the spiritual (in which case the sexual is passive). The mind cannot give active attention to both simultaneously.

I suspect that it is this fact which has given rise to the religious idea that they are in opposition—i.e., pursuing the sexual interest means that the spiritual is quiescent. This gives rise to such statements as: 'Ye cannot serve God and mammon.' (Matthew, 6: 24)

The fundamental proposition of this theme is that it is not a case of 'either/or'; it is a case of giving the right attention to the sexual 'downward flow' during the first 'half' of life (which is actively feminine, passively masculine) and then to the spiritual 'upward flow' during the second 'half' (which is actively masculine, passively feminine).

In this ideal process, using the electrical analogy, the circuit energy functions properly. All human purpose can be effectively accomplished in a completed life-cycle.

One of the best approaches I have encountered which unifies the two concepts sexuality and spirituality, and resolves the problem of their apparent opposition, is of Vedic origin. Here it is demonstrated that the threefold basis of all human motivation is the desire for happiness, knowledge and immortality.

The motivating force or spirit of this threefold desire manifests in all human activity and is the root of both sexuality and spirituality. Whereas in sexuality it is experienced as the desire for pleasure, information and longevity (immortality as the desire 'never to die'), in spirituality it is experienced as the desire for lasting happiness, true knowledge and immortality. Satisfaction of the former is sought in physical, sensual, factual, worldly terms; of the latter, in realisation of the true nature and identity of Man, and, thus, of the individual self.

The transformation or conversion of the former into the latter carries the individual right through the cycle of life from birth to death (or, to be more accurate, from pre-birth to after-death).

3 Physiological evidence and scientific proof

Neurophysical research in recent years has established that the two cerebral hemispheres function differently. This is not the case in the brain of any other vertebrate so that evidence for it did not emerge until certain effects were noted as a result of human brain surgery. (In particular, it was noticed where the *corpus callosum*—the neural 'bridge' connecting the hemispheres—was severed in people suffering from seriously disabling attacks of epilepsy.)

Observation of behaviour after such surgery led to the conclusion that the human brain has a 'bimodal' nature—that each hemisphere functions in a different fashion and can operate independently of the other. The left hemisphere tends towards 'a more conventional, linear and rational mode of cognition' and the right towards 'a more relational and intuitive form of thinking'.[1]

Since the discovery of this functional differentiation, there has been considerable research, analysis and comment on its nature. One summary is as follows:

> Each side of the brain is able to perform and chooses to perform a certain set of cognitive tasks which the other side finds difficult, or distasteful or both. . . . The right hemisphere synthesises over space. The left hemisphere analyses over time. The right hemisphere notes visual similarities to the exclusion of conceptual similarities. The left hemisphere does the opposite. The right hemisphere perceives form, the left hemisphere detail. The right hemisphere codes sensory unput in terms of images, the left hemisphere in terms of linguistic descriptions.[2]

From reading a number of reports describing and comparing the characteristics of the two halves, I have distilled in the table below some which are most commonly associated with the left and some with the right.

LEFT	RIGHT
extrovert	introvert
optimism	pessimism
particulate	'whole-istic'
analysis	synthesis
time	space

Physiological evidence and scientific proof

conceptual	visual
detail	form
linguistic description	images/imagination
categorisation	collation
linear	shapes, patterns
rational	intuitive
logical	relationship
remembering	recognition
numerate operations	music
reasoning	idealistic

Just how certain of these words are to be interpreted is not usually made clear. Certain pairs are evidently indicative of what might be described as movements in opposite directions—one 'outwards' and the other 'inwards'. The left is centrifugal in nature, differentiating and proliferating; the right is centripetal and integrating.

However, rather than analyse the characteristics too excessively (a proclivity of an over-active left hemisphere) it seems important to reflect on the lists and to obtain a feeling or overall sense in one's own experience of their different natures and the quality of their relationships (a proclivity of right-hemisphere functioning).

'Analysis' and 'synthesis' are useful concepts to help overcome certain apparent inconsistencies and contradictions.

For example, I take 'detail' to mean concern for the analysing or breaking down into components of a 'form'; in turn, 'form' can then be a 'particulate' feature or detail of a larger 'shape' or 'pattern'; in turn, patterns of forms are components or features of the whole design, the complete 'collation', the 'whole-istic'.

I would take 'remembering' to imply a 'linear' continuity of cause and effect sequence in 'time' whereas 'recognition' implies a 'spontaneous knowing' of a relationship.

'Numerate operations' require a 'logical, linear, rational' consistency whereas 'music' expresses random and unpredictable sequences of sound composition (which only become predictable and memorable once they have been notated in linear heiroglyphs for the purposes of repetition). The former accepts and obeys strict discipline and law; the latter continually attempts to express that which is beyond the limitations of law.

If 'reason' is taken in its common sense of the logical, rational and predictable, then it belongs on the left. If, however, it is interpreted in its more subtle and intuitive sense of 'sounding' acceptable—as when we say 'that sounds reasonable'; i.e., we are not certain that the proposition is logically or rationally valid but somehow know and feel it to be so—then it would more appropriately be placed on the right.

I then take 'conceptual' to mean the expressing in concrete, manifest terms—as, say, a 'linguistic description'—that which has been 'visual'-ised in an 'idealistic' inspiration on the right side.

The left puts into form that which may then behave in relation to other form, enabling it to be analysed and compared. The motion or behaviour of one form in relation to another gives rise to the concept 'time'. On the other side, the right, the relationship itself is perceived as a whole, which requires appreciation of the 'space' in which the behaviour is occuring.

In whatever manner one may 'analyse' and 'categorise'—or 'recognise' and 'visualise'—the differentiation between these two lists, it seems to me evident that it is correct for them to have been described as two different modes of thinking. Understanding the differentiation itself calls upon the facilities of both hemispheres. This is most important to recognise for it demonstrates a key principle. The analysing faculty of the left distinguishes the fundamental dichotomy or movement in two directions which motivates the whole creation (sexuality). The synthesising faculty of the right seeks to recognise, understand, resolve and re-integrate into a unified whole (spirituality).

According to one commentator:

> We can be much clearer in our minds about the strategies of the left hemisphere because we can think about them, using language, by a process of introspection. It is much harder to arrive at a clear conception of the modes of thought which are the prerogative of the right hemisphere because to a large extent they may be expected to defy analysis by symbolical verbal means.[3]

I find this comment both confusing and illuminating (probably the former in my left hemisphere and the latter in the right!). The confusion arises from the use of the word 'mind' and the fact that it is a word frequently used, even in the most erudite scientific expositions, almost as if it is synonymous with 'brain'. In fact, if pressed, no one seems to be at all sure what mind *is,* nor do they know how neurochemical impulses are translated into what we call 'our experience of the world'. That 'black hole' of incomprehension apart, who or what are the 'we' who are 'clearer in our minds'? What can 'think about' the strategies of the left hemisphere? The right hemisphere? Is it the right hemisphere that has a comprehension or conciousness of the left, and is the difficulty in having a clear conception of the right therefore due to its not being able to conceive of and comprehend itself? The statement seems analytically useful on the surface; but it begs a number of crucial questions which cannot be left unexplored.

Another commentator suggests that 'the integration of the two halves is a prerequisite for optimal achievement, balance and self-fulfilment' and, further, 'that we commonly have an imbalance due to our over-valuing the left hemisphere'.[4] What is not at all clear in this assertion—nor was it so in its full context—is in what terms the achievement and fulfilment is to be realised. Sexual or spiritual? For what purpose is the balance to be restored?

What then can be usefully deduced from this evidence that the two halves of the brain function differently? I suspect that eventually realisations of enormous significance for the evolution of man will come from it but I wish to use it here, in the interests of this exposition, in a particular way.

I would propose that the left and right hemispheres represent feminine and masculine modes of functioning respectively. Both operate, of course, in both the female and the male human being.

A further piece of physiological evidence came to my notice in 1979 when reading about a television programme called 'The fight to be male'.[5]

The gist of this presentation was to explain that 'the natural form of the human is female; a male is the result of interference with "natural" foetal development.' It proposed 'a remarkable battle in the womb' and the following paraphrase outlines the evidence for this view.

In the case of a female conception, the ovum is fertilised by a sperm carrying an X-chromosome. After a few weeks, the developing embryo has formed both male and female organs to a primitive degree. Then the gonads become ovaries and the male features are transformed or disintegrate.

In the case of the male, the ovum is fertilised by a sperm carrying a Y-chromosome, both male and female features develop to a rudimentary stage as before, but then the gonads form testicles instead of ovaries. The testicles secrete a hormone which absorbs or disintegrates the potential female parts before producing testosterone which then promotes development of fully male characteristics.

The curious fact however, which was discovered some years ago, is that if the female ovaries are removed at an early stage of embryonic development, the ensuing growth will *continue as female*. If, on the other hand, the testicles are removed from the embryonic male, the male growth discontinues and the sexual development *reverts to female*.

The implication to be drawn from this is that foetal development is biased towards becoming female and that this pre-disposition has to be 'fought against' by the action of one crucial male hormone.

A further point raised by this presentation—a point evoked by the discovery described above—concerned the dissimilarities between the male and female brain.

The popular theory has been that, although on average the male brain fully developed is slightly heavier than the female, there is no effective difference between them as far as intelligence and function are concerned. It was assumed that the adoption of male and female roles after about two years was the result of being conditioned to do so by environmental 'persuasion'. This theory is now being questioned by certain scientists following research which has established that young male rats develop a much larger complex of fibres in the 'sex centre' of the brain than the females do. (I take this 'sex centre' to mean the R-complex and the primitive hindbrain; in which case, 'sex centre' implies more than simply reproductive sexual behaviour.)

This disparity in the development of sex centres between male and female has not yet been established as being the case with humans. Recent research in East Germany with pregnant rats, however, has shown that stress has the effect of inhibiting the secretion of male hormone in the embryo and this has led to the contentious speculation that stress experienced by a woman during pregnancy, again inhibiting male hormone production, could result in retardation of a properly developed sex centre in male offspring.

These two physiological phenomena—the different functioning of the two hemispheres of the human brain and 'the fight to be male'—are very significant for this commentary on sexuality/

spirituality and I would like to pursue further implications of them.

These proposals are necessarily hypothetical. They could be said to originate in the right hemisphere as a result of observation (especially introspection), collation of non-linear relationships, intuition (a 'knowing' or recognition which cannot be 'proved' but which has a validity and certainty for the individual). They are based on a synthesis of remembered experience (this experience-recall being the crucial, reflective function of the left hemisphere) and are visualised in an integrative pattern. If the proposals prove useful, it will be because a concensus of others also recognise them.

Inevitably, this process is 'non-scientific' in the sense that the orthodox scientist is disciplined into accepting only that which is provable in terms of the left hemisphere. For a theory to be established as fact, it has to be demonstrated repeatedly and consistently under laboratory conditions. The scientist tends to analyse and categorise, confining himself to sensorily observable causes and effects. This method of establishing facts now seems to be reaching its finite limit, epitomised for example in the current problems haunting astrophysics and atomic physics.

As an example of the problems confronting atomic physics, I will use the following quotation:

> In quantum theory, we have come to recognise 'probability' as a fundamental feature of the atomic reality which governs all atomic and subatomic phenomena.
>
> The fundamental role of probability implies a new notion of causality. In quantum theory, individual events do not have a well-defined cause. For example, the jump of an electron from one atomic orbit to another, or the disintegration of a subatomic particle, will occur spontaneously without any single event causing it. We can only predict the probability for the event to happen.
>
> This does not mean that atomic events occur in completely arbitrary fashion; they are governed by statistical laws. The narrow classical notion of causality is thus replaced by the wider concept of statistical causality in which the probabilities for atomic events are determined by the dynamics of the whole system.[6]

This statement suggests that the conventional scientific method is nearing its finite limit and that logical thinking in cause and effect terms through chronological time has been projected as far it can feasibly go. In the terms I am using, the left side of the brain is now going to have to acknowledge to a far greater degree the faculties of the right, which does not require proof in conventional, scientific terms. Curiously enough, the above quotation uses words and descriptions which suggest that the atomic world functions very much in the manner of the right hemisphere.

Modern science has always regarded its methods as being objective and its results to be proven facts. It is now having to acknowledge that the scientist himself is an integral and inextricable feature of scientific theory. Thus science was never truly objective at all; rather, it is inevitably subjective. There is no such thing as an independent, objective world; it is always a world as each individual sees and interprets it.

For several centuries, it has been the practice of science to concentrate on the practical validity of a theory and to ignore the source of that theory. That something should work consistently and predictably has been sufficient justification in itself. All the way from Archimedes in his bath to Einstein lying under his tree, the mode of comprehension in the moments of discovery has been ignored in favour of factual information. But where did the spontaneous inspiration come from? The right side of the scientist's brain—and there is no logical explanation for its sudden manifestation.

As I see it, the left side of the brain, up to now defiantly satisfied that all physical phenomena are explicable in logical, scientific, 'objective', cause and effect terms, is presently and somewhat unwillingly having to face inconsistencies and inadequacies which require the faculties of the right side to comprehend and resolve. It is now increasingly apparent that the factual, physical explanation is foundering to such an extent that metaphysical considerations will have to be acknowledged and reinstated.

In the terms of this theme, this means in effect that the sexual is not sufficient in itself; the spiritual has to be taken into account. Subservience to the feminine, group ethos does not fully answer the need of the masculine individual.

4 Feminine-left and masculine-right characteristics

I would introduce here—in addition to, or in alternative terms to, those characteristics listed earlier as 'left' and 'right'—a number of important qualities or functions which I regard as distinguishing themselves as belonging to one side or the other.

The feminine left is directed towards procreation and physical survival from which arise dispositions towards continuity, repetition, possession and security. These in turn give rise to a legion of inclinations, preoccupations and behaviour traits; for example, habit, tradition, conservatism, protection, defence, productivity, expansion and longevity.

Allowed to continue in these dispositions to excess, without appropriate intervention by the masculine, the feminine gravitates through comfort and content towards laziness and inertia.

The masculine is rather more difficult to comprehend and define because, whereas the feminine tends towards the physical, the factual and familiar appearance, and the material form, the masculine tends towards the abstract, the ideal, the inner meaning, the metaphysical, the immanent and the visualised perfection. The masculine manifests properties which run counter to the feminine; for example, rejecting habit and repetition, wanting to change, improve, develop and evolve in qualitative rather than quantitative terms, even if it means the discomfort and uncertainty of exploring the unknown, confronting danger, being adventurous and taking the initiative or, if necessary, the offensive.

Allowed to continue in this disposition to excess, without reference to and consideration of the stabilising, practical influence of the feminine, the masculine tends to take off into impractical fantasy, desiring change for change's sake, indulging in selfish whims and causes which can lead to a purposeless destructiveness.

I would emphasise yet again that these dispositions are present in both man and woman (and boys and girls). A man may well choose a repetitive job and favour continuity and security in a physical, material sense; herein he exhibits his femininity. Conversely, a woman may well choose to pursue the adventurous and insecure in search of perfection, thereby exhibiting her masculinity. I am not suggesting that there is anything necessarily 'wrong' in these traits; they may well be appropriate to those individuals. It is a question of degree—the extent to which the other aspect is frustrated or denied.

To the above characteristics which are, broadly speaking, most readily discernible in the sexual, mundane life, I would like to add certain other more subtle or abstract concepts which may be associated with one or the other.

The feminine is centrifugal (moves from the centre outwards), proliferates, expands, multiplies, works in terms of continuous movement in linear, passing or historical time (being concerned with the past and future). The feminine is group—or family—identified, is prone to the horizontal or latitudinal, is parallel to and in closer contact with 'the earth'.

The masculine is centripetal (withdrawing towards the centre), contracts, reduces, resolves, eliminates and is creative/destructive. (Whereas feminine procreation denotes linear continuity and reproduction, masculine creativity implies evolution through destruction of the useless and the redundant.) The masculine works through the vertical with an in-and-out, penetrating and withdrawing pulsation, acting spontaneously in 'no-time', being only concerned with the immediate, the moment now (time present). It is individual, self-concerned and self-sacrificial.

For clarification and reference, it would probably be as well at this point to make a more comprehensive tabulation of characteristics, qualities, properties—including those mentioned earlier—which I regard as associated with either the feminine-left or masculine-right hemispheres and the ways in which they function.

FEMININE	MASCULINE
procreative	creative/destructive
continuity	commencement, cessation
duration	change, transitory
material	abstract
concrete	discrete
expansion	contraction
preserve, conserve	abolish, consume
centrifugal	centripetal
extrovert, exoteric	introvert, esoteric
horizontal	vertical
latitude	longitude
divisive	integrative
analysis	synthesis

Feminine-left and masculine-right characteristics

conception	perception
form	symbol
perfect	ideal
proliferate, multiply	reduce, subtract
consistent, constant	irregular
disperse, spread	concentrate, distil
fission	fusion
belief	idea
imitative	original
appearance	inner sense, meaning
sequence, cause/effect	spontaneous innovation
passing, historical time	immediate, moment, now
past, future	present
constant velocity	acceleration/deceleration
time	space
group, family, collective	individual, separate
public	private
conservative	progressive
application	search, discovery, invention
gregarious	solitary
detail, particulate	pattern, wholeness
convention, tradition, habit	develop, improve, evolve
possession, accumulation	acquisition, disposal
survival of the species	self-preservation
surrender	sacrifice
defence	offence
longevity	immortality
gravitation	'takes off', flies
security	adventure, enterprise, risk
earth, water	fire, air
categorisation	collation
rational, logical	intuitive
remembering	recognition, cognition
language, arithmetic	music, geometry
explanation	inspiration, visualisation
literal, factual	reasonable (as 'sounds right')
quantitative	qualitative
fate	destiny
soul	spirit

At first sight, and taken simply as static items divorced from their context, some of these characteristics may seem unexpectedly placed. Part of the reason for this may be the common associating of them with male and female.

For example, it might be expected that logic would be appropriately masculine and intuition feminine. Claim is often made these days for the superior wisdom of female intuition and derision is commonly levelled at female logic. However, it is proposed here that intuition is actually a faculty of the masculine-right hemisphere and its effectiveness in women is due to their ability to apply it in mundane circumstances, often overriding the logic from the left hemisphere, thereby attracting the accusation of being illogical. Conversely, men tend not to heed the intuition of their right hemisphere because their insights are not so easily assimilated into the conduct of everyday life. Such insights tend to be idealistic and impracticable so that it is easier and more comfortable to replace them through the strict discipline, predictability and security of left-hemisphere logic.

The sometimes misleading association of certain characteristics with one sex or the other is however not the complete reason for apparent inappropriateness in the lists. There are other factors which have to be taken into account.

The first and most important is that the lists are compiled from the sexual, worldly point of view. Some of the concepts have significant properties which only become clear when they are looked at from the spiritual point of view.

The second factor, related to the first, is that it is necessary to take into account the age or phase of life of the individual and his or her degree of consciousness.

And the third factor which affects interpretation is the behavioural context—whether that behaviour is moderate or excessive (obsessive), natural or perverse, positively fulfilling or negatively destructive. (The implication here is that there can be positive destruction. For example, it may be necessary to destroy slums in order to build improved housing.)

One of the best ways of testing the appropriate placing of the characteristics of this bimodal functioning is to observe the dialogues which go on in one's own thinking—dialogues which, incidentally, reflect the dual nature of one's relationship with other people and the world in general.

We are all aware of making choices between alternative courses of action and we will recognise the interaction of the two sides—the more so when they are in contradiction than when in harmony. For example, the debate between the side (feminine) which wants to opt for the comfort of the habitual and the familiar versus the (masculine) effort and insecurity implicit in taking an adventurous alternative; or working for future advantage versus present pleasure;

or feeling the need for company versus the enjoyment of being alone.

It would now be appropriate to bring together as many as possible of the disparate elements so far considered and I feel the best way of accomplishing this in a systematic manner would be to examine the individual life as it progresses through its various phases. Of necessity, of course, it will have to be a hypothetical model but, in general terms, it should be possible to recognise the interplay of sexuality and spirituality as it is played out in most people's lives.

In my view, in attempting to understand the relationship between these two phenomena, we touch upon the very core of the human condition and purpose. The whole mode of human living depends on the health and sanity of that relationship.

5 Conception to infancy

Although the moment of conception and the phases of embryonic growth are symbolically very significant, and indicate so much that is relevant to the fulfilled life of the individual, I will have to be content in this particular book with one or two salient points.

The female ovum waits relatively passively in the woman; the pulsating male organ penetrates the female, ejaculates millions of sperm into the dark depths of her and then withdraws. The sperm 'swim' and 'struggle' into the Fallopian tubes (left and right) until one (possibly two or three or more) makes contact with the ovum, penetrates and fertilises it. The male serves the female by sacrificing his most potent fluid for her procreative purpose.

The male chromosomes complement the female and a new, individual entity begins to grow and expand. The being or existence of the separate ovum and sperm, and then their coming into union at the moment of conception, brings about a miraculous stimulation and activity of 'knowlege'—the inherent or instinctive 'knowing' by the genetic combination how to form a physical human being. The ovum alone, unfertilised, would be unfulfilled and die; the sperm likewise, failing to achieve its goal in the dark 'unknown', would die. But their coming into union permits the enlivening *spirit* of life to activate the innate knowledge of growth. Spirituality begins for that new individual in that instant—that creative moment—of sexual union.

The characteristics of feminine and masculine interweave throughout this story of conception and embryonic growth in the womb. It is a hidden and secret growth towards birth of the individual. (It is perhaps a pre-birth story which is told *in reverse* during the hidden and secret disintegration after the death of the body.)

However, the point to be made at the moment is that spirituality begins for the individual within the darkness of the female and that it is the masculine 'spiritual knowledge' inherent in the newly-formed organism which enables it to grow and to fulfil the feminine purpose of continuity of the species.

This sexual, physical development is actively feminine (centrifugal expansion of the being) and passively masculine ('intuitive' or 'hidden' knowledge serving the feminine purpose).

Conception to infancy

In the early stages of formation, the embryo is not specifically male or female; rather, it is hermaphrodite, having the features of both sexes in primitive form. It is not until some weeks later that hormonal activity in the gonads causes sexual differentiation. As already discussed, the survival bias is in favour of the female. 'The fight to be male' starts at this point and will continue, in other terms, right through to the end of the adult life.

There are several 'critical points' in the development of the embryo but probably none so critical as that when the foetus is sufficiently advanced to be deemed 'independently alive'. In other words, the point at which it would be possible for it to survive removal from the womb. With modern techniques of life support and hygiene, this is reckoned to be somewhere in the sixth to seventh month of gestation.

In Western societies, where factions claim the right to have abortion on demand, debate focuses on the exact time limit up to which it is justifiable and safe to perform this termination of pregnancy. (Recent opinion has stated this to be about the twenty-eighth week.) Even more debate rages over the morality of deliberately killing a human foetus. The feminine, instinctive view would, of course, be in favour of continuity and survival, a view supported by the religious establishment which gives this stance its moral basis. However, those who are advocating it for their own convenience are manifesting negative masculinity. In other words, their personal convenience is directly or indirectly related to selfish pleasure or mundane advantage seeking, with its concomitant unwillingness to accept responsibility. So, although on the face of it the practice is often promoted by so called feminists in the interests of 'women's liberation', in the context of this theme it is really the masculine acting negatively—i.e., offensively killing or eliminating.

If, on the other hand, there is a sincere and honest medical reason for aborting the foetus, then this may be the masculine destructive capability acting positively and appropriately. However, I must add, all this is looking at the situation from the sexual point of view. From the spiritual point of view, in terms of the eternal and the everlasting, the debate and its outcome are of no real consequence. ('Allah leaves in error whom He will and guides whom He pleases.') The 'spirit' of the individual cannot be killed whatever may happen to the body.

About two hundred and eighty days after ovulation, or two

hundred and sixty-six days after conception, the baby is ready for birth.

At birth, the baby's dependence on the mother's blood supply for nutriment and oxygen ceases. Independence as a self-regulating entity is signified by the first breath.

Through the birth, the feminine aspect and purpose is being fulfilled as contribution to survival and continuity of the species.

In the masculine aspect and purpose, the moment of birth is a significant spiritual event, represented in the Latin tongue by the fact that the word for breath is *spiritus*. With that moment of breathing, that miracle of inspiration ('breathing in'), the inherent knowledge as to how to grow continues but is enhanced or advanced by an intelligence as to how to function and exist as an independent being. The various physical systems—such as the respiratory, the circulatory, the ingestion, digestion and excretory—'know' of themselves how to function.

But the deeply spiritual significance of birth is that an individual has, alone, now set out to attempt to fulfil his or her destiny. Inevitably, he or she will encounter his or her fate as a physical, sexual group-member; whether he or she will realise his or her destiny, which is an individual, private and spiritual undertaking, is another matter.

Physical and psychological development is complicated, to say the obvious. Not only are there many aspects of it but in many of them it is often unwise to generalise; so many qualifications and exceptions have to be taken into account. For the sake of giving some measure to the phases of development to be considered throughout the lifetime, I propose to use seven-year periods.

These seven-year periods are only useful markers. Changes are gradual and their inceptions and completions do not manifestly happen suddenly and at the same age from person to person. Some people are slower than average in passing through them, some faster; and some, for one reason or another, do not fulfil all phases. There are occasionally sudden manifest markers or symptoms—the first show of menstrual blood indicating the attainment of puberty, for example. Nevertheless, even such obvious markers are usually the manifest culminations of physiological and psychological changes which have been taking place unseen for some time.

This seven-year phase structure is therefore an idealised, hypothetical model. The earlier phases, being more physical in their manifestation, are more regular and pronounced and are therefore more easily recognisable and measurable. As they are more closely linked with the age of the body, it is more likely that events signifying change will more accurately and generally correspond with the seven-year average. At the other end of the spectrum, where the changes are more likely to be psychological, the phases do not so readily correspond with age. Due to various factors—environmental conditions, past and present way of life, medical support—age of death varies enormously. In modern, civilised communities with good hygiene, nutrition and sophisticated medical techniques, the average life expectancy has been considerably extended compared with societies less well provided for.

However, I am here primarily concerned with the quality of life rather than quantity of years lived, and do not regard the achievement of longevity as particularly relevant. I propose to use in this model the ancient life-measure of 'three score and ten', a period which encompasses ten seven-year phases. Even so, it should be borne in mind that, since the later phases are more diffuse, someone dying in his sixties will not necessarily achieve less in spiritual terms than someone surviving into his eighties.

Finally, it should be noted that, although I will be associating certain developments with certain phases, this does not preclude the fact that they cannot be present in advanced or retarded form in particular people during earlier or later phases of their lives.

The basis for the accompanying commentary is primarily my present and memorised observation and experience of life up to the forty-two/forty-nine phase but it also includes the teaching and influence of various traditions, in the form of both verbal instruction and written commentary. Some of the latter are of recent origin but some, especially religious scriptures, date back as much as three or four millennia.

For the first seven years—which I shall refer to as the period of infancy—being male or female is of little introspective concern to the individual. As a baby, he or she is very much the passive recipient of whatever influences and experiences happen to occur in the immediate environment. He or she may be told that he is a boy or she a girl, and treated accordingly, but during the early years the information has no significant meaning for the infant.

According to the tradition, habit and fashions of the particular society, the infant may be conditioned to behave and dress appropriately for one sex or the other but, at this stage, it is an imposed and learned expectation rather than a self-cognised and sensible differentiation.

The inherent 'spirit' as instinctive or 'hidden knowledge' within the physical being—as nucleic programming in every single cell of it—continues to inform and effect expansive growth and regulation of function.

Now, however, knowledge of a different nature begins to be introduced. It comes from outside the organism in the form of sensory impressions and information. Instinctively, the infant selects and commits to memory that which is recognised as important—i.e., that which is advantageous or disadvantageous to its comfort and continuation. It learns to accept, and then welcome, that which furthers its well-being, and to protest against and reject that which threatens discomfort and danger.

It would be useful here to refer back to the threefold motivation for all behaviour—the desire for happiness, knowledge and immortality. We could say that the desire for happiness is the first to become active. The infant's acceptance of pleasure and comfort, and its rejection of discomfort and pain, are the first manifest indications of this desire motivating response and action. Although knowledge as incoming information is playing its part, the infant is not actively seeking it; and, of course, the desire for immortality is only represented by the instinct for survival.

There is little sign at this stage of the bimodal functioning of the brain. It is still, as it were, in a 'hermaphroditic', unified state. Pleasure and comfort, pain and discomfort—all are related to continuity, security and survival. In the infant, there is no cognised differentiation between self-preservation and survival of the species. In other words, there are not as yet any conflicting interests between the feminine-left hemisphere and the masculine-right.

Consciousness at this stage could be said to be passive and unified; the baby has a total outward awareness when it is awake. Not having experienced a sense, or learned a concept, of itself as being particular and separate from its environment, it is effectively 'unconscious of itself'. We may perhaps surmise that, if it could express itself, it would not say 'I am here in the world' but would rather say 'It is.' (Or perhaps, flippantly, 'Is this it?')

We could say that the baby has being and is conscious but does not *know* that it has and is. In this state, we would have no evidence to assert that, to outward appearances, it is any different from the offspring of any other creature, certainly as far as the higher vertebrates are concerned.

Usually, this state of innocence and ignorance does not last for long in the receptive infant. Learning accumulates at a rapid rate. There is no evidence to suggest that males and females learn differently, even though, as already mentioned, there may well be a bias in the information offered according to gender.

Neurophysiologists regard the brain as being in a state of 'high plasticity' up to about six years of age. This suggests that, starting with a 'clean slate', the memorising faculty of the brain is keenly receptive and absorbs a high proportion of the influential information it is receiving through the senses. Since the brain has not developed a power of discrimination beyond the instinctive ability to differentiate between the physically advantageous and disadvantageous, it is therefore susceptible to a conditioning and moulding over which it has no control.

It is significant that in human beings—during embryonic growth from about the twenty-ninth week and during the early years of infancy—there is asymmetrical development of the brain hemispheres, with the left developing faster than the right. In the terms of this theme, this is to be expected. Inevitably, emphasis must initially be placed on the ability to survive physically and adapt to environment before anything more sophisticated can be entertained. In other words, the feminine-left bias towards ensuring the survival of sexually and socially mature members of the group must take precedence over the development of masculine-right individuality.

As suggested, the rudimentary power to differentiate and discriminate during the infant phase is understandably assigned to distinguish physical pleasure from pain, comfort from discomfort, primarily as representing that which is conducive to survival versus that which threatens it. One would expect impressions one way or the other to penetrate deeply and be long-lasting in memory. This would not only apply to actually enjoyable or disagreeable physical stimuli but also the quality of emotional charge being carried with the information received. This would accord with the accepted view of psychologists that memories of early experiences have a profound effect on later adult life. ('The child is the father of the man.')

This seems to link with the neurophysiologists' proposition that the brain develops an ability to distinguish between that which it deems expedient to commit to long-term memory and that for which a short-term retention will suffice. The effects of this two-layered commitment we experience as adults through our ability (whether deliberate or not) to remember some things and forget others. It seems that 'something' (an inner knowledge or intuition?) chooses between that information which it would be useful to retain and that which is either only temporarily useful or is of no use at all. (For example, when laying a table for guests coming for a meal, it is only necessary to remember how many places need to be laid until the task is completed. On the other hand, a longer term commitment is required in order to be able to recall continually that a wire of a certain colour means the danger of electric shock.)

It seems reasonable to suggest that early, deep and long-term memory is predominantly concerned with survival—establishing firmly that which promotes it versus that which threatens it. This in turn implies that long-term memory is initially committed to serving the efficient functioning of the feminine-left hemisphere. This commitment continually projects into thinking concern for physical continuity, duration, security, longevity and so on (all concerns, it may be noted, activated by the *fear* of discontinuity and elimination). This natural disposition corroborates the evidence that the left hemisphere develops faster than the right in the infant.

Leading on from this, I suspect that all information received and accepted during the infant years is directed towards ensuring that left-hemisphere functioning is effective, in both males and females. Confirmation of this seems to lie in the fact that the left side of the brain operates the right side of the body. Usually, both sides do not become equally active. As the infant grows, the tendency is for the right hand to become actively manipulative and the left to become passively supportive in the interests of survival and exploration. In other words, it is due to the emphasis being on the activation of the feminine-left hemisphere that the right hand takes on the active role. This could be expressed in another way: that the masculine-right side of the body learns to serve the feminine-left hemisphere. This in turn is indicative of the pre-ordained commitment of the masculine to the feminine and exemplifies the bias against the former in its 'fight to be male'.

It should be pointed out incidentally that in this commentary when describing feminine-left and masculine-right hemisphere differentiation, I am always referring to the case of the right-handed person. Logically, the inference would be that, in the case of the left-handed person, it is the right hemisphere which performs the feminine function. In other words, in something approaching one case in ten, the 'wiring' is reversed. And then there is the case of the ambidexter ('both right'; not, interestingly, 'ambisinister', 'both left'). These special cases are undoubtedly very significant but space will not allow pursuit of their implications in this book. It would, however, be worth mentioning one particular feature discovered during research into bimodal functioning.

It has been found that whilst the brain is 'young enough'—i.e., is still retaining a degree of plasticity—if there is some accidental intervention in the ability of the left hemisphere to carry out one of its essential functions, then there is the possibility that the right hemisphere will develop the ability to perform it instead. This is an extraordinary example of intelligent adaptability.

The significance of this, as I interpret it, is that it is again an echo of 'the fight to be male' and is highly reminiscent of the reversion to female of the 'emasculated' male embryo. It demonstrates that, if something goes wrong in the feminine-left hemisphere, representing an impairment of survival potential, then the masculine-right potential is sacrificed.

This theme of masculine sacrifice on behalf of the feminine is one which will recur continually in different contexts as we consider the later phases of the life cycle. It is functionally expedient and appropriate in the interests of sexuality—but disastrous in the interests of individual, spiritual fulfilment, where the feminine needs to surrender to the masculine in later phases.

The infant, therefore, is predominantly programmed, and then inevitably informed and conditioned, towards maturity as a sexual, socially-acceptable member of society. This takes place before he or she is aware of himself or herself as a spiritually-inspired individual—i.e., before the masculine-right hemisphere has even begun to exert its influence.

6 Childhood and consciousness

As the infant grows towards childhood—childhood being, say, the seven-year period from seven years old to fourteen—a degree of differentiation between the sexes occurs during the educative process inasmuch as the female is more disposed to absorb and adopt left-hemisphere learning than the male is. Being physically the potential vehicle for the procreation of the species, there is a bias in her for acquiring information contributory to worldly comfort, security and survival. In other words, she is programmed and thus disposed to receive and accept relevant information more readily. This would account for the reputation that girls have for being more advanced during childhood than boys, who are said to be 'later developers'. It will be seen to be significant that this lagging behind is redeemed after puberty when the masculine-right hemisphere becomes fully developed and active.

The absorption of useful information is at first in the interest of straightforward physical comfort and survival—food, drink, warmth and so on. After this, the learning is about life in the world and being taught the means of survival in society when parental protection is withdrawn. Apart from learning physical skills of considerable variety and complexity (standing, handling, walking, washing, dressing, speaking, and so on), all enabling that individual to function independently within the family group, there will be that mental training required to enable the person to communicate with, cope with, and function in, the outside world. Basically this involves learning the vocabulary, grammar and syntax of the language used in the immediate environment and being trained in the techniques of reading, writing and counting. All of these tools appeal to the feminine-left hemisphere functioning, with its proclivity for the linear, logical, sequential, continuing, repetitive, imitative, mechanistic mode.

On the other hand, it could be argued that it is the fact that this basic information is fed to the left hemisphere which causes the left to develop these methods of functioning. It is impossible to tell for sure which is the cause and which the effect. Either way, it is nevertheless the left which takes on the feminine function.

Although the bias is heavily towards the left in this initial training, there may well be some appeal to the right. In infancy, this could, for example, be in the form of stories—'fairy stories'—which attract the attentive listener despite their illogicality and fantasy. Frequently they involve adventure, idealised characters and behaviour, imaginary forms and they often disregard the terrestrial laws of space and time. Music and art may also appeal to the right. Drawing, for example, introduces the mystery of locality and spatial relationships. As distinct from two-dimensional linear, logical representation of the three-dimensional, children's drawing happily ignores such strictures. Games and playing can appeal to either hemisphere—imitating the actual belonging to the left, visualising fantasies belonging to the right. Up to a point, the infant does not decide what is real and what is unreal. Only later will he or she be persuaded as to what is real.

All the learning about the world—knowledge in the form of in-form-ation—directed at the feminine-left hemisphere in both male and female infants is preponderantly in the interests of survival and procreation. Hence it is concerned with sexuality (even though it may later be used in the interests of spirituality). It is a mechanical repetition or re-creation of the parental form and represents a conditioning of being.

In what way may this phase be said to have its spiritual aspect?

As suggested above, games of fantasy, mythological tales, introduction to music and art, all these may contain seeds which will later germinate as the masculine spiritual search for truth and individual fulfilment.

However such seeds are usually randomly sown and lie virtually dormant, increasingly buried beneath layers of worldly information. As I see it, the instruction in mundane techniques plus the instinctive drive for comfort and pleasure can either temporarily or permanently eclipse the individual spirit. This is an event which might be called 'negatively spiritual' and it is a concomitant of the masculine-right hemisphere still remaining relatively passive or quiescent after the feminine-left has begun to function actively. This might be expected to generate a degree of frustration and I suggest it accounts for much of the wilfulness, stubbornness, rebellion, disobedience, even destructiveness in children, especially in boys.

This entering of the negatively spiritual phase is one of the possible interpretations of such stories as 'the fall of man' in the Judaic Book of Genesis and the meaning, in the Christian parable, of the setting out of the prodigal son into 'the far country'. One of the crucial aspects of it is the search for identity. As far as the child is concerned, his or her identity is imposed through external influences.

The infant child is given and persuaded into his or her identity; it is not consciously requested by the child. As he or she learns to speak and understand the meaning of words, by associating particular sounds with specific forms or objects, what had hitherto been a unified, anonymous, panoramic world becomes fragmented into a multitude of separate things with different names. The active, left hemisphere divides, analyses, separates, particularises, categorises the undefined and limitless whole into a proliferation of identifiable forms. This commonly begins with naming the immediate and familiar—mother, father, sister, brother, cat and dog—and includes the assigning of proper names.

During this process, the infant inevitably learns the proper name which has been assigned to himself or herself. Because names are identified with objects and the infant is repeatedly called by a certain name, and thereby encouraged to believe that he or she *is* that body with that name, it is inexorably established that 'this is me' and 'I am called John . . . or Elizabeth . . . or whatever'. (Often the child will resist the identification for a while and say, 'John wants that' or 'Elizabeth doesn't want this', referring to himself or herself in the third person.) However, sooner or later the child comes to believe that his body is what he is and his name is who he is. He did not consciously decide that for himself. He was persuaded to believe it.

I am not intending to insinuate that this process is inappropriate or diabolical. It is proper and inevitable that it should happen for, without particular, localised identity, it would not be possible to take an adult place in the world. It does however have a far-reaching effect. It is the platform upon which personality is built and gives rise to crisis of identity in various forms later. This in essence is the spiritual aspect which has much to do with the search for *true* individual identity.

In parallel with this imposition of mundane identity, it should also be noted that all beliefs acquired during childhood are inculcated, for better or worse, through external influence. This again, of course, has far-reaching effect through later life. In particular, the beliefs about oneself tend to reinforce the assumption and nature of self-identity, hence crystallising personality. Whilst some beliefs may operate to the benefit of the individual, or be harmless enough,

Childhood and self-consciousness

others can become a debilitating burden and restriction. But one is speaking here in terms of worldly success or failure. As might be expected by now, what is advantageous or otherwise in the realm of sexuality may be the reverse from the spiritual viewpoint. The so-called strengths of personality in the world's terms can be most difficult to cope with in spiritual terms; and *vice versa*. For example, humility is not reckoned to be an advantageous ingredient in the pursuit of fame; on the other hand it may be an essential ingredient in the spiritual context.

In what way may we experience the assuming of mundane identity as being antipathetic to spiritual understanding? We may see a glimmer of this as I consider evidence for what I would call a shift in consciousness during childhood—in fact, it could be claimed to be a signal, or even the cause, of the subtle shift from infancy to childhood.

Why is an isolated moment, or incident, or scene of childhood recallable from memory whilst the duration of time and the experiences 'either side' of that moment are forgotten?

If I recall such moments—and it seems to vary considerably with different people how far back in their history they can go to retrieve them—they are often associated with excitement, joy, pain or fear. It is as if the bland, dimly conscious continuity of life were suddenly interrupted by an intense emotional charge or experience. I suggest that this infers an instant and spontaneous 'awakening' or stirring of the right hemisphere which disrupts the steady, 'low voltage', linear continuity of the left. It is, as it were, a stimulating, masculine penetration of the feminine.

I use the word 'awakening'—and thus associate the experience with an increased degree of consciousness or awareness—because such memories have an exceptional vividness. I suspect they do so because, at that moment, some pleasure- or fear-provoking factor has intensely increased the sense of self.

An interesting clue in this pursuit is to look at a photograph of oneself taken a long time ago. Somewhere in an old family album of ours, there is a photograph of me as a boy standing beside a new bicycle. I can recall vividly the joy and pride of that moment and can recall being there in that scene looking at the friend with the camera taking the photograph. But, apart from remembering the scene and recalling the emotion evoked in me at the time, when I look now at the person in the photograph, I see a stranger. Could that really have been me? Did I look like that? Yes, it must have been, and I must have done—for I know I was there.

Here we see 'the being there' enlightened by the knowledge of 'knowing I was there': matter/spirit, sexuality/spirituality. My left hemisphere accepts the logical, sequential memories which prove it to be a fact; my right hemisphere is not entirely convinced and is confused by what it intuitively knows to be an illusion or deception.

For the curious effect of this experience—if the right hemisphere contemplates it—leads to a strange comprehension. The past 'me', the physical object or image in human form at that historical juncture in my boyhood, is not the same as the older, physical 'me' now. And yet the 'I' then—the 'I' or inner self who was looking out through those eyes at the photographer—has *not* changed. That 'I' in 'me' then is the same self or spirit which is looking at the photograph now many years later.

I hope this is not too confusing! It is rather difficult to express because left-hemisphere conditioning commonly persuades us to elide the 'I' and the 'me' and to believe they are the same. Those who have experienced this seemingly 'schizophrenic' effect will recognise what I am attempting to describe. It is certainly not an uncommon experience, though it may well be expressed in a less schizophrenic way. For example, older people may often be heard to say something to the effect: 'I do not really feel any older than when I was a child.' This I take to be indicative of the undeniable recognition that, though the body may grow older and the appearance change, there is present in each individual throughout the lifetime an 'ageless witness' of all which befalls that person. Experience of the presence of this inner self begins in childhood, and it is the 'dawn' of right hemisphere, active spirituality.

However, for the moment, the point to be drawn is that such experience is clear evidence of the bimodal functioning of the brain hemispheres. The feminine-left hemisphere has learned to believe that this material person here has a consistent continuity and duration through historical time. The masculine-right hemisphere can understand through observation and experience that this logical, sequential deduction is an assumed half-truth and knows that the sense of self is only ever present *now*. The appearances of this physical person 'me' change and its personality changes but the witness of that change, the 'I', is constant and unchanging, unaffected by passing time.

The left-hemisphere reasoning, for example, will assume that the existence of the person who goes to sleep continues through until that person wakes up. Yet where was the conscious sense of self, the 'I', during that sleep? This is again clear indication of the left hemisphere's identification with the body's existence (being) whilst the right only knows of the presence of the conscious self or spirit (knowledge).

It is this constant self, which 'inhabits' the right hemisphere, which inspires the individual, spiritual motivation as it emerges as 'self-consciousness' in the child.

And so, perhaps in infancy, certainly in childhood, there are memorable moments which make the experiencer more conscious of his or her situation. These I would call indications of increased level of consciousness or the emergence, or 'liberation', of consciousness from the physically-existing being.

Although these moments are initially like flashes or bursts, especially in the early years, I suggest that they are related to a gradual and general shift of consciousness which begins to manifest in the maturing child. As I recall it, it is such a spasmodic and subtle intervention that it is difficult in retrospect to pinpoint when exactly it starts. It cumulatively constitutes what is called the sense of self-consciousness, which means a clear awareness of the self as a physically existing and identified being separate from its environment. This phenomenon represents a gradual enlivening or activation of the right-hemisphere functioning. A feature of it worth repeating is that it begins to take place when the left hemisphere is already established, active and dominant. This implies a further stage—this time psychological in nature—of 'the fight to be male', because the development of the masculine-right function will be against the already committed bias of the feminine-left. This is why the emergence of self-consciousness can have bewildering repercussions for the child. His or her individuality is now confronted with an established social conditioning.

I use the word 'bewildering' deliberately, though with particular regard for the reaction of the masculine in the male. The left hemisphere in a boy is likely to be committed to a lesser degree to the imitative, learning function than it is in the girl. Reciprocally, the girl will be less likely to be disturbed by the activation of her masculine-right hemisphere because her left hemisphere functioning will not be so deeply penentrated by it.

The emergence of self-consciousness could be seen as synonymous with the increasing ability to direct will. Up to that time, self-will has manifest primarily as mechanical, temperamental reaction of a defensive nature. With self-consciousness, self-will goes, as it were, on the offensive and actions are more likely to be autonomous and unpredictable. Particularly in the frustrated male, they may be overtly wilful, aggressive and possibly destructive.

Having been conditioned by outside influence—pre-programmed in the left hemisphere—towards the belief that the named physical entity is the identity (id-entity) of the person, the gradual increase in awareness which could be associated with activation of the right hemisphere brings about self-consciousness, a very distinct sense of self. This gives rise to a characteristic awkwardness of behaviour. This may result in a wide variety of responses ranging from an over-assertiveness or bumptiousness through to unsociable withdrawal. One gets the sense of an emerging individuality testing itself against, and trying to reconcile itself with, the already established socially inculcated programme, the adopted personality.

This being so, it then begins to look as though the left hemisphere is comparable to a computer. It receives information, is programmed by the person's social environment, memorises or stores what is relevant, and processes or responds if uninfluenced by right-hemisphere intervention—mechanistically, imitatively, reproductively. According to its accumulating memory of experience and information, it automatically and logically accepts or rejects in its decision-making process.

After the first six or seven years—after the period of high plasticity—increasing activity of the right hemisphere produces features of individualistic behaviour which are not, as it were, in the programme. I emphasise again that this is not meant to imply a sudden switching-on of the right hemisphere; stirrings to the right can intervene spasmodically from an early age, especially in the case of the male. It is rather that the onset of childhood signifies that it is becoming more insistent and consistent, promoting and establishing individual characteristics.

The spiritual process of individuality has begun to assert itself and it may manifest as sociable or anti-social behaviour. Conformance with the group ethos, sexuality, may now be tested and challenged by individual spirit or initiative, spirituality.

This interpretation of what happens in the early stages of the human life cycle invites the conclusion that the increasingly differentiated bimodal functioning in the brain hemispheres is in some way linked with increased consciousness. We do not *know* what consciousness *is*. Since it could be said to be *the means of our knowing* anything, that is not surprising. We cannot be 'conscious of consciousness'; we can only be aware of the effect of being conscious; what we know and experience is evidence of its presence. In other words, we can recognise the experience which we call 'self-consciousness' and we can know what it is to be aware of something; but we cannot say what the phenomena of consciousness and knowing *are*.

It does not, nevertheless, seem to me to be invalid, merely because it cannot be proved, to propose that 'degrees of consciousness' may well be associated with particular, observable modifications of brain function. Whether consciousness is the cause and hemisphere differentiation the effect, or *vice versa,* would be impossible to prove. They appear to be coincident and I suspect that, as in the earlier quotation concerning the theory of probability in atomic physics, it is not a case of cause and effect (the demand of left-hemisphere, logical, sequential thinking), but requires the new 'notion of causality'. This would mean that increasing degrees of consciousness are spontaneous, discrete 'jumps' of 'spirit' or knowledge (like the 'quantum jumps' of electrons in orbit round the atomic nucleus) which take place in the right hemisphere at certain stages of brain evolution. To comprehend and accept this as a possibility is in itself indicative of the intuitive capacity of the masculine-right hemisphere. As already suggested, twentieth century scentists are commonly committed exclusively to the feminine mode of functioning whereby the linear and finite must be shown to behave predictably and repetitively in order that any fact may be acceptably and conclusively 'proved'. Whereas earlier scientists—such as alchemists, whose work has been continually misrepresented by their latter-day counterparts—did not divorce themselves from metaphysical intuition, today's researchers and commentators are reluctant to admit and entertain such abstracts as 'consciousness'. As mentioned earlier when referring to inspirational moments of scientific discovery, spontaneous and 'unprovable' jumps of intuitional comprehension, inexplicable in logical cause-and-effect terms, are an anathema to them.

For example, in a recent, guarded, but only just academically respectable speculation on the evolution of human intelligence,[7] one commentator, having (surprisingly) invoked the Old Testament creation story into his orthodox, historical account of brain development, comes to a comment about death:

> One of the earliest consequences of the anticipatory skills that accompanied the evolution of the prefrontal lobes must have been the awareness of death. Man is probably the only organism on Earth with a relatively clear view of the inevitability of his own end. Burial ceremonies that include the interment of food and artifacts along with the deceased go back at least to the time of our Neanderthal cousins, suggesting not only a widespread awareness of death but also an already developed ritual ceremony to sustain the deceased in the afterlife. It is not that death was absent before the spectacular growth of the neocortex, before the exile from Eden; it is only that, until then, no one had ever noticed that death would be his destiny.

This evolutionary event—'awareness of death' and that, suddenly, someone 'noticed that death would be his destiny'—is accorded only passing comment. The entire book ignores or avoids any suggestion that the evolution of intelligence has anything to do with the phenomenon 'consciousness'. Rather, it perpetuates the Darwinian model which attributes evolutionary advance to the 'accidental' ability of a species to adapt more efficiently to changing circumstances than its potential competitors. There is no attempt to define what intelligence is nor why and how it increases. Thus the 'accidental' evolution theory conforms with the linear, historical, feminine–left view that the only purpose of life on earth is survival and procreation. Science assiduously discounts there being any other possible purpose; it is not interested in *why* we exist, only in how we came to do so, and may continue to do so.

This attitude reminds me, in passing, of an amusing anecdote told by James Thurber, in which a man gives his friend a bloodhound as a present. Some time later, the donor asks after the dog and, when the friend confesses that he has given it away, asks why. 'Well,' said the friend, 'it was never interested in where I was, only in how I had got there!'

The assumption that the human race is simply here to survive and procreate may be sufficient reason for existing for science but I find that 'something in my right hemisphere' protests strongly and regards the explanation as a blinkered half-truth. I am sure that many would agree that the 'sudden awareness of death as human destiny' was not just an incidental accident which happened to befall Man but an extraordinary and momentous event in the history of life on earth which gave Man a responsibility and purpose far beyond reproduction and expansion. It will be a long time, if ever, before any scientist is going to be able to explain the phenomenon of self-consciousness in biological terms.

In the experience of the human being, the realisation that one will die is a consequence of self-consciousness—awareness of being—acting on the inculcated belief that the self is the body. 'When the body dies, I will die.'

The realisation may well first occur in childhood and I am sure that in many children it has a most profound, inner, private effect. Individual, right-hemisphere, spiritual motivation begins in earnest at this point. Penetrating deeply into the feminine-left, sexual, social, group-continuity, survival-of-the-species motivation comes the fear of death and the urgency of self-preservation, not just as an instinctive response to threat but as an anticipated and inevitable event in the future.

Sometime around the age of six to seven, the infant enters the phase of childhood which is marked especially by the phenomenon of self-consciousness. And I have suggested further that this event is coincident with a marked activation of the masculine-right hemisphere, so that sense of selfhood appears to be a feature of consciousness associated with that hemisphere.

That the sense of self resides in one hemisphere or the other seems to be corroborated by the noted effects of brain surgery: 'Patients who have had prefrontal lobotomies have been described as losing a "continuing sense of self"—the feeling that I am a particular individual with some control over my life and circumstances, the "me-ness" of me, the uniqueness of the individual.'[7]

The use of the word 'continuing' is interesting. If this theme is correct, then sense or consciousness of self would be a feature of the right hemisphere but the continuing sense of 'me' would be the result of continual fabrication in the left hemisphere. This relates to earlier postulation that self-consciousness is an experience in the present moment in the masculine-right whereas assumption of worldly identity and the belief that 'me' is a consistent entity is the result of information processed in the feminine-left which recalls past events as a logical, sequential, historical continuity. It would not then be surprising, if the *corpus callosum*—the 'bridge' between the two hemispheres—is severed, that consciousness of self-existence in the present moment should be divorced from the sense of self-continuation through time.

Further, it is noted that sufferers from the 'mental discontinuities' of schizophrenia ('split-mind') often have 'crises of identity'. Although surgical intervention for relief in cases of people suffering from acute depression, bouts of homicidal violence, suicidal tendencies, schizophrenia and other severe 'madnesses' is understandable as a socially expedient remedy (and indicates a possibly irreversible failure of the feminine-left to be reconciled with the masculine-right), it is tragic to have to infer from what is being proposed in this book that such drastic measures must surely deny the 'victim' of any further evolution in spiritual terms during that life. He or she will never *know* his or her true identity and never understand his or her destiny.

The fact is that the onset of childhood marks the beginning of feminine-left and masculine-right rivalry within the individual. If one is active, the other must be passive. One is sure to have overall domination over the other (unless they dissociate or 'split' as in the mental situations described above) and, from the start of life, the odds are stacked in favour of the feminine-left. Future life is going to be either conflict, complement, compromise or conversion (in which dominance will be transferred to the masculine-right). It is now going to be a lifelong struggle for the *individual* to survive and evolve out of the *group dispensation*.

One or two minor pieces of information as evidence in support of this conflict occur to me in passing: the belief in earlier days that a deep vertical furrow between the eyebrows was a sign of actual or potential madness; the concept in Far Eastern tradition of it being possible to develop a 'third eye' in the centre of the forehead, which was perhaps based on the idea that a central, transcendental view was required in order to reconcile the dualistic views of left and right; the tradition that 'angels' have symmetrical faces. This tradition is related to the fact that up to a certain age, a child's face may be admired as 'angelic' partly because muscular tensions have not disturbed its symmetry. Later in life, it may be deduced, there is a tendency to assymmetry due to the conflict between left and right; for example, in the battle between 'what is expected of *me* by others' versus 'what *I* want to do.'

This left-right rivalry manifests in many ritual gestures at a social level. The right-handed handshake signifies, in so many words, 'I am willing not to be aggressive'. The Eastern two-handed handshake suggests a disposition to harmony between both hemispheres. In cheek kissing, the emphasis seems to be on the desire to make peace. Communist leaders are seen hugging and gesturing with the head to both sides, as if giving active and passive signs of bilateral accord. The central kiss on the lips is of course a direct exchange of profession of love.

In language, 'right' is associated with being correct; hence 'upright', 'rectitude', 'rights', 'righteous', and, significantly, 'in his right mind.' 'Left' derives from Old English roots meaning weak and worthless; in other languages, it has connotations of the sinister, the *gauche* and the deceitful. This would seem to indicate that true guidance should come from the right hemisphere whereas the left can lead astray. In terms of true individual spirituality, this will be seen to be the case.

The dawn of self-consciousness in the child can be bewildering and troublesome. The individual spirit begins to drive with new power and direction towards self-expression and self-ishness, trying to use the left hemisphere to effect its desires. However, it encounters the already inculcated beliefs absorbed from the social environment. Tensions begin when these learned conventions seem to oppose and restrict the will.

As already suggested, this confrontation is more likely to occur in the male because the female is more predisposed by nature to adopt the continuing *status quo* (though she may admire the rebellious male from afar!).

However, the social conventions and beliefs are not of course all negatively suppressive, no matter what the child may think. The society's traditional ways are, hopefully, more likely to be positively protective. The shell of an egg is a fair analogy; up to a certain stage of development, it is an essential protection and support; it should only be broken out of when the chick is sufficiently equipped to survive the next phase of growth. Therefore, it is important that an *intelligent* discipline is exerted on the child, especially the boy, because if the masculine is not to some extent 'trained' at this stage, there is the possibility that inappropriate licence will not only give rise to irresponsible and unsociable behaviour but also lead the individual into adopting selfish, pleasure-seeking habits which will be to his or her disadvantage later.

The emphasis is placed here on 'intelligent' because an excessively repressive, group discipline can lead to a frustration of the masculine-right which will then either erupt violently or be rendered impotent.

The nature of institutionalised education is therefore crucial. In a society which is devoted to sexuality and is virtually or actually agnostic (that is to say, spiritually deprived, no matter how influential any existing formal religious establishment), it is hard to find a reasonable balance between extremes of discipline and licence. Historically, the fashion will swing from excessive, and possibly sadistic, discipline (emasculating the spirit) to excessive liberalism (leading to barbarically wilful pleasure-seeking and self-indulgence). The key is whether the society permits aspirations other than its own economic perpetuation and expansion. If it does not, then education will tend only to be concerned with training economically-viable automatons. If it does allow genuine higher aspirations, then it will also serve individual fulfilment—which, in due course, will inevitably enrich and benefit the society in both economic and 'higher' forms.

I found a commentary on an aspect of Japanese cultural tradition to be a very useful view of this. It could be claimed that, by all reports, modern Japan has veered very considerably towards 'economic automatism' as a reaction to the disastrous failure of its militarism. It is to be hoped that the spirit of the old tradition depicted in this commentary still exists. When reading it, the concept 'Way' may be regarded, in the context of the educative discipline proposed above, as a balanced course between preparing the individual to be a responsible member of society and at the same time training him to develop towards individual spiritual fulfilment:

> In the pursuit of any given Way, the learner has to start by holding strictly to tradition—in other words, to the experience of that Way as transmitted and refined from generation to generation, and as represented in the form of concrete models, of oral tradition, or indeed of written tradition. He is permitted no freedom. The personal freedom of spontaneous activity is actually denied, as

being not the true freedom that is to be striven for. Only when the learner has conquered his own wilfulness and schooled himself—re-experienced the received tradition in its entirety—can he recognize what is of eternal worth for the Way in question. Only then, having attained maturity, can he go on to such personal creations as now arise spontaneously from within him.[8]

The feminine aspect of society—for example, its tradition—may then be protective, supportive, guiding and nurturing, being the platform from which the masculine individuality and enterprise may emerge and find freedom in the adult life.

Undisciplined, the masculine exploits the feminine for opportunist pleasure and gain; disciplined, the masculine reflects upon the inherited wisdom of the feminine and learns to serve it responsibly until such a time as it is mature enough to inspire and guide the feminine to higher purpose.

Apart from awareness of death, a further feature that emerges with self-consiousness is clear consciousness of one's own sex and therefore of the other sex also. Sex and death are curiously and intimately intertwined, emotionally associated with love and fear.

I am not suggesting that awareness of death and sex, and experience of love and fear, do not begin until childhood. On the contrary, Freudian theory is borne out in that infants may be observed to derive pleasure from tactile stimulation of erotic areas and may early in life engage in a kind of sexual play with partners of either sex. They also of course show affection and are frequently frightened. What I am trying to convey is the change of gear, or the added dimension, which takes place with the intervention of self-consciousness, bearing in mind that it implies an awareness of oneself as a separate and individual person.

Up to that time, the self has been, as it were, integrated with the world. Sexual pleasure and affection are self-preoccupied, receptive happenings and reactions; fear is automatic response to pain, the unknown and the unexpected threat. Something which has died may have been seen but that death is not associated with the possibility of 'my' death.

But self-consciousness causes a profound shift. Awareness of being separate introduces objectivity. Sex becomes consciously associated with attraction to, and love of, another person which in turn adds a heightened dimension of desire and anxiety. Fear reaches deep as the possible death of oneself is comprehended.

7 Brain development

In these childhood developments and considerations, we are now witnessing the full exercise of the brain and it would be appropriate to give an outline sketch of the features of it and the order of their coming into operation.

The most primitive or ancient part of the nervous system is the spine. What we call the brain begins in prehistoric evolution with a kind of extension or swelling at the top of the spinal cord which is now called, biologically, the hindbrain and midbrain. This assembly incorporates in vertebrates all the mechanisms and controls necessary for the body's functioning—regulation of the heart, blood circulation, respiration, digestion, excretion, etc.—and for its survival in terms of self-preservation and reproduction.

This most ancient part of the brain is then surmounted by the oldest part of the forebrain, a feature which can be traced back to the evolution of reptiles several hundred million years ago. This part has been established as being responsible for display activities such as hostility, competitiveness, ritualistic behaviour, territorial dominance and the establishment of social hierarchies.

The first part of the forebrain is then in sequence surmounted by the limbic system which contains, for example, the thalamus, the hypothalamus and the pituitary gland, in the human being. It is the seat of the more primitve emotions such as anger, fear, sentiment and affection. It may also be so for rather more subtle and sophisticated emotional experience, which we assume to be exclusively human; for example, joy, awe, ecstasy, love. Since it is known that the pituitary is the 'master' gland of the endocrine system, it may also be appropriate to associate mood and 'state of mind' with this area of the brain.

In the limbic system there is also a structure called the hippocampus which is much involved in memory retention. There are also areas associated with oral and sexual functions. (Perhaps the erotic excitement aspects of sexual experience rather than the purely reproductive function?)

Finally, surmounting the limbic system, there forms the neocortex, massively developed in the primates compared with less intelligent creatures. Amongst the manifold functions controlled from this region—including receipt and processing of visual and auditory information, recognition and expression of language and symbols (speaking, reading, writing, mathematical calculation)—two of the most essential characteristics of cortical function, arising from the ability to objectify, are the capacities to take initiative and to be cautious. These capacities are linked with the ability to imagine and anticipate which in turn generate, as a consequence, the experience of anxiety and worry. In man, it is the ability to objectify which gives rise to the capacity to think and comprehend in abstract. I propose that objectifying and comprehending in abstract are direct correlatives of the experience of consciousness and that they are associated in particular with the right hemisphere.

Leading on from this I would propose that, as far as is known, the ability to 'increase' consciousness is peculiar to man and that it is intimately connected with what he calls religion and spirituality. In other words, the 'freeing' of consciousness is an aspect of human purpose which is quite distinct from the earthly purpose of his 'lower' nature which he shares with all other creatures—procreation, sexuality.

It should be noted that, in parallel with the evolutionary development of the brain described above, the indication is that spirituality is a development out of sexuality. This implies that the emergence of spirituality requires acceptance of, and fulfilment of, the lower sexual nature.

As embryo, as infant, and then as child, the individual exhibits behaviour associated with all the 'earlier' features of brain functioning. As embryo, the hind and midbrain functions are established—blood circulation, respiration, ingestion, digestion, excretion—all conducive to reproduction and self-preservation, all instinctively 'known'. Birth into the world brings the early forebrain system into play with its 'outward' projection or expression in the form of aggression, acquisitiveness, competition, possessiveness and ritual performance (which is related to marking out one's territory and sphere of influence; the area which is one's own to operate in and from which one tests and challenge the environment).

Infancy also brings the limbic system into play. The outward projection of behaviour and emotion bounces back and generates an inner response—either positive, giving rise to happiness and affection, or negative, giving rise to anger and fear. Meanwhile, the cortex is receiving knowledge in the form of information through the sensory mechanisms, a process we call 'learning about the world'.

All this may be said to happen automatically, providing there are no malformations in the organism. It takes place similarly in male and female, though one may discern, derived from the characteristics already described, a certain divergence or dichotomy—between active and passive, and hence between a masculine and feminine differentiation which will become increasingly pronounced as the years pass.

In general terms, all the processes are directed during the early years towards procreation and survival but, bearing in mind the masculine/feminine characteristics already proposed, the division would be as follows: masculine—self-preservation, competition, hostility, aggression, acquisition, status, anger, leader, display; feminine—reproduction, ritualistic behaviour, possession, territory, hierarchy, sentiment, affection.

What were called the subtle or sophisticated emotions of the limbic system—joy, awe, ecstasy, love—may be derived from the inter-sexual relationship but I suggest that they are essentially trans-sexual or transcendent and may thus be regarded as belonging to the spiritual realm. One might say that orgasm is the nearest one may come to the spiritual experience in physical, sexual terms.

I emphasise that it must be borne in mind that *all* the above characteristics are present in the cerebral differentiation in both male and female and that both sexes are intially disposed towards procreative sexuality and physical survival.

The primitive masculine characteristics may be seen to contain the 'seeds of spirituality'. Self-preservation, for example, is the primitive form of the motivation towards immortality; competition for status is a rudimentary representation of the desire which will be required later to spur the search for true individual identity; fear is the fundamental emotion which stimulates or energises the urge to undertake the spiritual quest.

It may also be discerned that the feminine is essential for conversion or transformation. Self-preservation may only become self-sacrifice through and after service to the feminine procreative purpose; competition for worldly status can only be translated into spiritual leadership through compassion for the feminine; selfishness can only be converted to altruism through dedication to the feminine. Fear ('Fear of the Lord') can only be transformed into love ('Love of God') through union with the feminine:

Related to the above, it would now be worth introducing two further threads which will help to establish the grounds of this theme. Both of these features also reach right back to primitive roots in the evolution of man.

The first derives from an account[7] of squirrel monkey behaviour. The male performs an aggressive sexual display, especially in the company of other males, which is intended to challenge for leadership and to establish status. Although this ritual involves display of the erect penis, it is not sexual in the sense that it is necessarily done to impress the female as a prelude to copulation, nor is it indicative of his copulative potential. Lesion in one small part of the monkey's forebrain can eliminate the display behaviour whilst leaving the reproductive faculty unimpaired. '(Display) is probably derived from sexual activity, but it is used for social communication and separated from reroductive activity. In other words, genital display is a ritual derived from sexual behaviour but serving social and not reproductive purposes.'

I would deduce from this that, although display may have sexual connotations in its service to the feminine reproductive aspect, it also has masculine spiritual connotations—the establishment of individual status and identity.

This phenomenon reminds me of the experience in the Oxford Street clothing store which I mentioned at the beginning of the book. It indicates that the search by the shoppers was basically motivated by either one or both of two distinct concerns—the feminine, utilitarian concern for protection and comfort and the masculine, individual concern for competitive display and status. Apropos that episode, and the South American Indian one as well, it becomes evident that the connection between clothing and modesty is an artificial and superimposed convention, usually promoted by the religious establishment in the name of decency but really nothing to do with spiritual aspiration. The supposed association of hiding the body with modesty and decency is at best absurd and at worst, provocative, troublesome and inhibiting.

One of the most pathetic sights I saw in South America was a young Indian woman who lived with her tribe close to a Roman Catholic mission. The priests were deliberately attempting to replace the tribe's traditional and 'barbaric' way of life with a more 'civilised' mode of living. By giving the tribe food and other gifts, the Indians were well on the way to becoming totally dependent on the mission's support. They had been introduced to the concept of doing work for the mission in exchange for food and they had also been prevailed upon to wear clothing (though whether they had been given and could comprehend a reason for doing so I cannot tell). The men wore old shirts and shorts and the women a kind of simple shift which was tied round the chest above the breasts and fell to about knee length. This particular woman I saw one day was attempting to carry out a traditional thread-spinning task which involved rotating a stick by running it up and down her thigh with the palm of the hand. Since the garment prevented her doing this and kept getting in her way, she had rolled it up and was keeping it clear of the front of her body by holding it with her upper arms under her armpits.

The second thread or piece of relevant evidence is derived from the fact that neuroanatomists have discovered that the nerve and muscular mechanisms responsible for the swelling and erectile response in the female and male genitals are quite different from those involved in the orgastic climax—which for the male results usually in the ejaculation of sperm. The latter function involves the autonomic nervous system (more primitive, less controllable by self-will) and the former the parasympathetic nervous system (less primitive, subject to greater control or interference from the cortex).

This separation of the erotic prelude or foreplay (sensual pleasure-seeking and display) from the orgastic climax (self-abandonment, procreative) is highly significant for this theme. It is strong evidence for what I have called the masculine, individual, pleasure aspect of sexuality being differentiated from the feminine, group, procreative aspect of sexuality.

It throws light on several psychological difficulties which are encountered as the child progresses through puberty and adolescence to adulthood.

In passing, it places a perspective on masturbation, especially self-masturbation. The emphasis here tends to be on the male because he has to cope with the inexorable formation within him of that which has to be ejaculated. Having no commensurate, climactic emission, the female does not have the same compulsion to find relief; for her, masturbation is a casual, pleasure-seeking activity only.

Understandably, modern psychiatry has veered towards the view that masturbation is acceptable, because, in social conditions where intercourse is not readily and conveniently possible, permission to relieve tension is considered preferable to the possible repercussions of repression.

Nevertheless, masturbation, by the male especially, has long association with sin, and guilt about it can be very deep-seated. Even definition of it in *The Concise Oxford Dictionary*—'Practise self-abuse'—carries clear bias towards its being wrong. Obviously, the establishment religious censure can be very influential in moulding social attitudes towards such practices, especially if such influence is orientated in favour of the feminine, group-survival dispensation—i.e., towards social order, discipline of the group, marriage and procreation of the species.

But, in terms of pleasure-seeking as distinct from reproductive responsibility, the guilt may have deeper, more primitive, instinctive roots. The implication of seeking sexual relief and pleasure through masturbation is that it is indirectly at the expense of the feminine procreative, and may even amount to an active rejection of it.

It is not my intent to pass judgement one way or the other. Even if it were a 'black and white' issue, it is still essential for the individual to come to his or her decision according to circumstances. I would go so far as to suggest that danger lies in excess. It is possible that excess could lead to a habit so strong that it may impede the individual's later ability to reconcile the masculine-feminine in himself or herself (through failure to take on commitment and responsibility to the feminine) and also, concurrently, the ability in the male especially to establish heterosexual relationships beneficial to the female.

Exploitation of the feminine by the masculine (self-indulgent pleasure-seeking at the expense of oneself and of another) and rejection of the feminine by the masculine (through fear of emasculation, castration or impotence) are directly related to the perverse masculine drive to kill and destroy negatively. This applies in the female as well as the male, though it is more likely to manifest in the latter. (I am, of course, speaking above primarily psychological rather than literal effects.)

With the inception of self-consciousness in the human being during childhood—with its increasing, concomitant awareness of sex differentiation—all the aforementioned features of brain function seem to intensify. It is as if the whole system changes gear in aticipation of puberty. The division between the sexes widens as the masculine-right hemisphere, activating the feminine-left, begins to pressure and interfere, questioning the social expectations and beliefs inculcated during early years.

Self-consciousness, emanating from the right, heralds the beginning not only of stronger, will-directed search for self-gratification but also the ability to objectify and think in abstract. It also stimulates and awakens the creative imagination and prompts spontaneous ideas and fantasies.

It may give rise to strange and illogical remarks—illogical, that is, in the sense that they are often made suddenly and unexpectedly, totally out of the context of whatever is going on at the time. I know, for example, a girl who, when she was about six years old, was enjoying a relaxing bath when she suddenly said to her mother: 'I don't really think I am born yet . . . I am waiting to be born. . . .'

I am sure it is important that the parent, or any adult to whom such remarks are made by children, should not ignore such an observation, and should certainly not dismiss it as simply amusing or absurd. It is not easy to answer but at least the child should be able to appreciate that he or she has been seriously listened to.

Most likely, the passing question or reflection of this nature will not be expressed to anyone. They may well, for example, occur privately, as when the child is lying in bed about to go to sleep or has just woken up—i.e., when the left-hemisphere functioning is more quiescent than during daily activity.

Often the remarks or reflections will have something to do with self and identity, revolving around such questions as 'Who am I?', 'Where did I come from?', 'What happens when I die?'

Their sudden intervention in the child's mind can be bewildering, even fearful. They are of the deepest spiritual importance. If they are expressed to someone, then that person should provide reassurance at least. The child needs above all to be able to trust; the fear will then be assuaged; but the child will not forget the nature of the response. The presence or absence of response and reassurance will be deeply impressed in memory.

Fear of the unknown and the threat to the existential being evoked by the sudden intervention of an inner question such as 'Who am I?' signify the 'conception' in the carnal human being of the 'regenerate' man. It is like a masculine impregnation from the right hemisphere which sows the seed of the new individual in the feminine left. It is the prerequisite fertilisation which will gestate and give rise to the birth of spirituality at puberty.

'Who am I?' . . . masculine, spiritual; 'I will die' . . . feminine, fatal. Contained within these two expressions is the whole panoply of the twin-aspected life. The masculine, spiritual challenge to aspire to the great quest of life—self realisation; and the feminine response which invokes the desire to ensure continuity through procreation of the species, generation after generation.

However, the child, experiencing these first stirrings of the right hemisphere, is not equipped to comprehend the import of what he or she is experiencing. The activity of mundane life all around is analgesic at this impressionable age. The fear or bewilderment will soon be covered over by the everyday concerns of achieving pleasure and avoiding pain. The spark of desire for the knowledge of real identity is submerged under the flood of information about the world. The child heads inexorably for the engulfing emotions of puberty and the need to establish personality.

8 Puberty and education; success and failure

Physiologically, the manifestations of puberty are well-known and obvious.

'Spirit', as instinctive knowledge, continues to control the systems and automatic functions whilst informing the final burst of growth towards maturity.

The body changes shape and the pubic hair gows. In the female, the breasts develop and the pelvic girdle expands preparing the girl for motherhood. These changes of configuration tend to produce an hour-glass shape which can be accentuated by slimness of waist. In the male, facial hair grows and the voice breaks (though these effects vary in degree from race to race). The tendency is for the overall male shape to be tapered like an inverted triangle from shoulders downwards. The muscles in the male are usually less sheathed with fat than the female so that she tends towards a softer and more curvaceous appearance. Also, she has a lower centre of gravity, indicative of her being 'closer or more committed to the earth'.

I listened last year to a radio programme[9] in which four experts discussed their experience and understanding of puberty as they encounter it in their professional work. It was generally agreed that puberty represented a 'metamorphosis' during which the capacity to reproduce emerges, signalled in the male by the forming and emission of sperm and in the female by the release of ova from the ovaries and the start of menstruation.

The events leading up to these anatomical transformations and climactic discharges are complicated and mysterious. A number of glands are known to be actively engaged in its evolution—for example, the pituitary, the adrenal and the pineal—but it is not known what causes or triggers the co-ordinated and amazing effects of their secretions.

Listening to these experts, I was fascinated by the information they were broadcasting. I think 'fascinated' is an appropriate word because listening to information about a mysterious experience which we all go through absorbs our interest in a 'spell-binding' fashion. This I take to be the hunger of the left hemisphere for what is assumed to be real knowledge. The feminine left is imbued with the desire for the truth but looks for it in worldly information.

At the same time, however, there was another part of the mind—the masculine-right—which was objecting strongly.

In retrospect, the kind of commentary or assessment of the programme derived in response to the information could be reconstructed as follows:

These experts in this field of research into human behaviour admit that they do not know what *causes* puberty. They imply by what they say that it is only a matter of time and more research before the cause will be understood. This strikes me as demonstrating an amazing optimism, even an absurd ignorance. Why do I suspect such delusion? Because observation and experience have taught me that what are called 'causes' are inevitably simply effects. I might say that rain causes me to get wet; but being wet is really an effect of being in the rain; it does not explain what causes rain to be wet.

What is the point in looking for the so-called *cause* of puberty?

It may be that in due course a finer, subtler and more elaborate explanation (description of effect) of puberty will be formulated than the present one couched in terms of hormonal secretion of glands, etc. But after proposing that there is feature X which precipitates activation of the glands, it will then be deemed necessary to discover that which causes activation of feature X. We are back in one of those ever-receding processes—which will perhaps eventually take us through to molecular and atomic explanations. And the same impasse will be reached as that in subatomic physics. Cause and effect will eventually elide in a 'statistical law of probability'. Just as it is probable that for no known reason an electron will periodically make a quantum jump into another orbit so the conclusion will be ineluctably drawn that puberty is just a statistically probable phenomenon which occurs after a certain duration of life.

Such is the limitation of feminine linear and sequential thinking which eventually has to admit a characteristically masculine "negative-positive"—that the cause can never be known. It is only possible to describe effects and deduce laws which then allow for a certain predictability of behaviour.

The feminine has to surrender in the end to the inexorable realisation—and I emphasise this principle of surrender of the feminine as being crucial later in the spiritual context—that the

Ultimate Cause cannot be known in the way that a fact of information may be learned and subsequently recognised. Explanations are delusive fabrications of self-will. They obscure the reality of the situation. They are man-invented, become fashionable, serve temporarily, fall into disrepute and are then discarded. To be fascinated by them and to believe them is to commit oneself to illusion.

'We are, *in effect,* none the wiser.'

This commentary demonstrates a certain over-reaction and frustration in the masculine assessment. It shows how exasperation can escalate into rejection of the feminine. The essence of it is objective and correct but emotion has lent it a corrupting arrogance. The masculine tends to dismiss the intrinsic value of the feminine contribution—that explanation or description of effect is crucial to understanding the law and the realisation of limitation and untruth. It is nevertheless crucial that the masculine does not mistake explanation for truth.

Referring back to the earlier table of characteristics of left and right hemisphere functioning, the above commentary throws some light on the rather curious assignment of optimism and pessimism to left and right respectively.

The feminine left tends to exhibit an over-confidence that problems can be resolved in mundane, logical and material terms; it is only a question of more research and more information, for example. This frustrates the masculine which sees this as a route to either temporary respite, compromise or even 'nowhere'; it becomes angry that the feminine can be so short-sighted and naive. This frustration frequently escalates to anger and violence if the masculine is unable to provide a more effective answer!

It would be more appropriate for the masculine to become more compassionate. The feminine is doing what it is programmed to do. The masculine should be more aware (become more conscious) that its superior view has been born of its observation of the feminine. In other words, the masculine's comprehension can only arise as a result of its objective appraisal of the feminine functioning. It is only through the feminine searching for a describable cause that the masculine can take the quantum jump of realising that the Ultimate Cause cannot be described as a fact.

It is only through elimination of all that God *cannot be* that it can be understood what God *is.*

Puberty and education; success and failure

The physical process of reaching puberty is of course gradual but fulfilment of its purpose is usually accepted as occurring around the age of fourteen—usually earlier in the female than the male, thereby again indicating the more urgent degree of commitment of the female towards the procreative purpose. Or, perhaps one should admit, the greater reluctance on the part of the male.

Although fourteen is the average, the age of puberty can range between twelve and sixteen. It is generally accepted that adverse environmental conditions—such as dietary deprivation or stress—can be retarding factors. There appears to be no suggestion that environmental influences can advance the process but it is noted that there is a direct correlation between 'degree of maturity' in the child of four of five and the onset of puberty. I infer this to mean not just physical development but the intelligence, 'brightness' and awareness of the child—its transition from being a purely receptive (feminine-left) organism to its actively exploring and engaging with its environment (masculine-right). If so, I suggest that there is indication here of the direct bearing of spirituality (intelligence, consciousness) on sexuality (procreative maturity).

Although the physical development is gradual, the first emission of sperm and the first blood of menstruation are sudden and momentous events. No matter how well forewarned, the sensations of the first emission and the first sight of blood are dramatic, personal experiences. In that moment, a new dimension of desire and fear is precipitated—a 'mattering' of life and death, sperm and blood.

One way of expressing this new dimension of desire and fear is in terms of success and failure.

In spiritual terms, the desire in the masculine is for success whilst the fear in the feminine is of failure. (It is worth noting that a desire is directional quest *for* something; a fear is a static apprehension *of* something.)

In terms of sexuality, this manifests in reverse. (If the reason for this reversal is not already anticipated by the reader, then it should become apparent when we come to the second 'half' of the life cycle.) The desire in the feminine is for success whilst the fear in the masculine is of failure.

To pursue this manifestation in terms of the physically differentiated male and female, I am now having to propose a psychological differentiation also. This I would call a psychological tendency to 'polarize'. For example, what manifests as active desire in one corresponds to a passive fear in the other. The differentiation is subtle but definite; perhaps in the context of desire and fear it is most easily distinguishable.

Thus, in the male, the feminine desire to succeed in impregnating the female is passive in relation to the active masculine fear in him of failing to do so. This active fear is related to self-preservation—the possible loss of virility and individual identity, both of which are inherent in the ejaculation and self-abandonment of orgasm; hence the fear of possible impotency, emasculation and castration. Compared with this fear (which the female must assuage and overcome), the actual desire to procreate is passive. This is not to say that the desire for erotic pleasure is passive. As already pointed out, the neural and muscular mechanisms associated with erotic pleasure are quite different from those employed in the reproductive aspect of coition. The ability of the female to assuage the male's fear and to entice him to copulate is essentially dependent on her disposition to stimulate him erotically in the first place. This leads, incidentally, to the projection that the employment of contraception during intercourse is a means of satisfying the 'mutually-masculine' desire for pleasure whilst avoiding the feminine procreative responsibility.

In the female, the feminine desire to succeed in being impregnated is active in relation to the passive masculine fear in her of failing to be so. The desire is normally manifest in her seducing the male to give his virility for her reproductive fulfilment. Concomitant with this, there is the passive masculine fear in her that she will be rejected and abandoned. This passive fear can become active if, in the spiritual aspect, she fears that her individuality is being exploited or violated; in that condition, her sexuality is suppressed and gives rise to 'frigidity'.

	MALE		FEMALE	
	masculine	*feminine*	*masculine*	*feminine*
SPIRITUAL (Individual, private)	desire for success (active)	fear of failure (passive)	desire for success (passive)	fear of failure (active)
SEXUAL (Social, public)	fear of failure (active)	desire for success (passive)	fear of failure (passive)	desire for success (active)

Puberty and education; success and failure

Needless to say, these two threads of sexuality and spirituality are so subtly interwoven in the psyche that it is very difficult to disentangle and distinguish them. However, if it is persevered with and recognised in experience, then I think it throws useful light, in principle, on the nature of the left-right dichotomy within each individual and also on the nature of male-female relationships.

In the broad terms of sexuality (procreative, social, public), it suggests that it is the feminine which dominates, leads and succours whilst it is the masculine responsibility to serve and support. In the spiritual aspect, these roles are reversed; it is the masculine which dominates, leads and succours and the feminine which serves and supports.

This is corroborated by two aphorisms I have among collected notes. The first is an observation in general worldly terms (and I do not know to whom it is attributable): 'A man thinks he ought to be a success; a woman thinks she will be a failure.' The second is in individual spiritual terms and I believe it to be attributed to Gautama Buddha: 'Man looks for God; woman looks for God in Man.'

Bearing this psychological 'polarisation' in mind, it is now possible to pursue the sexual and spiritual implications of puberty.

Whatever the deep psychological significances of the onset of puberty—reaching right back to the hind and midbrain principles of self-preservation and reproduction—the behavioural and emotional changes are more obvious. 'Childish things are put away.' Fear of mortal death and the desire for immortality recede into the background as the business of fulfilment in the world is actively undertaken.

Inevitably, adolescence is dominated by sexuality in the sense that the influences commonly brought to bear on the individual persuade him or her to conform to the social norm. Put in simple terms, this means that the dominant concensus of persuasion is towards indoctrination of the belief that fulfilment is to be found ultimately in terms of successful marriage and child-rearing. I am not saying this is the only influence, especially in recent decades in modern industrialised nations; but it is still traditionally the dominant one.

Its strength lies in its appeal to the feminine, in both male and female. Conforming to the traditional pattern provides security. The feminine is reassured by the familiar; finds comfort in habit, personal possessions and the repetition of rituals; follows regime and routine; enjoys receiving encouragement and affection, dresses for warmth and comfort, seeks to establish its own unthreatened territory, its home. The establishment of a secure base is a natural and beneficial prerequisite for the stable development of the individual which should follow; in particular it inculcates by example the importance of providing such safety and protection for succeeding generations. The possible danger of it is that it may be excessively maternal and lead to smothering or emasculation of the masculine.

In adolescence, the masculine in both male and female begins the search for identity and status. Since the weight of persuasion tends to be towards finding this identity and status in the world's terms, emphasis is placed on developing the strengths of personality, compensating the weaknesses, and focussing on the means of achieving the highest possible status. The masculine calls on the individual to venture 'alone' into new territory, to explore in numerous ways, to find and test new relationships, to be inventive and take initiatives, to compete against others, to dress in order to signal and create effect, to display gain and superiority, to take on personal responsibility and leadership in group activities.

Primary education for the child is 'preparatory'—directed particularly at preparing and moulding the individual to accept the social norms of behaviour and teaching the basic left-hemisphere techniques and skills of communication. Discipline is effected through the fear of consequence and the promise of reward. Learning is repetitive and imitative memorising of information.

In secondary education for the adolescent, the preparatory methods continue but gradually fade out as the emphasis moves, or should move, to 'public' schooling. Here the focus should be directed towards the importance of working with others in order to become a useful, responsible and contributory member of society. The appeal and stress here is on self-discipline.

A rather subtle, paradoxical and insidious situation can arise in secondary education (and tertiary) where the social environment is agnostic and committed to material gain (feminine). Emphasis *appears* to be put on the individual's development (masculine). The boy or girl is seduced by a 'liberal' environment (little discipline, no uniform, a 'do what you want to do' attitude) into believing that unbridled self-expression (cf. p.54) is the way to self-fulfilment. The bait or bribe is that achievement will result in personal status, wealth and prestige—the proposed ingredients of that self-fulfilment.

Puberty and education; success and failure

In fact, paradoxically, the result can be the reverse effect. The so-called individual self-fulfilment turns out to be no more than a seduction into conforming with the economic machine; undisciplined self-expression turns out to be a pleasure-seeking self-indulgence. This can lead to a frustrating bewilderment because the process has not revealed true self-identity; this frustration can then result in due course either in anti-social behaviour or self-violation.

Unfortunately, in an agnostic, material-gain society, the alternative—a rigid and repressive discipline, such as pertains under certain communist regimes, for example—the resulting effect can be just as disastrous—emasculation. In this situation, any attempt to exert masculinity is called 'dissidence' and is rapidly suppressed.

Balance and correct priority in secondary education—in fact, in all phases of education—can only derive from true understanding of masculine-spiritual purpose. Here it is understood that service to society—for its own sake, not primarily for material gain—is the essential prerequisite for later individual development and fulfilment. The masculine must first serve and support the feminine in order to realise its own true masculinity.

The stability, efficiency and health of the society or group is the essential base from which to explore the means to true self-fulfilment. The danger is that *excessive* persuasion towards fortune and fame (feminine 'desire for success' playing on masculine 'fear of failure' in terms of sexuality) is likely to be counter-productive in spiritual terms. Excessive pursuit of fortune can become obsessive and corrupting, and I very much doubt whether worldly fame is conducive to discovering true identity. Neither fortune nor fame have been proved to be deeply or lastingly fulfilling in themselves and evidence suggests that the pursuit and maintaining of them give rise to debilitating anxieties and tensions. Nevertheless, it should be pointed out that the emphasis here is on the consequences of *excess*. It is inevitable that someone taking his adult place in the world will be tempted and fall initially for their seductive promise. As I shall be proposing later, it is the very disenchantment and disillusion resulting from the failure of these pursuits to provide happiness that constitutes the first real, conscious movement towards spirituality.

Good secondary education should begin to provide the means of being able to cope with the difficulties which are inevitably going to arise in adult life, especially the disenchantment and disillusionment which will occur in various forms and guises. Essentially, this aspect of secondary education will begin to cater for and exercise the powers of the masculine-right hemisphere.

Self-consciousness gives rise, as already mentioned, to objectivity. This means the ability 'to throw in front of'; i.e., the ability to observe 'from a distance'. This is very important because it implies that 'something' which observes has separated out from or transcended that which is under observation. I would call this observer the 'I'—the inner witness, the source of consciousness. I have also suggested that this feature is a very significant development in spiritual terms and that it is associated with masculine-right hemisphere functioning. The emergence of the 'I'—which could be described as 'a withdrawal of consciousness from involvement in matter'—enables a variety of functions in the right hemisphere to operate and I see it as the responsibility of secondary education to exercise them. It is now possible to encourage abstraction of meaning from information. The study of history or literature is now not just a case of memorising facts and stories but drawing deeper meanings from them. Mathematics and science subjects are not just figures, formulae, theoretical models and processes but demonstration and comprehension of relationships, patterns and laws. This kind of mental exercise encourages the faculties of reasoning, comprehending, considering and synthesising.

I remember reading of a master who said to a pupil who was complaining that he did not see much point in learning what he considered to be useless information: 'You are not at school just to learn facts; you are here mainly to gain a sense of value, a sense of proportion and a sense of humour!' That sums up the essence of educational responsibility to the right hemisphere. The continued learning of information, skills and techniques will no doubt have their applications and uses in later working for a living but they are of secondary importance as far as the individual's happiness and understanding of his life are concerned.

The well-being of the masculine-right hemisphere can be much enhanced during this phase by the appreciation and practice of music, art, poetry and drama. And even though the deep personal questions of life tend to be submerged under all the pressures and diversions of everyday life, there will be some who will want to explore such questions through beginning to take an interest in the work of philosophers, theologians, psychologists, sociologists and so forth. It is a pity if the individual cannot find access to and is not encouraged to consider such material. In this respect, transitory and arbitrary programmes on radio, television and cassette, etc., are of little value; what is needed is personal verbal exchange with teachers, and written texts which can be considered and referred to when the appropriate time is available and the desire strong. This enquiry is essentially private and personal; generalised, impersonal 'feeding' does not satisfy this quest.

The problem is that in a society heavily committed to investment in training economically-viable members, such pursuits as those mentioned above do not have direct practical application to increasing material wealth and are therefore considered at best fringe luxuries and at worst dispensable superfluities. Ironically, they may even gain a reputation as being 'effeminate' interests. In this bias, we may see again a reprise—this time in psychological terms—of 'the fight to be male'. What society tends to regard as manly pursuits in the socio-economic context are really the masculine serving the feminine sexual, procreative purpose. The truly masculine, spiritual purpose is manifest in the work of many of the great philosophers, poets, writers, composers, dramatists, artists and so on. Because the desire for spiritual understanding is active in the male right hemisphere, the majority of outstanding, creative contributors in these fields have been men.

It could be said that such men have frequently tended to work through the inspiration of their right hemispheres at the expense of, or in ignorance of, the feminine left, which is why they have often been social misfits or failures, have gone mad, have suffered domestic upheaval, run into debt, and have ruined their marriages, relationships and themselves through debauchery, drugs, alcohol and other self-destructive practices. It could be said in many of these cases that the feminine-left hemisphere functioning has been unable to cope with the power of the ideas emerging in the masculine-right.

Whereas primary/preparatory education prepares for secondary/public education, the latter prepares for tertiary/university education. This should be based on personal study, self-discipline, creative mental exercise, individual tutoring and group debate. Its horizons should ideally be the limits of the known world, its perspective wide-ranging and all-embracing, and its concerns universal. As the name university implies, such institutions should provide for exploration of the knowledge of the *universe;* they should provide an opportunity for the individual to search for the meaning of life, and not confine him or her to concentrated study of particular and isolated subjects. The essence or spirit of university should call upon Man's most noble and profound spiritual aspirations—to understand Man himself, the world, and how the two are related. 'What is the Universe; who and what am I; what is the nature and purpose of the relationship?

Thus, primary education works through personal, instinctive motivation; secondary education works through group, social, emotional motivation; tertiary education works through universal, individual, intellectual motivation. The first is, in principle learning information through imitation; the second, learning through feeling the meaning; the third, learning through objective reasoning. Of course, it is not so straightforward and clear-cut as that, and each phase will embrace continuation of the one preceding it; but it gives indication of the progression of emphasis. The whole process leads from others being responsible for the person through to the individual becoming self-reliant. It also leads to the emergence of right-hemisphere intuition—a knowing undeniably for oneself, the deepest and purest meaning of conscience. The three phases could be said to be hermaphrodite, feminine and masculine respectively.

As distinct from education as learning how to become an economically-viable member of society, this process should equip the individual to find the way to his or her spiritual destiny through 'waking up to reality'.

If a society ignores this responsibility to the individual, primary education will drift into an easy liberalism or permissiveness, secondary education will extol the virtues of glamour and gaining wealth and prestige, tertiary education will indoctrinate with self-gain ideologies. This alternative results in a failure of individual responsibility (masculinity impotent) and social anarchy (femininity exploited).

9 *The ideal and the perfect; romance and love*

With the onset of puberty, it is as if the emphasis or centre of gravity moves from the primitive hind- and midbrains to the subcortical limbic system. The predominantly instinctive behaviour of infancy and childhood proceeds to an increasingly emotional phase with the emergence of self-consciousness. As already acknowledged, this gives rise to manifold effects. It is not easy in the linear, sequential discipline of writing to convey the simultaneity of these numerous aspects but I trust that the reader will bear this limitation in mind and be able to synthesise an overall picture from the analysis.

Essentially, the effect of the physiological changes at puberty is emotionally experienced. Emotion means a 'flowing out from oneself' so that the overall changeover from childhood to adolescence is one of transition from being inwardly concerned to being outwardly concerned. Self-consciousness is at first very subjective but at puberty it becomes more mature and objective so that it becomes better described as consciousness of self. This promotes steadily growing commitment to the belief in being separate as an independent being. Concomitantly, subjective emotions—which might better be called 'inmotions'—such as embarrassment, fear, uncertainty, frustration and anger tend to be projected or objectified. This gives rise to the tendency, for example, to blame negative feelings on objects 'out there'. The sense of self projects a heightened sense of others and hence the need to share with them, to compete with them, and, negatively, the temptation to blame them for frustration and failure. One of the principal distillations of this situation is a more naked sense of vulnerability and incompleteness which makes desire and fear more urgent and vivid.

The feminine looks to find security through possession of that which will satisfy the desire for completeness. Since the feminine in both male and female is now committed to belief in a particulate, physical world 'out there', it is inevitable that the desire to possess is directed at identifiable, material objectives, or perfection in sensible form. The feminine looks for completion in a centrifugal desire for expansion, total possession, continual reproduction and repetition.

Whereas the feminine in the female becomes actively motivated in sexual terms by desire for success, the masculine in the male becomes actively fearful of failure. The sense of vulnerability in the masculine reaches right back to the primitive urge of self-preservation. Again, being committed to belief in a world of particulate and independent entities, the desire to succeed as an individual focuses on the need to compete. Instinctively the masculine 'knows' that the fittest survive and therefore self-preservation is translated into the need to prove supremacy in whatever field of activity it happens to be engaged in.

I feel sure I do not have to elaborate in detail on the above proposition. In material, sexual, worldly terms, the feminine desire for security and completeness through acquisition and possession and the masculine fear of self-eclipse giving rise to the urge to compete and gain power are manifest right through the manifold expressions of human activity. All this worldly traffic in the interests of economic and social stability and the gaining of power are, as suggested earlier, ultimately associated with, and are played out in, the arena of sexuality. They are all fundamentally based on the feminine purpose of procreation and survival of the species. Rather than embark on more elaborate commentary of this general feature, it is more to the point of this theme to concentrate now on the sexual relationship of male and female. It is in this particular aspect that we may see the possibility of the spiritual conversion whereby the sexual human being aspires to truly spiritual manhood and womanhood.

Commonly (certainly up to recent times), the female is preponderantly committed to the feminine desire for completeness through physical procreation. The masculine fear of failure however is of course present in her and this manifests, for example, in the need to compete with other females. In the human situation of more or less equal numbers of men and women, this need to compete does not so much lie in the sheer necessity of finding any male to impregnate her so much as one who will serve and support her in nurturing the resulting children. The masculine element in her thereby modifies her search in that she needs to attract the ideal man for whom other females may also be competing.

The male on the other hand is ordinarily haunted by the fear of failing to prove his virility, and hence the compulsion to

The ideal and the perfect; romance and love

compete with other males to convince himself and others of his supremacy and ideality. In his pleasure-seeking self-centredness, this would most easily be recognised if he could achieve being able to make love to every female within reach. In a situation where there are as many men as women this is not only very difficult but in feminine-orientated society, especially where monogamy is the rule, pressure and restriction is applied to persuade the male to take responsibility for serving and supporting the resulting family group.

This is potentially highly frustrating because the male's instinct is to be as a bull with a herd of cows or a lion with a pride of lionesses, his mating procilivity only being restricted by natural, external controls of population. This frustration has to be resolved in the human situation where the external controls are far less evident, especially in wealthy industrialised states where they have been largely overcome. The excess male libido therefore has to be diverted or re-directed.

Generally speaking, it is transferred into economic competitiveness, i.e. the persuasion to achieve supremacy in work and career, or competitiveness in pastimes, e.g. sport. In this transfer of sexual energy, we may see the beginnings of the idea that it may be *converted*. As an extension of this, there is then a particular feature of human activity—that the purely sexual energy may be re-directed into non-economic, non-physical pursuits. In other words, further refining of sexual energy leads to the elements of aesthetic content being introduced into human aspiration, most notably, for example in purely intellectual and artistic pursuits. To the extent that such pursuits are *not* applied to the enhancement of blatantly economic gain so they are more likely to be purely spiritual in nature.

Apart from the (usually) predominant masculine fear of failure in the male, he also of course carries the feminine desire to acquire and possess. It is not difficult to see therefore that his sexual competitiveness, diverted towards this feminine aspect of himself, can find outlet in the desire to possess wealth. Economic success in work and career endows him with money and power. This in turn gives him the sense of superiority that he requires over his fellow-males. It may even allow him a certain degree of ability to indulge his frustrated sexuality. If he is not able to do this in actual sexual terms, then he may well indulge in other 'instinctive' outlets such as food, for example. Apart from these 'feminine indulgencies', there are also masculine ones, such as gambling and hunting to kill purely for sport. This diverted means of satisfying the masculine fear of failing to establish male status and superiority can hardly be accounted satisfactory. At best it provides precarious and transitory pleasure; at worst, and in the longer term, it is notoriously corruptive and obsessive, and covers a suppressed or actively desperate discontent and unhappiness. I would suggest that this is a self-destructive proclivity deriving from ignorance of the spiritual aspiration.

In passing, it occurs to me that the above considerations may throw further light on a pair of the hemisphere characteristics listed earlier—that the feminine is centrifugal and the masculine centripetal. At first, this suggested to me that one would expect the female to tend towards outward promiscuity and the male towards inward satisfaction with one partner, whereas, of course, it is generally accepted as being the reverse. It is, however, the feminine which looks for stability, continuity and duration and it is the masculine which is spontaneous, impulsive—perhaps then, the opportunist. On further reflection therefore, I can see the respective proclivities is being justified in that the feminine, from the centrifugally produced circumference would regard the single-centre, ideal-man focus as being symbolic of security. On the other hand, the masculine, from its centripetally established self-centredness, would regard the whole domain around as accessible as a means of reflecting back its god-like autocracy and superiority. Thus the female only needs to concentrate on the single impregnation to be fulfilled whereas the male would derive satisfaction from exploiting a plurality of females.

I would emphasise however that the above commentary is only in terms of the overall feminine context of sexuality. In the spiritual aspect, the masculine in both male and female represents the one central deity (centripetal) whilst the feminine is in service to the whole creation (centrifugal).

The sense of vulnerability and incompleteness, which begins in earnest during adolescence, stimulates the search for status and security. Though this may find its expression in a thousand human activities, it is the purely sexual one that carries the naked power; all other forms of attempt at fulfilment *in worldly terms* tend to be subsidiary to, or even substitutes for, fulfilment in sexual terms with a partner. This is particularly so for the adolescent. He or she may have been introduced to, and have found a strong sympathy for, a

The ideal and the perfect; romance and love

form of artistic or intellectual expression—interests which will be highly important in later spiritual development. But usually, and naturally, these will tend to be passive or subsidiary to the sexual drive which focuses on fulfilment through a partner. Apart from the possible aesthetic interests therefore, the adolescent concentrates attention and activity towards finding and attracting this partner.

What we might call 'a mystical alchemy' takes place in this quest and fulfilment of partnership. The process whereby one accepts or rejects another defies logical or rational analysis. This is because, though it is likely to be played out in sexual terms, it is in essence a direct reciprocal of the spiritual quest. It involves a 'supernatural magic' reminiscent of the transactions of the gods and goddesses in Greek mythology or the lovers in Shakespeare's *A Midsummer Night's Dream,* suspended somewhere between heaven and earth.

One ingredient of this that must be considered at this point—associated with the masculine-right's functions of imagination and visualisation—is the ability to conceive of there being perfection.

It seems to me that this perfection is rarely, if ever, imagined in formal detail. The feminine left may make attempt to express it as the ideal—in artistic representation, for example—but it remains vague and elusively unrealised. This is especially so in terms of human relationship and in particular in that of the ideal or perfect sexual partner. Some assessing function, comparing the immediate experience of another person with a diffuse and hidden pattern of criteria, rejects or accepts that person as being potentially ideal or perfect. (The female looks for the ideal, the male for the perfect. The masculine conveys the idea which must be perfected or 'made through' the feminine.)

This spiritual quest for the perfect or the ideal does not seem to apply to the majority of lesser creatures where mating is simply a matter of responding to sensory signals, especially smell; any pairing will do providing the conditions are conducive. And yet some creatures pair off and remain together. How can such a selection of mate be said to operate? If the selection is purely fortuitous then why do they choose to remain together? Can a swan, for example, be said to look for an ideal or perfect mate and do they, once paired, 'decide' to stay together? Can there be said to be a 'spiritual' element in their fidelity to each other? And whilst on the subject of other creatures, what may be said of the fact that certain more intelligent animals—

the dog and the horse, for example—are amenable to becoming domesticated whilst others are not? May there be a 'spiritual' element in their forsaking the natural, wild state and acceding to man's desire that they should obey, work and be companions for him? Is this in a lower estate the parallel of the monk who forsakes the affairs of the world to devote himself to a higher ideal?

Whatever the explanations may be in the lower kingdoms, the pairings of people, sexual or otherwise, seem to be conditioned by self-generated criteria of the ideal or perfect partner or friend. These may range from admiration of physical attributes with aesthetic and/or erotic associations, through physical and mental talents, abilities and interests to intellect, wisdom, character and disposition. The permutations of these ingredients are of course enormous and it is perhaps fortunate that one's ability to visualise the ideal and the perfect is not too detailed and critical. Somehow, all the signals go into the brain's 'computer' for assessment and out comes a positive or negative decision. The decision may of course be tentative, awaiting qualification in the light of further experiential evidence! If this assessment process continues to produce positive response then the partnership or friendship strengthens and endures. In the case of the exchange at the immediate sexual level, and possibly spiritual also, a certain spell or dream operates and the attraction, or repulsion, is spontaneous and immediate, often ignoring and overriding the slower analytical process, which may vainly protest! Such assignations of love, sexual or spiritual, operate at a masculine, archetypal level and are not to be gainsaid at the level of mortal machinations. Thus, lovers are often deemed foolish in the eyes of their fellow men.

Undoubtedly, the perfect and the ideal concepts are conditioned by worldly experience as the feminine hemisphere attempts to depict and formulate their manifestation. The impression I gather is somewhat analogous to the genetic pairings of chromosomes at conception. Each person inherits a range of characteristic, instinctive strengths and weaknesses which are to some extent modified and imposed upon by experience in life. In encounter with another person, this range of factors is paired off with the complementary range in the other. According to the degree of compatibility—whether through similarities or compensating differences—there will be a commensurate degree of mutually supportive, constructive and stimulating communication. If this does not happen, the encounter will either be sterile or even hostile.

However, the point to be made is that this selection process is ever-haunted by a persistent demand that ideally it should be a guide to the perfect. Maybe this is something which is subtly or overtly inculcated through parent and teacher. We are told, for example, that we have behaved well or badly. In relation to what? In relation to the idea that we could consistently behave perfectly. Or we achieve a certain percentage of marks in an exam paper; this implies that we have fallen short of being one hundred per cent perfect. Whether we are simply conditioned to it or not, it must still be based on what appears to be an exclusively human idea—that there is a perfection to be attained. This is a spur to human endeavour and the belief that it may be achieved in worldly terms is like a mirage in the desert luring us ever onwards.

With the onset of puberty and the arousal of sexual energies, the search for the ideal and the perfect becomes a strongly emotional charge. The adolescent does not readily compromise and does not heed possible consequences. The male searches for his perfect heroine, his goddess, and the female for her ideal hero, her incarnate god.

This is of course the essence of romance. It is the masculine-right which conjures up the dream-ideal in response to which the feminine casts the spell of perfection. This dream-spell may overpower any sense of reason in the masculine-right and smother any common sense 'reality' learned by the feminine-left.

It may seem surprising at first to consider that it is the masculine-right in the male which projects the dream since it is commonly women who are said to be romantic. But this is not so according to this model. The inexperienced masculine in the male envisages the quest in sexual forms—even though this search is spiritual in essence, it being a representation of the desire for truth and true identity. The masculine uses familiar imagery to give expression to the self-reassuring need of the male to see himself as hero or god-like knight setting forth to find the heroine or maiden-goddess imprisoned in her earthbound limitation and committed to mundane labour from which he will successfully rescue her and transport her to his kingdom where she will be happy evermore. The feminine in the female reciprocates and reflects the male role in this romantic dream of liberation through casting around her the enchantment which will attract the ideal male in her direction.

If paradise were meant to be on earth, then the romantic dream fulfilled in sexual terms would be enough. But it is only half the story. The feminine in the male (the black knight) does not have courage in the heart and is reluctant and fearful that it will fail in this undertaking, and will itself fall into bondage. It is safer and easier to indulge in selfish pleasures, especially using women for that purpose when opportunity occurs; it is more comfortable and secure to 'stay at home' within his own defences (his castle).

But the feminine in the female (the evil witch) is powerful and applied, desirous of that which will bring it fulfilment in earthly terms, regardless of the danger to which it will expose the innocent and romantic masculine. It casts its spell of fascination, encouraging the masculine to believe that the dream can be perfected. This feminine only desires to bind the masculine to its service; the masculine dream can never come true in these feminine terms.

I admit that the above may sound somewhat exaggerated and over-dramatic but I venture to suggest that the adult married male may well feel the threat with that degree of intensity (as indeed may the masculine in the female when it feels bound and frustrated by the domestic situation). The desperate threat of emasculation that this bondage can create reminds me of the macabre fate of the male praying mantis. The female often responds to the sexual overtures of the smaller male by biting off his head. The decapitated male, *in extremis,* manages to complete the act of copulation. As if to underline there being no further use for the male and to complete his suicidal annihilation, the female then proceeds to eat what is left of him.

In strongly disciplined feminine societies and groups, where pre-marital intercourse is, theoretically at least, forbidden, and the opportunity for sexual indulgence is therefore less easy to come by, the romantic dream is more effective in carrying the masculine to commitment. In a permissive environment, the feminine fulfilment and security is threatened by the masculine licence to hunt simply for pleasure. This in turn threatens the whole structure and fabric of a social stability based simply on procreation and economic expansion for it undermines the bonds of marriage and family.

Nevertheless, however illusory the romantic dream may be and however doomed it may be to fail under the rigours, stress and demands of mundane life, it is spiritual in essence and should serve a significant purpose during adolescence. Experience of romantic love, with its accompanying ecstasies and despairs, should prepare the individual for the perception of the nature of true love, with its accompanying trials in spiritual instead of sexual terms.

In the infant and child, love tends to be represented by affection. I use this word to indicate an instinctive, spontaneous response of gratitude and attraction towards that which is providing reassurance, comfort and security. This display may well contain both an unconditional self-surrendering to the source of the giving and also the self-interested motive of eliciting continuation and repetition of that giving. In principle, it is an intuitive, instinctive reflex mechanism associated with self-preservation. In it are the roots of the desire to acquire and possess and the fears of loss and rejection.

With self-consciousness, and hence the feeling of being separate, there comes the more intense sense of vulnerability and incompleteness. Desire to possess and fear of loss intensify and it is in response to the latter that negative emotions such as anger, jealousy and covetousness can be raised to a new pitch of power. This increases the general level of anxiety and tension in the psycho-physiological system; and it is worth noting that *fear* is always at the root of aggression.

With puberty and sexual maturity, the focus of attention changes as self-consciousness objectifies to become consciousness of self as a separate and independent individual. Whereas the child looked 'inwards' to parent, home and the familiar to provide the means of assuaging the sense of vulnerability and incompleteness, the adolescent turns 'outwards' to look for the satisfaction to be provided through contact and exchange with the sexual partner and the world in general. Having identified with a particular person as the potential source of this satisfaction, and having received sympathetic response, the dance begins. The sense of vulnerability intensifies even further and the desire to possess, combined with the fear of rejection and abandonment, promotes a certain madness. Thus the nature of love at this stage can be powerfully possessive and the threat of loss can provoke fearful emotions of hate, anger and jealousy. Though this kind of love and hate with its associated emotions may well continue through the later phases of adult life in the sexual context, the more stable adult is better able to cope with it, either through development of reason in the right hemisphere of the cortex or through the ability to devise defences and diversions. For the young adolescent there is little protection and such experiences deeply impress. It is hardly surprising—given that the ectasy and joy of it tends to be outweighed by anxiety, pain and disappointment—that there is temptation to resort to artificial means of tranquilisation and to alternative forms of pleasure-giving stimulation or escape.

Yet, for all the emotional turbulence of love in the sexual context, the experience of wholly concentrated identification with another in a romantic and totally self-contained dream can elicit the essential characteristics, in 'embryonic' form, of true, spiritual love. These features are, for example, worship, devotion, self-surrender and self-sacrifice.

The spur of love, in whatever context or form, is the desire to satisfy incompleteness. At first it seems that the incompleteness can be satisfied by acquiring and possessing the finite totality (centrifugal, feminine); this proves to be an impossibility. This form of love may however be converted. Ideally, and apparently paradoxically—though understandably since it is a conversion or inversion of the original—fulfilment of spiritual love resides in the 'opposite' direction. This requires the realisation, through disillusionment, that completeness derives from not desiring to possess anything. It is a sacrifice and surrender of all, including one's so-called self, to the dimensionless, indescribable, unlocatable, incomparable, ineffable centre or source—the deity (masculine, centripetal).

The fulfilment of this spiritual alternative is, I suggest, a direct reciprocal of the sexual where the reflection of the mystical union with the godhead is represented by self-abandonment at the highest pitch of human love where each is willing to annihilate himself in merging with the loved one.

The deep and tragic poignancy of human love is that it is earthbound and timebound. Its most ecstatic heights are confined to the momentous and momentary climaxes—the 'little deaths'—of erotic love; its tragic end is in mortal death—in romantic extreme, in the suicide pact of lovers. But this is to perceive human fate from the aspect of sexuality only. The spiritual aspect is quite different. Here the individual surrenders himself or herself to the Unknown and Almighty Source in an ecstasy of annihilation—a voluntary and therefore 'suicidal' dying to mortality. Mortality is an involuntary fate, immortality a voluntary destiny.

Emotionally, fear is assuaged, desire satisfied and security enhanced in the acts of worship and devotion—in any context, religious or otherwise.

I have already mentioned adulation in the context of romantic love but of course the 'object' of worship may take many forms other than the ideal or perfect partner. The principle is the same however—the desire to satisfy the sense of incompleteness through identification with the superlative.

During adolescence—and earlier—this worship is understandably likely to take effect at the physical/sexual end of the continuum—towards the virile, athletic and brave hero and the nubile, enchanting and beautiful heroine.

These heroes and heroines perform, display and compete in numerous arenas, one of the most prevalent and obvious being in sport, particularly for the male aspirant. It is no doubt appropriate that so many competitive games involve balls, goals, penetration of defence, accuracy of aim, etc. The hero in this context is of course as likely to be admired by the male as the female and elicit the worship of the younger male especially. This takes us back to discussion of the primitive brain and the display behaviour of the squirrel monkey. The male in competition is as likely to be reassuring himself of his superiority among males as intending to impress the females. It is the excellence of the winner that the younger male admires and wishes to emulate. This aspect also accounts for the active dislike among many women of watching sport; they see, as it were, nothing in it for them! It also accounts perhaps for the opinion that athletic heroes make poor lovers; that would be the case if their motivation is male dominance rather than reproductive fitness.

Another opportunity for worship is provided by the performers of popular music and dance. In this case, the female more actively participates as the pelvic rhythms and romantic lyrics are overtly redolent of the ideal sexual union and hence reproductive fulfilment. A far more spiritual content is evident in ballet, for example, where the emphasis is on self-discipline, co-ordination and integration of the body and romantic enactments (primarily in classical ballet).

Yet another opportunity is presented through the fictions of stage, television and cinema screen. (I use the word 'fiction' in the sense that the spectator or audience experiences emotions vicariously. No matter how 'true to life' the situations and people depicted, they are not actual and real for the spectator. This applies also to documentary, news or information programmes.) These fictions provide a continual parade of heroes and heroines, cowards and villains, who fascinate, enchant and repel as they triumph or succumb in their adventures and trials. Entertainment supplies heroes for both females and males, and heroines for both males and females, i.e. both sexual and spiritual images for both sexes.

In passing, the insidious problem created by these vicarious, two-dimensional enactments (even the stage requires an illusion or falsification of space and perspective) is that it may become more comfortable and secure (passive, feminine) to spend excessive time and life sitting, watching and living through the adventures and trials of others than to experience and learn to cope with the actual, three-dimensional challenges of one's own life (active, masculine). Inevitably, excessive reliance on entertainment, as a means of escaping from the responsibility of the present moment, leads to atrophy. It develops a gradual anaesthesia and insulation which, in turn, forces the media to concentrate increasingly on supplying more and more sensational and stimulating images. This means focusing increasingly on the most primitive emotional content— such as sex, violence, death, catastrophe, competition.

This is not to suggest that all entertainment is totally negative. On the contrary, in moderation it can be beneficial relief and relaxation, especially humour and music, for example. And there can be educative and spiritual element in genuine attempts to inform, instruct and demonstrate the lessons to be drawn from the drama of life.

Unfortunately, no matter how well intended and sincere the inspirational, intellectual content (masculine), it is very difficult for it to survive against the attraction of the vicarious, fictional, emotional excitation (feminine). Even in this context, it is possible to discern 'the fight to be male'.

10 Transition from sexuality to spirituality

As indicated by the nature of the physiological effects, the emphasis in puberty and adolescence is on sexuality. The former signifies the ability to reproduce and hence signifies continuity of society or survival of the species. The bias is thus strongly towards feminine domination; even the finest specimen of virility, for all his manly display, is only physically of use as an agent for insemination, as a worker and a defender of the interests of the feminine, procreative pupose. (This is not to say that the masculine spiritual is absent or without influence during this phase, but it is weak and subsidiary.)

Puberty, as signal of the threshold of adulthood, has always been regarded throughout the history of human society as a most important event. This is understandable when it is considered that the strength and continuity of the group population—and its food resources in the environment—are dependent on fertility. It is also understandable that, beginning with the early societies whose religiousness involved pleasing and placating the spirits of nature, there should have been a continuing association of the first emission of sperm and the first menstruation with celebrations and initiatory ceremonies of a religious character.

The sexual, spiritual significance of puberty as an important juncture in the life cycle continued to be acknowledged as societies became more technologically advanced, as activities and occupations became more diverse and sophisticated, and as more elaborate theologies and religious foundations evolved. Though the feminine, sexual, reproductive aspect continued to be included and the mother-goddess, fertility tradition was usually retained in some subsidiary form, the emphasis in the West, generally speaking, shifted gradually to the spiritual significance as inferred by the evolution of the monotheistic, father-god image.

There are many ways of explaining and expressing this complicated transition from feminine to masculine as it emerged in various forms but I must confine myself to the particular terms and principles of this theme and emphasise simply the actual fact that the transition or transformation took place.

Whereas the early focus was on the female goddess of fertility and there was often symbolic representation of the sexual male in service to the feminine ethos (for example, the erect phallus as monolith, totem pole, etc.), this gradually shifted to the concept of the male god of creation and after-life (sometimes with the non-sexual, spiritual female devoted to god worship and service as vestal virgin, virgin mother, and so on).

I suggest that this evolutionary transition or metamorphosis through human history is enacted in the individual life as the sexual, feminine concern and domination of the earlier phases of life should, in the ideal model, change to a masculine, spiritual concern and domination in the later phases.

I would add that to date this transition appears to have taken place through history in only a minority of individuals (bearing in mind that adoption of the monastic life does not conform to the model. That course constitutes rejection or abandonment of the feminine sexual, not fulfilment and transformation of it.) In my view, there is in this present age the possibility of its happening on an unprecedented scale. It is as if the centre of gravity of humanity as a whole is now going through its spiritual adolescent phase. This would mean that the masculine, hitherto dominated *en masse* by the sexual, feminine ethos, will begin to experience genuine, individual, spiritual inspiration which, in turn, will bring about a human renaissance on a scale commensurate with that which has been enjoyed by the materialistic, communist ideology.

As in the adolescent experience of the individual, this renaissance will not be without its turbulance and suffering. Many of the restless phenomena we currently witness in society today—social revolutions, causes and ideologies, claims for rights of equality and opportunity, crises in the expansionist economic system, feminism, homosexuality, abortion on demand, sexual permissiveness, the quest for alternative life styles, alternative technologies mindful of ecological conservation, societies, groups and movements searching for peace, truth, individual understanding—all these are indicative of the quest for self-realisation and are in parallel with the adolescent predicament wherein the masculine individuality seems to be in conflict with, and is being smothered by, the feminine group tradition.

I hope that by now in the development of this theme it is not really necessary to emphasise that this is not a 'male chauvinist' argument.

Male chauvinism is essentially based in sexuality and is exploitive of the female. This proposition transcends that level of behaviour and is saying in effect that we are witnessing a situation which may be likened to the struggle of the spiritual masculine in both the male and the female during adolescence. It is indicative of individual idealism struggling and stirring in an historically feminine-dominated ethos. The anxiety manifest, for example, in the current stance being actively taken by both the feminist and the male homosexual in Western society may be seen to be based on the fear by the masculine in both the female and the male that there is a danger in present society that the individual self (masculine) may be suffocated or smothered by current obsession with material gain, group survival, state control and invasion of privacy.

I further suggest that this proposition is substantiated and indicated by the parallel evolutionary developments of the brain which were discussed earlier. The early phases were dominated by the ancient hind—and midbrain instincts of reproduction and self-preservation. This gave way to increasing influence from the developing, emotional limbic system (whose spiritual expression was the emergence and maintenance of the 'faith' religious). There is then the massive development of the cerebral cortices; first dominantly by the left giving rise to scientific, finite, linear, logical philosophies and systems of thought. This in turn is influenced by the growing power of the right hemisphere with its emphasis on objectivity, intuition, synthesising intelligence and, above all, individual consciousness.

Again, I point out that this describes a gradual shift of the psychical centre of gravity. It is not to say that there were not in the past individuals whose right hemisphere functioning was fully developed. But it could be said that they were apparently few and far between and hence their influence during their lives tended to be small and local (partly also because there were then only limited systems of mass communication). Their inspirational words and works have often survived and serve good purpose centuries after their deaths. The European Renaissance of three or four hundred years ago is an example of such evolution though, of course, it had to be expressed mainly through the emotional, faith-religion ethos of its time.

As far as the adolescent individual is concerned, he or she finds himself or herself in an emotional situation in which the dominant influence, learned by the left hemisphere, draws towards the feminine purpose of proliferation on earth. It is strongly implied by the group system that growth of intelligence through secondary and tertiary education should be directed towards economic expansion (to enable an ever-increasing population of human beings). This is felt to varying degrees, according to sex and the nature of the individual, to be a threat to the free exploration and expression of individual aspiration. This threat with its accompanying frustration will be increasingly experienced during the succeeding phases of life, unless the individual can find a resolution of it. It will reach its highest pitch of intensity in mid-life.

The intervention of the right-hemisphere working is not, of course, totally negative; nor is it necessarily stifled. Signs of its presence are manifest in the adolescent's expression of his or her desire as an individual to do something worthwhile with his or her life—something more challenging and aspiring than commitment to mere physical pleasure, comfort, wealth, procreation and longevity. There emerges, through this development, evidence of an inherent disposition to benefit others. This is represented in its feminine expression as the desire to serve the well-being of one's fellow-men (e.g. being a doctor or a nurse) and in its masculine expression as furthering knowledge and wisdom (through exploring, discovering, inventing, modifying existing deficiencies in the present system in any context).

These aspirations are fundamentally spiritual in nature and they have no doubt played their part throughout history in moulding the religious feature in society. The religious establishment, in its feminine aspect, endeavours through upholding a tradition of morals and laws to encourage the altuistic disposition of man. Whether it provides for the masculine, spiritual aspect—individual fulfilment as distinct from group stability and enhancement—is quite anther matter.

Consciousness of self at puberty and during adolescence, with its concomitant sense of vulnerability and incompleteness, and its arousal of deeply searching question as to the nature and purpose of life, demand a response which it is the responsibility of the elders in society in their wisdom to provide for.

Given that a crucial feature of right-hemisphere functioning is to convey the ideal and that in response it is the left-hemisphere

Transition from sexuality to spirituality

responsibility to perfect that ideal, it is not difficult to deduce one possible reason for the emergence of a concept of a reassuring, fulfilling, abstract, omnipotent, masculine deity.

According to the strength of the religious establishment in general, and the commitment to it of the parents or guardians in particular, the child may be introduced at an early age to the religious ethos of its environment. This will have little meaning for the child but it may well be reassured and become accustomed to the repetition and security of atmosphere, music, chanting, prayer, ritual and ceremony.

At puberty, the boy or girl may then be initiated into adult membership. In the Christian tradition, where it is called 'confirmation', the individual is expected to vow *consciously* his or her loyalty and devotion to the principles, concepts, doctrines and beliefs pertaining to the teaching and example of Jesus of Nazareth. This man demonstrated through his life and acts the ideal manner for the human being to fulfil his or her destiny, through love and service to mankind and acknowledgement of the Almighty God. This is a commitment which, it is promised, will guide the perfect mortal life and lead to the ideal salvation. It speaks of the spiritual or divine essence in every man. It is traditionally one of the faith religions in the sense that the fulfilment is achieved through having the faith or courage to believe steadfastly that such resolution is feasible through devotion of the 'heart' (emotion, love transformed).

As far as the adolescent is concerned, he or she may or may not be attracted to the formal religious representation (though in centuries past, and in present-day societies where intellectual education is not advanced, there may be little or no option or alternative). In principle, the manifest religious establishment is more likely to appeal to the feminine because its formal tradition, its continuity through generations, its historical precedence, its repetitive rituals and ceremonies, its emphasis on procreation (marriage and family), its statutory laws, doctrines and beliefs, its group worship—all correspond with the disposition and characteristics of the left hemisphere. The need for reassurance, security, comfort and stability is met through such religious practice—which is why I suggest that the religious *establishment* plays a *feminine,* serving role in society—appropriately so.

For the adolescent female also (hence the phenomenon of religious 'mania' in some girls) there is added attraction if the deity is presented as a benign and compassionate father-figure (and if, as in the Christian tradition, there is a 'hero' or ideal man). Conversely, the adolescent male—indeed the 'adolescent masculine' at any age—is less likely to be attracted since his disposition is to establish his individual virility, superiority and god-like status. He is therefore less inclined to be sympathetic towards an authoritarian father-figure and will be inclined to feel threatened and suffocated by the feminine ethos of rigid, formal, conformist, religious practice. Much depends on the ability of the elders to expound and teach the truly masculine content of the religious message—whether it will help him or her as an individual to understand and fulfil his or her own destiny.

The spiritual feminine in the female finds its ultimate security, fulfilment and happiness of being through passive self-surrender. (Surrender implies passive submission.) The spiritual masculine in the male actively looks for inspiration and the real knowledge which will enable it to convert its selfishness into self-sacrifice. (Sacrifice implies an active elimination of self-will.)

In this process we may see again the parallel with the physiological model of brain development. Primitive spirit worship is response to *instinctive* desires and fears (hermaphrodite); formal faith religion is response to *emotional* need (feminine); spirituality is response to *intellectual* quest (masculine). The first is primarily self-survival (physical), the second group-survival (emotional) and the third individual 'survival' (intellect).

Whereas infancy and childhood were predominantly preoccupied with the desire for happiness, during adolescence the second aspect of the threefold desire begins to operate conciously—the desire for knowledge. Whereas in the first fourteen years knowledge was mainly in the form of 'uninvited' information, such knowledge is now enriched through the search for meaning in experience. As yet, the third aspect, the desire for immortality, is still relatively dormant—though it may well be present in the beginnings of the spiritual quest.

For, at the moment of sexual maturity, the drama of life and death begins in earnest—symbolised by the release of mature male germ cells and the spilling of female blood—as consciousness of self introduces realisation of the death of 'myself'. The scene is set for the masculine-feminine, male-female, spritual-sexual interplay. This can be readily appreciated and experienced as a polarised state in which the dual factors are either in opposition and conflict or sympathy and complement.

But is it simply a case of one condition or the other as a static and unresolved conflict or harmony? Is it a case of them being in an overall pattern of continuing imbalance in which cyclic movements cause alternation within a closed-circuit monotony of disintegration and re-integration, rejection and attraction? Or, considering the individual life as a whole—or even the evolution of humanity as a whole—may a gradual shift or conversion, a spirally-evolving movement through the vertical, masculine, third dimension be discerned? Does the development of the cerebral cortex and the growth of intelligence and consciousness signify a transition and progressive resolution of the duality?

Undoubtedly, in the terms of this theme, the first 'half' of human life is dominated by the feminine, physical, sexual, procreative dispensation. There may be (could be, should be) a transformation taking place through the feminine whereby the second 'half' becomes increasingly dominated by the masculine, spiritual, creative/destructive dispensation. Could this lead to resolution of the dichotomy in the human condition through realisation of the truly 'abstract, individual, divine androgyne'?

We shall see as the theme matures that, inevitably, the spiritual culmination—realisation of immortality—must reside in absolution through union with the 'almighty, asexual, creative/destructive spirit'.

It may sound paradoxical but, whereas Man's earthly, sexual, procreative purpose is self-perpetuation, his heavenly, spiritual, creative/dissolving purpose is self-annihilation (which, in its positive aspect, is Self-realisation).

In this context, it may be appreciated that society is bound to regard suicide as a crime; from the feminine social and religious aspect, it amounts to a rejection and abandonment. From the masculine, spiritual aspect, it is a tragic self-denial, and could be likened to a 'spiritual abortion'.

The complete human life cycle begins with the embryonic, unified, earthly bisexual, proceeds through bifurcation as a duality of sexes and finally ends in reunion as the heavenly androgyne.

As far as adolescents are concerned, they ordinarily find

themselves engulfed in a maelstrom of desires, fears and emotional reactions, with which they have to cope as best they can, both publicly and privately.

In the past, societies have usually sought to restrict the sexual licence of the young, partially no doubt because the consequences in terms of population increase would have been economically intolerable. However, theoretically, and in the absence of any other stricture, a modern society which sees the gratification of pleasure as Man's only purpose or compensation in life can afford to become more permissive, given the means of contraception and the emergency support of readily-available abortion. It would now, for example, be possible to allow totally unbridled sexual expression in wealthy and sophisticated societies. This would perhaps relieve an enormous amount of tension (except in the case of those who for one reason or another could not participate). But are there, nevertheless, other factors beside the economic one which persuades society that such licence would not be beneficial in the longer term?

As far as group-survival is concerned, there could certainly be the fear that, given access to unlimited pleasure, there would tend to be increasing abandonment not only of the reproductive responsibility but also of the responsibility to support, care for and educate the offspring, through the family-unit system especially. There are undoubtedly signs of this in industrialised societies today, especially where the religious influence is weak.

I suspect that the really effective deterrent in the longer term is observation of the effect that such licence has on the individual. Even though the society—and, in particular, the religious element—may not be able to explain this, if it has any integrity and compassion in it at all, it will instinctively comprehend that failure to instil the need for control, moderation and self-discipline in the individual will lead eventually to an undermining and corruption of spirit which results in apathy, depression and disintegration through some form of self-violation. Briefly, the chances of possessive love being transformed into altruistic concern and spiritual love will be drastically reduced.

We do not yet have experience of the above trend taken to its extreme. As I say, there are signs in industrial nations that there is a strong drift towards it and it may be that we are destined to witness extreme consequences. It will be as well if there are some alert enough to monitor and record those consequences. History teaches us that lack of discipline, greed, indulgence, licentious behaviour, aggression, violence and folly are common features in societies following the decline of their empirical expansion, i.e., during the masculine contraction or withdrawal phase after one of feminine extension of territory, influence and power. This is why the capitalist West shows signs of impotence in the face of Communist expansion. If the masculine spirit of the former does not turn from its obsession with pleasure and gain, it is likely to suffer the same fate as the male praying mantis; the feminine, communist, ruthless monster will 'de-capitalise' it and consume it!

Thus, it is as well that this alertness is focussed on what is currently happening in Britain in particular. Whereas in former times the post-empirical disintegration tended to take place in the upper echelons of society where the power was held, leaving the lower classes basically unimpared in terms of economic, agricultural viability, it seems that in this twentieth century situation, the whole nation could be involved in the self-destroying process.

Nevertheless, at present, law and regulation still operates to a degree, and the economic stricture especially still exerts through education a restraint on the adolescent phase. No matter how eager the boy or girl is to be at large in the adult world to seek fulfilment in one form or another, the society still insists that he or she will undergo sufficient compulsory training in order that all members will be prepared to play a contributory part in the economic viability of the state.

The tensions therefore remain in the individual—created by the friction between 'what I want to do and cannot' (masculine urge versus feminine resistance) and between 'what I have to do and do not want to' (feminine requirement versus masculine withdrawal). I remember the situation being described to me with a very apt analogy: 'It is like driving with one foot on the accelerator and the other on the brake!'

The accelerator is driving powerfully towards an as yet undefined but ideal paradise of bliss and perfection where one will be able to do just what one wants to do (masculine); the brake is that externally enforced pressure and restraint which requires conforming with the established order and acceptance that there are obligations to others (feminine).

The struggle begins in earnest during adolescence. It seems to be mostly conflict. Can the romantic dream ever be reconciled with the mundane and pragmatic demand? Will they ever complement each other, or one be made the same as the other?

11 *The age of majority*

I come now to the age of majority; traditionally, in England, the age of twenty-one (completion of three seven-year phases). I prefer to retain this measure despite the fact that 'officially' it has been reduced in recent years to eighteen.

I take this 'advance' in the age of majority to be analogous to the fact already noted that, though the average age for puberty is earlier in the female than the male, and though it is generally accepted as being at the age of fourteen, it tends to be more advanced according to the 'brightness' of the child at the stage of four or five.

Thus, taking into account that the highest point of sexual potency in the male is reckoned to be eighteen or nineteen, and the fact that the learning aspect of secondary education becomes more applied and intensive in a modern, industrialised society, the adolescent is ready much earlier than twenty-one to exercise an economic contribution and make a political choice.

The latter is a reasonable proposition providing party politics—as is usually the case—confines itself preponderantly to policies and practices concerning the distribution of wealth and power within society.

Even so, it is worth noting that the eighteen-year old is likely to base his judgement on self-survival/instinctive and group-survival/emotional grounds rather than objective, reasoned and altruistic grounds. This advance in voting age thus tends to be of advantage to the feminine-left, socialist elements in politics. It should nevertheless be added that a large number of adults do not develop throughout their lives beyond the 'adolescent' level of assessment and judgement.

The reduction of the age of majority is, in effect, an economic and sexual, and therefore feminine, development. It does not take fully into account the tertiary, masculine component which allows the influence of a more mature and reasonable intellect. In other words, it ignores the spiritual aspect which should introduce, hopefully, a truly individual, independent, reasoned and altruistic ingredient. By the age of twenty-one, this element should have begun to temper the selfish, instinctive, self-preservation motive and the emotional, group-survival reaction.

Before considering the course of the young adult phase, I would like to introduce two or three further ideas which I hope will help to structure, and thus render more easily comprehensible, the rationale of later developments.

The first is a schematic picture (opposite) of some of the principal features of development in the first thirty-five years showing a threefold, staggered relationship between various components.

I should emphasise that this picture is schematic and that it only in the physical-left that the 'body-clocks' give a consistent and generally valid measure in chronological time. The mental centre is usually so dominated by the physical-left in the early years that there tends to be a 'dragging' effect on the spiritual-right.

This means that in societies where the masculine, spiritual influence is weak, there is likely to be a retardation and therefore a delaying or prolonging of the phases on the right side. At worst, where 'the fight to be male' is lost, spirituality/individuality is 'aborted' and the person remains a 'crystallised' personality, reverting to become a simply mortal, psycho-physical, 'feminine' organism.

However, the importance at this stage is to indicate the staggering of the three aspects of development, with the feminine/physical/procreative/economic 'life' having a fourteen year start on the masculine/spiritual/creative/intellectual 'life'. In between, the 'mind' or the mental function, becoming receptively operative at seven and actively operative at puberty, begins (schematically) during adolescence the task of coping with demand from 'both sides' and begins to lead 'two lives'. Thus it is at this point that the person actively forms definite personality traits according to the interaction of the 'inner', private, individual nature (masculine/spiritual) with the 'outer', public, group demand or expectation (feminine/sexual). Here the ideal is confronted by the pragmatic.

This leads to 'mental puberty' at twenty-one where the polarisation is truly established and the 'adolescent' individual sets out into the world. By twenty-eight, the person is actively leading 'two lives', frequently an uncomfortable situation in which the externally-acquired life may be in conflict with the inner sense of what would really be true to the individual. The battle is now seriously engaged because the individual, vertical, idealistic impulse is weak and tends to be frustrated by the horizontal, cross-flow of the committed sexual-economic current. At this stage the latter has a

The age of majority

AGE	PHYSICAL	MENTAL	SPIRITUAL
0	*Physical birth* Infancy: first seven years of physical growth	(Reception of sensory impressions; mental 'embryo')	(Instinctive, unconscious knowledge)
7	Childhood: second seven years of physical growth; primary education	*Mental 'birth'* of the person; passive, reactive formation of the personality	(Self-consciousness; spiritual 'embryo')
14	*Puberty* Adolescence: third and final period of physical growth; active inter-sexual relationship	Active, positive formation of personality; secondary education	*Spiritual 'birth'* of the individual; consciousness of self—the 'I' Spiritual infancy; romantic dream of the ideal and the perfect
(18)	Sexual, economic threshold of adulthood		Growth of original, intellectual, individuality; tertiary education
21	*Physical maturity* Physical 'plateau' leading to gradual decline of potential	*Mental 'puberty'* Distinct cerebral hemisphere differentiation and functioning	Spiritual 'childhood'; testing of individual aspiration against group expectation; self-knowledge
28	(Marriage)	*Mental 'maturity'* Personality fully formed; leading 'two lives'— private and public	*Spiritual 'puberty'* Ideally, active formation of true individuality; becoming 'true to oneself'; self-understanding
35	(Parenthood)	('Marriage of two minds')	*Spiritual 'maturity'* Disillusion; illumination; self-realisation

linear strength as direction towards achievement of security and worldly identity in future time. The feminine is in full flood which makes the ability of the masculine, spiritual to penetrate that much more difficult.

This leads to another principle which now seems relevant and worth proposing—the threefold aspect or phasing of a process. These are its inception or beginning, its continuation or maintenance, and its ending or completion. Respectively these are masculine-creative, feminine-procreative and masculine-destructive or resolving.

It is represented, for example, in the cycle birth-life-death. It is also evident in the sexual act of masculine penetration, feminine fertilisation and masculine withdrawal. This principle is the basis of the wave-motion characteristic of directional movement in nature. The steady, feminine, linear, continuous, horizontal motion is impinged upon by the impulsive, masculine, vertical, penetrative thrust, which drives the direction downwards towards the trough or nadir of the wave (the deep, dark 'womb' of the earth or the waters—both feminine). This is followed by the withdrawal of the masculine, creating a 'vacuum', causing a rising, upward movement, which, passing through and beyond the horizontal, linear mean, ascends to the crest or zenith of the wave (towards the high, bright 'birth' in the air and fire of sunlight—both masculine). Thus do all processes obey the cyclic, rhythmic law of fall and rise, or rise and fall. As far as this theme is concerned it is sexuality which first rises and then falls whilst the spiritual first falls and then rises (ideally!).

The commonly ignored phase of this threefold evolution is the third one, especially in the physical, worldly context. Usually there is appreciation of the creative act and the need to maintain and continue the resulting effect—for example, sexual intercourse and the bringing up of the resulting child. But seldom is the inevitability of the ending or withdrawal given due consideration and weight. Thus, to follow the sexual act, resulting-child example, there can be retardation of the child's development through the failure of the parental obligation to 'let the child go'; i.e., parental 'hanging on' to the child through a desire to continue the father-mother role delays, or even aborts, the ability of that child to become adult (not physically, of course, but mentally and spiritually).

In principle, if the continuing is painful or uncomfortable, then it is the feminine (in the male and the female) which tends to fear that

The age of majority

it will never end; the masculine may become desperate and destructive. If the continuing is pleasant and comfortable, the feminine tends to hope that it will go on for ever; the masculine may become lulled into a false sense of security. In fact, the timing of the end is as regulated as the beginning, even though both beginning and end are 'hidden' and unpredictable in the two-dimensional, past and future, feminine, chronological time projection. In other words, both conception and death are subject to 'out of time' masculine impulses.

The point that needs to be made, however, is that the law, as mentioned earlier, dictates that the ending is dependent on the quality, worth and usefulness of the continuing. Hence, in the continuing, it is the feminine responsibility to serve as well as possible in the circumstances and to be prepared to surrender at the culmination. The masculine responsibility is to make the best possible use of the continuing and to convert the ending from being a negative destruction into a positive absolution.

This is especially relevant to the conduct of human relationships, temporary or lasting, intimate or formal. It is the quality of the continuing which dictates whether the termination will be destructive or positively resolving.

Thus, in the context of a man and woman contracting to marry, the process of establishing the marriage will depend on the quality of the relationship. If the feminine in the female or the male holds a continuing poor opinion of its worthiness, it will regard masculine withdrawal as a destructive rejection and abandonment. If, on the other hand, it receives encouragement and appreciation of its worthiness, then it will accept the inevitable masculine withdrawal as completion and resolution of its desires and fears.

Conversely, the masculine, if it has a false and inflated opinion of its own value, will fail to engage the feminine appropriately and will eventually destructively reject and abandon its responsibility when it fails to receive the adulation that it believes to be its due. If, on the other hand, the masculine effaces itself and allows itself to serve and give due appreciation to the value of the feminine (which it must do in order to realise its own *true* worth), then it will withdraw with a sense of desire and fear alleviated and of its purpose being completed.

This is applicable in the worldly, sexual terms of love and death; it is also so in terms of the spiritual individual and his or her inner reconciliation of the left and right hemispheres. For it should now be becoming apparent that what is happening 'within' the individual is enacted in the 'outer' life. Thus all internal conflict and resolution is projected as external friction or reconciliation. There is, ultimately, no one to blame but oneself!

The threefold process of the individual, sexual/spiritual life begins with the masculine seeking out, being attracted by and penetrating the feminine. Having conceived, married and served the feminine in the continuing relationship, the masculine then withdraws or retires, having resolved the feminine desires and fears, 'taking the feminine with it', as it were, rescuing it through absolution from the bondage of its earthly existence and commitment. In return the feminine, through its experience, provides the masculine precisely with what it needs to find the way back to the creative cause—the 'divine and almighty source'.

This herioc and chivalrous adventure and quest is echoed in many myths and tales—in that of Sleeping Beauty, for example—and in many religious allegories—in the Judaic Old Testament story of the Exodus and the Christian story of the life of Jesus Christ, for example.

The essence of this cycle may be summarised in saying that the feminine needs to know that it is loved and the masculine needs to learn through the feminine how to love.

Of course, much can go wrong in the world of mortals! The masculine may be mesmerised by its ideal dream or fantasy and remain idealistic, failing to engage and obey the pragmatic laws. It may fail to acknowledge the need of the feminine and fail to penetrate it with intent to fertilise. It may fail to sacrifice its self-interest to marry and serve the feminine. It may become enmeshed in the feminine desires and fears and fail to withdraw. It may withdraw prematurely and selfishly and fail to absolve the feminine. The feminine may fail to attract the masculine, to acknowledge its masculinity, to surrender and abandon its earthbound commitment, to obey and follow the masculine as the latter retires.

Herein is enacted the dance of birth, life, love, death, destruction and salvation. And it begins in earnest for the individual when he or she reaches the threshold of adulthood and sets out to take a place in the world.

12 *Marriage*

As suggested earlier, the physiological, evolutionary story begins in the unified spinal cord which swells at the top and bifurcates into primitive procreative and self-preservation faculties (though of course the spinal cord serves both of these motivations). As at the beginning of the embryonic growth, the being is androgynous, or exhibits 'a unified bi-sexuality'. This 'unified duality' then evolves into a polarised duality as the being becomes one sex or the other. Each sex is 'half an androgyne', not a separate and complete creature in itself.

I believe this emphasis to be important because it suggests that physically the male and the female are not independent and complete but only 'half-complete'. This is recognised at puberty as the quest begins to reunite the duality through the joining of one half to the other. This is enacted at the physical level in the act of sexual intercourse—at its most ideal or perfect as a mutual orgastic climax with mutual intent to conceive a child—a perfect reproduction of the partners' complete self-image.

At the psychological, emotional level the de-polarisation or mergence of the duality is expressed in the act of marrying whereby each wishes to find resolution of his or her desires and fears through the 'missing half' of himself or herself. Unfortunately, rather than resolving deficiencies, the mundane situation may exacerbate and entrench them, especially if the marriage is not undertaken in a spiritual context, i.e., it is not made or consummated 'in heaven'.

I remember very clearly, many years ago, a man I regarded (and still do) as being a 'spiritual mentor' saying: 'A wedding does not mean you are married; it means that you have made a contract *to* marry.' This is a most important and subtle point because it implies that becoming truly married is an extended process which must be worked for if it is to succeed in fulfilling both partners.

As distinct from this approach, there seems to be a fairly common assumption that one day one is not married, then one goes through a wedding ritual, and suddenly one *is* married. Each wakes up on the first morning of the honeymoon and says inwardly, 'I am married' and then tries to assess whether the gamble has been a success or a disaster! If each partner waits and hopes that the other will turn out to be perfect or ideal, then the chances of the contract being fulfilled are drastically reduced—which is why there are so many divorces, and marriages which are wars of attrition or uneasy truces of expedience.

The undertaking of a vow *to* marry is, in the spiritual context representative of a personal commitment. In its feminine aspect, symbolised by the wife's vow, the left hemisphere commits itself to obey the right *after,* in the masculine aspect, the right hemisphere has sworn to serve the left, symbolised by the husband's vow.

In other words, the feminine-dominated procreative marriage in the sexual, worldly sense, at the beginning of adulthood, is at the same time a masculine-dominated, spiritual commitment by the right hemisphere to 'marry' the left. Thus the physical and emotional intent and achievement of temporal marriage is representative of the individual's resolve to come to peace with himself or herself through the merging or unifying of the left and right sides of his or her own mind. This is necessarily a long process and the marriage contract, temporal or spiritual, is a lifetime's commitment; or, more accurately, until 'death' eliminates the duality. This is not necessarily mortal death; it means a 'dying' to one's desires and fears, a dying of one's false self to the true Self.

The actual physical partner in marriage, because he or she becomes a reflection of oneself, is the means whereby the inner, spiritual resolution is achieved and established in each individual. Whereas, in the physical sense, the fruition is a child, in the individual it is the 're-birth' of the spirit as the 'regenerate' man.

When it is said then that a marriage is 'made in heaven', I take this to mean that the procreative, sexual, economic, mundane commitment (feminine) is subsidiary to, and dependent upon, the aspiration of each partner to help the other achieve individual, spiritual fulfilment (masculine). If this is so, then I suggest it throws some light on the so-called 'choice' of partner.

There seem to be two basic approaches to this selection. One is a kind of calculated, arranged, 'computer' system (feminine-left). This is evident in the courtship situation where the mundane pros and cons are deliberately assessed: 'Has he enough money and career prospects?'; 'Will she make a good home-maker, cook and mother?' On the basis of this assessment, the answer to whether the marriage is a good prospect or not is, in the main, couched in practical, material, quantifiable terms. It is the logical, analytical, feminine approach, taken to its extreme in certain cultures where the parents arrange the marriage and the participants may meet, almost for the first time, at the wedding ceremony. They will almost certainly have had very little opportunity to assess each other emotionally and may have no right to refuse the contract made on their behalf. I assume that the theory in this approach is that, providing the economic base is secure (and perhaps the 'signs' are benign) then, in spiritual terms, it is possible for the individual to be fulfilled through marriage to more or less anyone of the opposite sex, given that each has made the vow of commitment to the other.

The second approach is of course where the partners are free to choose whomsoever they please. There may well be some acknowledgement of practical considerations in this selection process but, by its nature, this masculine approach tends to be based on 'head over heels', impulsive, spontaneous, irresistible enchantment. Inevitably it involves the right-hemisphere, romantic dream of the ideal and the perfect. I suggest that the 'theory' behind recommendation of this mode of conjunction is that, providing the mutual enchantment exists and has substance, then practical demands and problems will resolve themselves in the due course of events.

Both approaches could be said to have their advantages and dangers and it is not possible to judge that either is totally right or wrong. The severest criticism could justifiably be levelled at the extreme forms of either. In the calculated, arranged marriage, the romantic element will need to find response and to play its part after the contract has been made. If it fails to find such response, then the danger is that the association will remain purely procreative and economic and will be bereft of romantic, spirituality inspiring content. In this event, the masculine in either partner may well seek elsewhere in extra-marital associations for the missing stimulation and fulfilment. Conversely, in the romantically based marriage, the practical, mundane requirements of physical and economic survival will still have to be met. If they are not satisfactorily and continually solved then the danger is that the romantic dream will rapidly fade. For the feminine this will mean continual threat to security and an ennervating frustration and anxiety, especially so in the female if the situation is a threat also to her desire to bear and bring up children.

The odds are of course heavily stacked against survival of the romantic dream. This is inevitable in that it is, in essence, spiritual and not sexual. When it first arises, and is visualised vaguely in the right hemisphere during the adolescent phase, there has not yet developed in that hemisphere sufficient power of discrimination and evaluation—for there has not yet been sufficient experience to inform those powers. It is inevitable therefore that the ideal dream should be drawn to and find expression in the comparatively superficial, sexual terms of perfect form, display of personality, opportunity for indulging in pleasure, and so on. This applies in the general sense of how it is envisaged the future married life will ideally be conducted or, in particular, how the perfect partner will satisfy desire and enhance self-image. This is fatal inasmuch as no perfection in romantic or material terms will ever be lastingly established in worldly terms, since it is the nature of form to be ever-changing.

One way or the other, however, the conjunction serves Nature's purpose—in luring the masculine into furthering the feminine procreative purpose. This the feminine is most likely to accomplish—as far as the reproductive as distinct from the pleasure-seeking content is concerned—during the late-adolescent/early-adult period. From then onwards the reproductive factor begins to decline, and partnerships are increasingly inclined, in worldly terms, to be based on mutual pleasure-seeking and economic expediency, and the desire for companionship through fear of loneliness.

It is interesting to note that in one of the dictionaries I use *(The Concise Oxford Dictionary)*, the definition of 'adolescence' states that it is the period between childhood and manhood or womanhood. The former is given as being from fourteen to twenty-five and the latter as being from twelve to twenty-one. The lagging behind of the male is thereby proposed as continuing well into the third decade of life. This would suggest that the romantic dream of the ideal and the perfect will generally persist later in the male than the female. This may be suggested as accounting for the fact that the female, by her early twenties, is likely to be more insistent than her partner that the practical aspect of providing home and material support for herself and offspring should take priority over impractical, wishful dreams and schemes.

In other words, she will more readily translate her spiritual aspiration into material form, seeing her status and proof of success in terms of her ability to establish the perfect home and family.

It is most probable that the feminine in the male will be persuaded to follow this inclination. He will then inevitably be committed to satisfying his masculinity through achieving success in terms of the acquisition of self-esteem, wealth, status and power through work and career. If the feminine in him is strong compared to the masculine, then this may prove to be a tolerable state of affairs—at least through the next phase or two of his life. On the other hand, if the spiritual masculine in him has gained noticeable strength—or it does so later—then he will begin to suffer frustration.

If the feminine in the female is strong then of course she will quite contentedly espouse the responsibilities of wife and mother. If, on the other hand, the masculine is strong in her then she may devalue or forsake the domestic role in order to pursue self-enhancing and self-satisfying work and career. This is not to suggest that such female pursuit is necessarily 'selfish'; on the contrary, especially in the female, it may well be altruistically motivated, particularly if she aspires to a serving, caring, enriching role in, for example, a religious, artistic or social welfare context. In other words, it is more natural for her to express her spirituality in service to mankind. This, in turn, contrasts with the masculine, emotional, spiritual expression of the male which is individual and creative. It is for this reason that the masters of painting, sculpture, inspirational literature and musical composition have always tended to be men.

All the above, incidentally, suggests that so-called 'feminism' is something of a misnomer. It would more appropriately be called 'masculinism' in that it is attributable to the stirring and striving of the masculine in the female. Thus, 'women's liberation' in actually 'masculine liberation' in the female.

The above demonstrates the point I made at the beginning of the chapter—that permutations of factors begin to proliferate in the sexual/spiritual, feminine/masculine, female/male interplay when one reaches the adult phases where all are actively operating, sometimes in complementary, sympathetic, harmonious and positive relationship, sometimes in conflicting, antipathetic, discordant and negative relationship. Vacillation towards one condition or the other is going on all the time in the waking and dreaming states, whether the enactments are superficial, minor and transitory at a personality level or whether they are deep, enduring and repetitive experiences deriving from inherent character.

However deep or shallow, and however complicated or simple,

this continuing interplay has an oscillating rhythm which could be seen as commensurable with the motions and elements of the sexual act. If so, it may be justifiable to extend the analogy by suggesting that, since the motion and friction of intercourse is usually the prerequisite of attaining orgasm, so the movement and conflict in the mental arena may be observed as the essential, precursory stimulator of energy necessary for spiritual 'orgasm'. Certainly no evolutionary gain was ever born of idleness and inertia.

Any appraisal of a situation depends first of all on whether one is considering the sexual or spiritual aspect of it. And I further propose that it is not possible to consider one in ignorance of, or with deliberate exclusion of, the other.

The spiritual, being concerned with the individual, will involve consideration of that individual's state—the current relationship between the left and right hemispheres in him or her, taking into account age, stage of development and background experience. Problems of conflict and, thus, failure of reconciliation between one side and the other, give rise to pervasive, inner, private anxieties and frustrations. These, in turn, are projected into and affect the sexual, worldly conduct. Here they manifest and intervene in that individual's human relationships, especially in the romantic, sexual partnership, whether casual or committed.

In directly sexual terms, the problems manifest as variations of the fundamental malfunctions of impotence (masculine-desire-frustration) and frigidity (feminine-fear-anxiety). Indirectly, these are projected into all that individual's worldly relationships—whether they happen to be with the same or the opposite sex and whether they are friendly or hostile. This means that psychologically—in the mental arena, with spiritual aspiration on the one side and sexual demand on the other—there is a continual struggle against mental impotence and frigidity, or rigidity. If it is accepted that the prime purpose of human life is fulfilment of the individual destiny, then this struggle is the mental counterpart of 'the fight to be male'.

The above may seem an unduly negative view but I submit that the negative is bound to predominate in the sexual, worldly context because the spiritual aspiration emerges consciously in the being some time after it is already disposed to the carnal commitment. For the individual's relationships and transactions to be positive and creative, giving rise to happiness, harmony and love, it is necessary for the spiritual element to gain in strength in order to control the selfish, indulgent, reactionary activities of the wilful, sexually-dominated mind, which is continually falling into contention with the world.

This does *not* imply the desirability of suppressing or renouncing the sexual element (a course which has at times been advocated by so-called 'puritan' influences in society, especially the religious). Far from it. It simply calls for a restraint and moderation based on consciousness of the needs of the partner in the relationship. This consideration can only be exercised through the intervention of the altruistic, spiritual influence from the masculine-right. This principle of consideration should of course ideally extend to all relationships—thereby transforming the primitive, instinctive urge to acquire and possess into one of giving and dedication.

Since it is the intent of this book to propose that the complete life involves a sexual/spiritual transformation or conversion, this taking-to-giving conversion indicates the nature of the ultimate transformation—that of converting self-preservation (leading to unwilling or 'untimely' death) to self-surrender or self-sacrifice (consciously accepting death).

If the individual is working at, and succeeding in, the resolution of the private dichotomy within himself or herself then that reconciliation will be projected into the public domain, in particular into the intimate, marriage relationship. It gradually results in the individual taking responsibility upon himself or herself instead of attributing blame to this, that or the other cause 'out there'. The evolution of this positive aspect is, needless to assert, difficult to accomplish because it requires a virtually total conversion of what one has learned to believe.

For example, it requires realisation that true masculinity and femininity have nothing to do with proving oneself in worldly, sexual terms. The assertive, dominating, confident, power-wielding male and the alluring, provocative, glamorous, sex-object female are two popular images which are effectively devoid of spiritual content. Given the current pleasure-seeking, economic-expansion obsession in general, the conversion of values is not easy to pursue with conviction. This is especially so, as I have already said, due to the 'fourteen-year start' afforded to the physical-sexual conditioning before the masculine spirit becomes active. Even though parental and institutionalised education may introduce restraining discipline and intelligent persuasion during the primary and secondary phases, the young adult still has a formidable task ahead if he or she is to convert instinctive desires and fears, and control wayward emotions.

In one respect, it would not be so formidable if the romantic dream were properly appreciated. This depends on the availability of the spiritual guidance in the environment. If it is there, and wise enough, it will facilitate translation of the dream into a realistic appreciation of the true and transcendental nature of the ideal and the perfect. Unfortunately, in the absence of such guidance, the purity and meaning of the dream can easily become sullied and distorted by ignorant instruction and infelicitous childhood experience. For the right hemisphere evolves the dream and visualises it through the forms accumulated by the left hemisphere. Thus the dream gravitates to expression in familiar worldly images; this is inevitable and appropriate so long as those images are not excessively grotesque and frightening.

If the left hemisphere has suffered negative and destructive response to its instinctive desires and fears during infancy and childhood, then the dream of the ideal and perfect will be unduly modified by exaggerations and suppressions. These may so corrupt the dream that it becomes fantasy, especially sexually-based, destructive fantasy. (I use the word 'dream' here to imply something passively harmless and potentially instructive or constructive whereas 'fantasy' implies something actively dangerous and dynamically destructive.) The more bizarre and extreme the fantasy (negative-masculine) the more unlikely that it will be able to find innocuous expression in the actual world (positive-feminine). Thus are sown the seeds of madness, in which the private inner world is partly, or even totally, excluded from the public convention.

To summarise the situation as the individual is likely to experience adolescence and early adulthood in sexual terms, it will tend to be turbulent, with the romantic ideal beset by desire and frustration and perfection haunted by fear and anxiety.

This was encapsulated in a comment I read recently by an eminent American psychiatrist who specialises in sex therapy: 'It may be said that sex is composed of friction and fantasy.'

In its negative aspect, that might be said to be the case for worldly life in general!

Marriage

Finally, it would be appropriate to add emphasis to the indication in this chapter that marriage, apart from its procreative aspect, is a highly symbolic commitment. Whether or not a person actually marries a physical partner, the crucial significance is that in early adulthood there should be the inception of a process wherein the masculine-right and the feminine-left hemispheres contract to 'marry', a process whereby the inner disposition and the outer performance become compatible and harmonious. Otherwise, the inculcated social expectation will be in conflict with the inner nature and the individual, frustrated in being able to be 'true to himself (or herself)', will not emerge. The 'regenerate man' will be aborted.

13 *Celibacy*

Are there any means whereby this turbulent labyrinth—this 'strangest of mazes'—may be avoided should one wish to do so?

One method is to renounce the sexual, worldly commitment. This can be done to varying degrees. At extreme, it requires total abstention from sexual relationship, celibacy, withdrawal from the world, and so on. This brings us back to the monastic way of life, and the questions concerning monks with which I introduced this book.

In what might be called its negative aspect, such extreme renouncement constitutes deliberate denial of the feminine, procreative purpose. This rejection may denote a fear of emasculation through dissipation of energy by becoming enmeshed in the feminine-dominated dispensation. In its positive aspect, there must be a conviction—born, surly, of a masculine idea—that all the individual's energy should be devoted to the spiritual quest. What is required is a committed espousal by the feminine-sexual of the ultimate, masculine-ideal—the 'deity'. Translated, this means that 'union with the divine' must be at the expense of physical union in sexual intercourse.

In principle, celibacy means that it is deemed inappropriate to divert attention and energy (exemplified by ejaculation of sperm) in order to serve the reproductive aspect of human life. However, in order to harness and control the feminine, sexual desire to procreate and the masculine desire for sexual pleasure, it is necessary to subject the left-hemisphere functioning to a strictly circumscribed regime—enacted through a highly ordered life with continual, repetitive habit, office and ritual. Every hour of the day, week and year must be more or less totally and predictably occupied. This will leave no time or space, theoretically, for friction and fantasy, sensuality and wishful dream. The feminine-left is thereby disciplined to surrender to, and devoted to worship of, the abstract, masculine-ideal—the 'deity', whilst the masculine remains free and unencumbered to contemplate and merge with the 'divine perfection'.

Of course, there are varying degrees of withdrawal or enclosure, ranging from totally withdrawn, isolated communities or individuals (in some cases, even sworn to silence) to less extreme situations where the masculine function still serves the worldly feminine to a degree by helping, and giving support and comfort, to those in trouble or need.

It is not appropriate to judge the theory and practice of celibacy as being right or wrong, generally or absolutely. It must remain a matter of experience and conviction for the individual who undertakes it—for no man is in a position to judge the true spiritual worth of another's life. He may have an opinion about it but that is not guarantee of veracity. A man or woman may be deemed in worldly opinion to have led a virtuous or misguided life; but that is not guarantee of its having been a truly spiritual or non-spiritual life.

As one for whom the possibility of celibacy never arose—since it never presented itself as a prospect during my youth—and as one who therefore took the conventional, worldly path of marriage and family, the persuasion to take vows of celibacy seems to me to be now outdated. I consider it to be so in the sense that it may once have been appropriate—during the phase which I have called the emotional, 'adolescent' phase of human evolution, when emphasis in the dominant faith-religious was on worship and devotion. Now that the emphasis has moved on to the intellectual, scientific phase of evolution, celibacy seems unreasonable in that it could deny fulfilment of the individual in terms appropriate to the present age.

In the structure and model of this theme, celibacy *appears to be* a 'by-pass' because it attempts to avoid the danger—and abandons the responsibility—inherent in the threefold principle of the masculine needing to 'enter' the feminine, to 'fertilise' it and *then* to withdraw. By failing to accomplish this threefold process, the masculine rejects, denies and abandons the feminine instead of fulfilling and absolving it. In other words, celibacy is an attempt to remain unified by refusing to enter duality. Though individual integrity may be retained or preserved by abstention from worldly commitment, the resulting individuality will not have been naturally and fully earned and may therefore be incomplete and impotent.

In whatever way the celibate male may be able to explain and justify his rejection of the female, or *vice versa,* the really important issue is what effect such measures may have on the individual himself or herself. Whether sexually celibate or not, the essential, psychological, spiritual 'marriage' must be the espousal within of the right and left hemispheres of the brain. The right hemisphere, when it becomes mature and active during early adulthood, must enter into a contract of 'marriage' with the left, in order to accomplish fulfilment of the feminine, first 'half' of life as a member of society. It must however, in order to accomplish fulfilment of the masculine, spiritual responsibility, begin to withdraw during the second 'half', thereby consummating the sexual/spiritual conversion or transformation.

When the 'marriage' of the right and left hemispheres is achieved—'harmony of the hemispheres'—no worldly desires or fears remain. There is therefore no sense of vulnerability or incompleteness in worldly terms (though there will be in spiritual terms) and the person begins to become truly individual (or indivisible since right and left have become 'as one'). Spiritual withdrawal is not then a rejection, separation or divorce, forced by circumstances; it is a natural and voluntary retirement.

Retirement from worldly commitment means retracting from the communal activities and concerns. The individual simply has no further interest in them, having outgrown them. It is a question then of preparing for death as a 'liberation' rather than an abrupt termination.

To divert for a moment into speculation, it is obvious that if celibacy had ever been proved to have (or were it ever in the future be proved to have) undeniable benefit in terms of after-life reward, then it would have become increasingly widespread. If that had been the case, then, theoretically, it would eventually have led to the extinction of human life on earth because reproduction of the species would have died out. As this has not happened, we may suspect that the masculine-inspired idea of feminine/female suppression or rejection has not been proved spiritually viable.

Reversing the idea, and as reaction to it, would it be possible for a masculine/male suppression and rejection movement in sexual terms to arise and succeed? Are we in fact seeing signs of it in the world today? (As a small and symbolic pointer to what I mean, I recently read in a national women's magazine an article which was titled 'Is it time your man had a vasectomy?'[10])

Theoretically, such a movement could now be carried to an ultimate situation. Due to developments in science and technology during this century, the sexual, physical male human being could be made redundant and dispensed with.

It would be possible now for women, convinced that psychologically they are no different from men and have equal capacity and ability, actually to fulfil their procreative function without the presence of males. Having secured well-stocked banks of deep-frozen male sperm before actual elimination of men from the planet, the continued reproduction of just female humans could be achieved. Through techniques of artificial insemination or through implantations of ova fertilised in the laboratory, combined with a now more or less certain method of sex selection, it would no longer be necessary to suffer all the problems created by the existence of men. (It might, perhaps, be necessary occasionally to produce a few 'laboratory' males and allow them to mature in order to renovate and replenish the sperm supply.)

With the aid of automated machinery, this exclusively female population could survive indefinitely, and some would no doubt claim that the world would then become a far more ordered and peaceful place to live.

Would it in fact be a perfect way to eliminate controversy, conflict and war?

I leave that as an open question!

14 Family relationship and private life

During the adult period from twenty-one to thirty-five, developments take place on several levels in sexual-spiritual, feminine-masculine and female-male relationships.

Whereas the first three seven-year phases are predominantly physical-sexual-personal, the second three from twenty-one to forty-two are predominantly mental-emotional-social. The third triad of the three seven-year phases, from forty-two to sixty-three should be predominantly spiritual-intellectual-individual. (Physiologically, this represents a progression from dominance by hind—and midbrain, through the limbic system to the cortices.)

It is during the second twenty-one years that a sixfold, dualistic, sexual-spiritual interplay becomes fully active and operational. This may be represented by the two-triad scheme below.

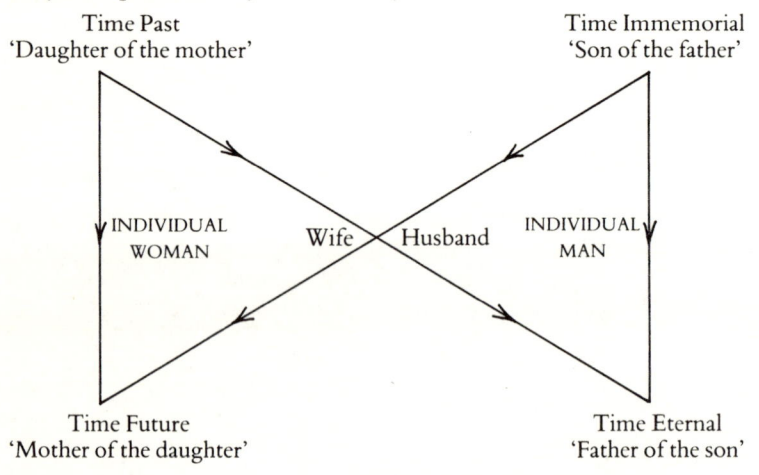

```
      Time Past                              Time Immemorial
'Daughter of the mother'                     'Son of the father'


          ↓ INDIVIDUAL                       INDIVIDUAL ↓
            WOMAN      Wife   ✕   Husband      MAN


      Time Future                              Time Eternal
'Mother of the daughter'                     'Father of the son'
```

The full sexual-spiritual interplay of the child-spouse-parent progression is played out dualistically in the world as the daughter-wife-mother role of the female interacts with the son-husband-father role of the male. Physically, it is focussed on the family group and the balance of the whole system depends on the condition of the wife-husband relationship in marriage.

Much may be drawn from this sixfold scheme as inter-sexual enactment in the world. For example, one may see that 'the daughter of the mother' has a diagonally direct projection through her conjugal role to find her spiritual ideal in 'the father of the son'; if she fails to find it in the husband-father then she will look for it in her actual son. On the other hand, 'the son of the father' has a direct projection to the sexually perfect as 'the mother of the daughter'; if he fails to find it in the wife-mother then he will look for it in the actual daughter. One may surmise that the strong traditional taboo against parent-child incest is not only on account of the biological repercussions (a genetic distortion on the procreative side) but also because of the spiritual implications (a distortion of individual evolution).

One may also deduce that the mother-daughter relationship is 'extra-marital', as is the father-son. Projected, this may account for the husband-mother-in-law reaction. The husband may resent his wife having a relationship (mother-daughter, psycho-physical, imitative and reproductive) which 'by-passes' him and which he feels may be detrimental to his wife's 'spiritual evolution' through him. Conversely, the wife-father-in-law situation may involve sexual threat and jealousy or resentment of a relationship (father-son, psycho-spiritual, 'divine' inheritance through the male line) which she may feel by-passes her.

In other words, the mother-son and the father-daughter relationships are both sexual and spiritual whereas the mother-daughter relationship is sexual only and the father-son spiritual only.

This perhaps accounts for the fact that, in the Christian tradition, in the Holy Trinity, emphasis is placed on the direct, spiritual, masculine legacy from Father to Son. The third member, the Holy Spirit, is usually expressed in neutral, non-sexually identified terms, though some Syriac texts of the third century refer to the Spirit as being feminine in nature. Referring to the diagram, it can be appreciated that in the male triad the third point is in conjunction with the female. This suggests that the third point (where the 'holy spirit' operates, in the 'mystical union' or 'spiritual marriage') may be regarded as a 'husband-wife' or androgynous factor which relates 'father to son'. It suggests that the feminine ingredient not only allows 'the father to pass inheritance to the son' but, in spiritual terms, also allows or enables 'the Son to return to the Father'.

The above extrapolations and speculations apart, the basic model may be applied to the psychology of the individual—to the left and right hemisphere relationship, as in the diagram overleaf.

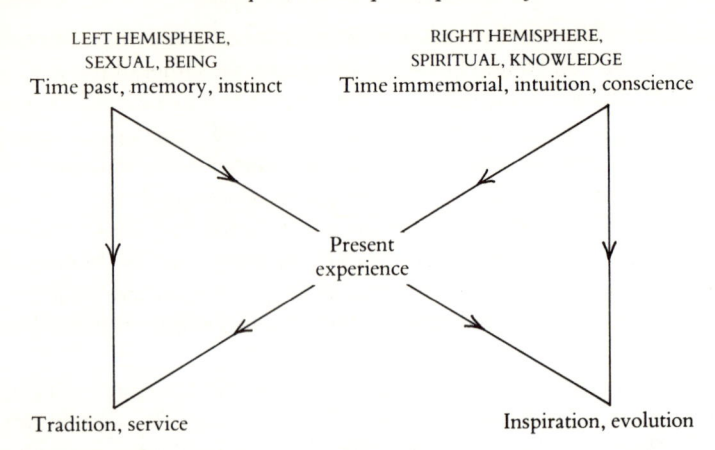

```
LEFT HEMISPHERE,              RIGHT HEMISPHERE,
SEXUAL, BEING                 SPIRITUAL, KNOWLEDGE
Time past, memory, instinct   Time immemorial, intuition, conscience
```

```
                    Present
                  experience
```

```
Tradition, service                      Inspiration, evolution
```

It may be deduced from these relationships, both worldly and individual, that, when functioning positively within tolerable limits of co-operation, left and right hemispheres work together through the present moment of experience. Feminine, left-hemisphere instinct aided by masculine, right hemisphere conscience maintains traditions and provides service. Right-hemisphere, masculine intuition, supported by left-hemisphere, feminine memory produces inspiration for evolutionary progress. It could be said that at the conjunction of the two triads, the present moment—perhaps what Tibetan tradition calls 'the third eye', which is depicted in the centre of the forehead—the seventh factor, which could be called the divine, the spirit of consciousness, enters, controls and directs.

As they stand, the two diagrammatic schemes, social and individual, are ever-repeating and fateful, from generation to generation in the former and from moment to moment in the latter. Their masculine evolutionary (or 'devolution-ary') capacity depends on the seventh factor, the 'divine intervention' or 'penetration'. (For example, as the cause of the beginning of a life and the cause of the ending of it.)

This factor I have called consciousness. There is no possible way in which a human being can command consciousness. The degree to which it is present is beyond his will to dictate. Thus the individual's evolution or devolution is not a matter he or she can decide to effect. All he or she can 'do' is learn through experience to work towards balance and harmony between the hemispheres and thus become responsive (masculine) and receptive (feminine) so that the 'divine' may penetrate and operate. (This could be a possible interpretation of the Christian parable of the 'wise virgins' awaiting the arrival of the 'bridegroom'. Matthew, chapter 25.)

In a general sense, this means that the female becomes passively receptive, which requires her to surrender her will, whilst the male becomes actively responsive, which requires that he sacrifices ('makes sacred or holy') his will.

In this way, the individual evolves to fulfil destiny rather than devolving as a victim of his or her fate.

Commonly, the contract to marry is undertaken during the first phase of adulthood. The romance and 'madness' of courtship progresses to the responsibility of co-habitation. The magic and sensual ecstasy of copulation is given fully approved rein and, in so-called 'advanced' societies, with the aid of contraceptive techniques, may be indulged in according to mutual appetite.

However, particularly in the advanced society, the psychological demand and 'shift' precipitated by the transfer from unmarried freedom to commitment to one partner can often have considerable effect on the sexual relationship.

Referring back to the diagrammatic schemes, time-past parental influences or left-hemisphere instinctive fears and experiential memories may not only cause problems during adolescence and prejudice the ability to make the marriage commitment but, after marriage, may become increasingly stimulated and affect the condition of the partnership. It could be said that there will be as many permutations and expressions, and hence case histories, of this as there are marriages. Once again, I will have to confine myself to what would be called 'the normal course of events'.

Ordinarily, the procreative momentum is strong enough, and the romantic dreams of the ideal and perfect persistent enough, for the partnership to commit itself to attempting to have children. Again, the demand caused by this event is considerable. It requires further surrender and sacrifice of self-will.

I emphasise the word 'attempt' (to have children) because the act of intercourse—with reference to the diagrams—is an intimate conjunction, in effective manifestation, of the two triads. The act itself is preparatory/responsive/receptive and an essential juxtaposition of male and female but it does not in itself guarantee conception of a child. The seventh, 'un-command-able', factor is present in the moment of fertilisation. The condition of the male and female consummation allows the divine intervention. As indicated earlier in the book, spirituality begins at conception. The 'being' is inspired by the 'knowledge' as to how to grow into a new individual.

Perhaps if this were more consciously appreciated by the parents, there would be less tendency to later, inhibiting possessiveness. Of all negative, time-past, parental influences this can be among the most insidious since it can severely retard evolution of the individual, both sexually and spiritually. I refer of course to a demanding and claiming possessiveness towards the child, not a caring and intelligent responsibility towards it. The latter implies a gradual 'letting go' of the child so that by the age of majority he or she is 'free' as an independent adult.

The birth of offspring creates a family. In principle, this event is manifest fulfilment of the feminine procreative purpose. Schematically, the physical birth of the new generation at the time the parents have reached physical maturity means that, when the offspring has in turn reached physical maturity, the parents reach the end of their mental/emotional phase—i.e., at 'forty-two' when the procreative ability in the female recedes—and the spiritual, third phase should begin.

The point is, however, that the parents' mental/emotional phase is closely in parallel with the phase of rearing the offspring. Traditionally, the female aspect of this requires her to take responsibility for nurturing and caring for the offspring within a domestic, family environment of which the care and maintenance is traditionally hers. Her mental/emotional phase is thus enacted in close contact with the child. Meanwhile, the male moves outside the intimate, physical family 'circle' to find the means of supporting the group, his mental/emotional role being enacted in a leading, directing and teaching role.

Certain elements in modern, advanced and sophisticated societies, particularly among women, have in recent years seen fit to question the female domestic role which they view as a male-instituted obligation restricting their evolution as individuals. As previously suggested, this is a 'masculinist', not a 'feminist', attempt to revolutionise social attitudes.

In many ways, it is understandable that this movement should take place in an ethos which promotes fulfilment primarily in material gain, pleasure-seeking and social status terms. I suspect that

Family relationship and private life

it ignores two features of the mental/emotional phase enacted through marriage, motherhood and family.

First it is commonly implied by the 'liberationists' that serving the husband, the children and the home is a one-way, all-giving commitment; hence the negative complaint that it constitutes a restrictive and limiting denial for the female. This assumption and conditioning tends to eclipse the fact that the phase is not an obligation but a responsibility. This means that the family environment allows (or should allow) a two-way, responsive process wherein the wife-mother receives back through her giving what she needs for her future individual, spiritual fulfilment—a kind of mental/emotional feed-back giving stability and security.

This brings forward the second, ignored feature—that fulfilment of the individual in spiritual terms is antipathetic to fulfilment in worldly terms of gain and status. Fulfilment in the wife-mother context is conducive to the true individual fulfilment in the third, spiritual phase of life, whereas the acquisition of fame and fortune may well not be.

This is not to say that spiritual fulfilment is precluded by omission of the marriage/parent commitment or by the achievement of worldly fame and fortune. It is to suggest that the 'liberationist' argument is suspect in what it regards as real, female fulfilment— even if it can be said to have defined what it means by it. Marriage and parenthood are conducive, but not essential, to fulfilment in that through them there is a direct reflection of the second diagram (p.118) in the first (p.116). And fame and fortune are antipathetic, not precluding, because they can become obsessive pursuits which are then difficult to surrender in the spiritual phase, which is not 'of this world'.

So, the feminine in the female finds resolution of her desire for success in sexuality through becoming a mother; this ensures that her fear of failure as a procreative agent in service to the creation remains passive or dormant. The active fear in the feminine of failure as an individual is assuaged in the accomplishment of marriage; the masculine, passive desire in her for success as an individual is satisfied (or ideally should be!) during this mental/emotional phase through being an 'inspiration' to her husband. This is appropriately indicated in the term 'helpmate'.

It is even more appropriately implied in the Judaic Old Testament phrase (Genesis, chapter 2) where Eve is created 'an help meet' for

Adam because it implies the female/feminine role of enabling the male/masculine 'to meet himself/itself'. In other words, the masculine understands its own nature through reflection in the feminine. Without the feminine, the masculine cannot realise the true nature of its masculinity, either in the male or the female.

The above paragraph throws more light on the inappropriateness of certain militant 'feminist' ideas. Since the feminist assertions and claims are really the masculine in the female attempting to express itself and achieve individual status in the sexual, social, economic world, the militant feminist forsakes her spiritual role as helpmate to the male (either privately in the family or publicly in caring, social service of some kind). This powering of the will in mundane interest, instead of the surrendering of it, must surely attract mental/emotional and psychosomatic, physical repercussions. It will, for example, give rise to severe anxieties beneath the forced public performance because not only will the feminine in her be denied its natural security but the masculine in her will fail to realise its spiritual destiny.

As I suggest, the cause of this emergence of the femininst is due to the masculine in the female but I would add that this in turn is caused by the failure of the masculine in the male to play its appropriate spritual role. The accusation by the feminists that the male has been and is over-dominant is justifiable in that he has in the main excessively exploited in the realm of sexuality and has failed to acknowledge and understand his masculine, spiritual responsibility.

As a result of this, there is now an increasing sense of impotence, desperation and bewilderment in the male as his efforts to lead, direct, advise and teach in the world's affairs increasingly founder. Inevitably, the masculine in the female is tempted to try to rectify the situation.

As the female achieves marriage and turns her attention to caring for the family, the onus is placed on the male as husband and father to provide support for the family. Needless to say, there are many occupations in a modern, industrialised society in which he may accomplish this. The spectrum of work ranges from feminine-sexual on the left through to spiritual-masculine on the right. The vast majority, as might be expected, are at the former end because of the dominant socio-economic demand of life on earth.

In principle, at the feminine end are the physical, manual occupations, particularly those 'close to earth' such as those involving the growth of food and retrieval of resources such as fuels, fibres, building materials and so on. These engage such feminine characteristics as cyclic periods, continuity and repetition. These occupations are followed in the spectrum by all manner of manufacturing processes which have feminine, procreative, economic expansion, production-line characteristics. And then there are many administrative occupations which employ the intellect in the feminine interest—banking, accounting, insurance, etc., being concerned with trust, security and economic stability. Here the focus is on manipulating quantities of 'work-tokens' (money), using the lawful, predictable, logical, sequential performance of mathematics. Then there are the teaching, medical, welfare, communication, law, order, government and armed service occupations, all of which basically serve the feminine-dominated group survival, expansion, social security and defence interests.

As and where it may, the masculine attempts to exercise its characteristic functioning within this array of social occupation. The individual idealism, intitiative and enterprise can, to some greater or lesser extent, be expressed in some form throughout all of it in a positive, healthy society. New ideas, intelligent decision-making, leadership, invention, responsibility, taking intuitive and adventurous risks—all these features require the exercise of masculine-right knowledge and inspiration.

In principle, the employee tends towards the feminine-left end, the employer exercising the masculine in the interests of the feminine tends to be somewhere in the middle of the spectrum, leaving the more sparsely populated right end occupied by a minority of truly 'self-employed'. This right end depends very much on the using of initiative and enterprise, employing artistic and creative talents and skills derived from right-hemisphere intellect, intuition, inspiration, visualisation, etc. (There are, of course, a fair number of so-called 'self-employed' who survive either by parasitically exploiting and extorting from the labouring left or who are only 'self-employed' in the sense that they are not paid by someone else but are nevertheless occupied in the feminine-left work.)

The more socialist or communist a society, the more it tends towards the feminine-left. Centralised, committee government, nationalised industry, unions exercising collective power, all tend to render the masculine, creative initiative and decision-making faculties impotent.

Conversely, the more capitalist a society, the more its dependence on masculine, individual, independent enterprise, choice and freedom—which should benefit society as a whole, but may selfishly exploit it. Inevitably, the more the centre of gravity of the society as a whole moves towards the feminine-left, the greater the threat to the individual. On the other hand, in the absence of spiritual responsibility, the more the centre of gravity moves to the right, the greater the threat to the weaker members. 'Democracy', in the feminine sense, is rule by the consensus of mass opinion; in the masculine sense, it should ideally be the ground in which masculine inspiration can thrive.

The masculine-spiritual element tends to become emasculated in a pleasure-seeking, status-conscious society, for spiritual activities are generally not directly wealth-creating and they tend to be either ignored, tolerated, adulterated or scorned.

In the absence of spiritual direction and content, the creative arts struggle against economic strictures and are frequently debased in the process, wallowing in all manner of decadent, irrelevant, pretensious and self-indulgent extremes which are of no real value or inspiration to anyone. Intellectual, academic study is confined to a self-important, self-selecting *élite* whose published works contribute nothing of practical benefit to anyone excluded from their closed-circuit, sterile machinations. The leaders of society, especially political, talk and argue unproductively, achieving barren compromises, counting negative criticism and obstruction as positive accomplishment, squandering resources, believing reactionary policies to be evolutionary advance, all of which alienates them from a bewildered and frustrated or apathetic public. The more the masculine fails to respond to the feminine, the more trapped in its own fantasies does it become.

To return to the hypothetical, ideal marriage and family situation, the male will assuage his active, masculine fear of failure in the sexual aspect by proving his potency as a father. This ensures that his desire for success in husbanding the female procreative purpose is satisfied. The active, masculine desire in the male to succeed in individual, spiritual terms finds outlet in the mental, emotional phase through establishing status in whatever career or occupation he is following. This keeps passive for the time being the feminine spectre in him of failing as an individual.

So, schematically, the male-female relationship with family responsibility continues through 'twenty-eight' towards 'thirty-five'.

During this period, each individual is leading 'two lives'—or, better, a 'double life'. There is the left-hemisphere-dominated, outer, public life in which the requirement is to conform with the traditional, social order. There is some scope in this for the exercise of personality but, generally speaking, this performing self, sometimes called the ego, is a vulnerable creature of circumstance confined by economic demand and group law. The other identity is the right-hemisphere, inner, private self—the potential real 'I'—who dreams and visualises, speculates and contemplates. This is the voice of conscience, the source of intuition, initiative and inspiration. This masculine 'I' or real self is 'younger' and less forward than the world-conditioned ego and it is continually frustrated by feminine-left domination in its 'fight to be male'—an adversity which it must overcome if the being is to become truly individual.

Strictly speaking, there are not *in reality* 'two selves'. The ego-self and the real self do not exist simultaneously. At any moment, one is not living the public life *and* the private life together. Whilst one is active, the other is passive. Most of the time, at least in the first 'half' of life, is spent living the personality, public performance. It is as if the individual, real self is drawn or lured into the worldly dispensation (the masculine thereby serving the feminine) where it is enmeshed or bound in a make-believe, illusory world where actuality is mistaken for reality.

In the process of disillusionment, as the real self asserts itself, it withdraws, as it were, from maintaining the fictional ego-self which gradually loses its power and dissolves. Thus, ideally, does one become 'true to one-self'. There is then no separation between the inner life and the outer life and the ego-self is seen for the pretender or usurper that it always was.

For the sexual-feminine in the female in particular, the romantic dream of adolescence translates quite smoothly into the actual, practical responsibility of being wife and mother.

If she suffers anxiety it is usually because her passive, masculine, sexual fear of failing to be an ideal mother and home-keeper (social) is haunting her or because her active, feminine spiritual fear of failing to be a perfect lover and wife (individual) is haunting her.

This can provoke an active desperation, irritability, aggression and irresponsibility on the one hand or a passive, withdrawing, hysterical, apathetic inertia and frigidity on the other. In other words, in the female, strengthening of the real self can cause both public outburst and private paralysis.

However, as suggested above, in positive circumstances, it is more likely that the real self in the female will lend its power and strength to, and thus more readily merge with, the ego-self in order to fulfil nature's procreative purpose.

For the male, the situation is likely to be different. Whereas, in the female, the individual self is passive and contributory towards the ego-self engagement in the procreative, economic purpose, the increasingly powerful real self in the male finds itself, as it were, committed to an ego-self, motivated by fear, busily engaged in attempting to establish wealth and status in the world.

It seems that, in a large proportion of men, the real self never becomes strong enough to overcome the worldly temptations and blandishments. For some the battle is never really engaged because the real self does not effectively gain enough strength to withdraw or emerge (the emergence of individuality being dependent upon and concomitant with withdrawal from blind, worldly pursuit). The real self is thus not able to survive and is suffocated, smothered or otherwise overcome by the momentum of the world-conditioned, feminine ego-self.

This battle inevitably manifests as considerable tension, stress and frustration in the male. Beneath the conforming, obedient and lawful behaviour—the public face—the inner, private turbulence begins in earnest as the individual attempts to convert the sense of himself being trapped into one of individual freedom and triumph. If the real self is strong, then the resistance of the ego is likely to be so also. The inner conflict may then erupt in aggression and violence, especially directed at the feminine in any form. The inner tension and frustration may well manifest as hatred and exploitation of the female especially.

Particular and typical manifestations of this inner conflict and frustration may be rejection of, and withdrawal from, the domestic situation, obsessive pursuit of career, dissatisfaction with work, divorce, drug taking (medically prescribed or otherwise), alcoholism, gambling and so on—many forms of projected, desperate, provocative behaviour as a means of relieving and escaping the tension within.

It is not possible here to enter into detailed commentary on all that may go astray. It is my intent to pursue in principle analysis of what is happening, how it may be understood and how it may be resolved. I do not suggest that the situation is 'wrong' in the sense that it should have been avoided. It is far too prevalent in the world today to have arisen without purpose in the grand scale of human evolution.

I surmise that the process of 'fall' into illusion (and the suffering therein) is inevitable and that it constitutes the challenge and trial of life as witnessed and experienced by those living in the present age. Paradoxically, it may be that the friction created by this conflict and opposition produces the stimulation and energy to find the solution.

15 *Beliefs; actuality, reality, illusion*

Before pursuing possible ways of comprehending the resolution of inner conflict, it would be useful to interpret two or three other phenomena and introduce certain concepts associated with them.

One of the key mental phenomena involved is the process of believing. Especially important is the forming of beliefs about oneself.

During infancy and most of childhood, the person is 'unconscious' in the sense that he or she is at the mercy of haphazard circumstances and experience. The infant-and-child learns from a seemingly arbitrary external influence of impressions, information and instruction. Having no developed intellectual power of discrimination or evaluation in the right hemisphere, there is virtually no objective censorship of what that person is led or persuaded to believe. Absorption and accumulation of belief establishes assumptions, attitudes and opinions—the basic framework through which personality operates. The construction of this framework and façade is of course inevitable and necessary in that the child has to develop a base from which to be recognised and to be able to operate as a member of society. Regardless of whether it happens to be a positive and beneficial base or a distorted and negatively prejudiced base, the important feature is that either way it is an assumption—an added or superimposed covering. The formation of this covering or protection is the product of an interaction of inner characteristic and outer influence. The result is arbitrary, partial and, above all, *artificial,* in that it is not a *consciously* selected and constructed identity.

The significant point about this process—as touched on earlier in the book—is that the feminine-dominated environment influences and persuades the being to become identified with his or her *physical* presence or existence. Hence, the belief is embedded very early on that 'This is me' (the identifiable body). Upon this assumed identity, the whole personality-fabrication is built.

This process is accomplished early in life by the feminine-left hemisphere functioning. The sexually-differentiated physical entity is thus committed to finding fulfilment in terms of materiality, continuity, procreativity, cause-and-effect logic, historical time, survival through physical endurance, mortality, and so on.

When self-consciousness emerges, the inclination strengthens, due to the body-centred belief, to seek fulfilment in pleasure-seeking pursuit. This further entrenches the ego-self. With the emergence of consciousness of self, however, during adolescence, there arises a more objective and detached assessment. It is then that one may recognise that 'one has beliefs about oneself'.

It is interesting to note how in that expression the word 'about' is used. 'About' means 'around' or 'outside of' which indicates very clearly that the believed identity surrounds or is superimposed upon the real-self, the true identity. This suggests that the feminine-left assumption usurps the power of the consciousness in the masculine-right to form the ego-personality—a false or artificial 'pretender'.

It is often noticeable that part of the disturbance in the adolescent is due to the persuasion to form a definite personality on the one hand in conflict with the inner knowledge that it is a pretence on the other. The former will usually prevail, though, especially in the case of boys, there is often considerable reluctance, even active resistance, to conforming to social convention and requirement. (I recall in my own experience being somewhat bewildered by the fact that I was expected to know and choose what I wanted to 'be' and to 'do' with my life.)

Generally, throughout adolescence and early adulthood, the absorption of the real-self in maintenance of the worldly ego-self is almost total and it is the left-hemisphere personality which traffics with the world. But, schematically, at about 'twenty-eight', the power in the right hemisphere increases, powering intellect, reason and intuition. I take the meaning of 'intellect' here to be, as its Latin roots imply, the power to 'gather, pick out or read between'; hence intellect incorporates the ability to discriminate and evaluate between alternatives.

This increased power in the right hemisphere I have suggested as being associated with increased consciousness. This infers an increased objectivity because of the withdrawn or detached view of the observer—the real-self. Hence, during this phase of adulthood, there may well be increasing unease and discomfort, even a crisis of identity, because the individual becomes more acutely aware that his or her ego-personality is a fabrication and illusion. Of course, the mental disturbance may not be described or manifest in those terms. It is more likely to be a restlessness and discontent which is then blamed on other people and situations—boredom with work or career, feeling trapped in the domestic commitment, and so on.

The inner, real nature begins to assert itself. There may be a frightening sense that through accident of personality and persuasion one has denied real talents and abilities.

As already suggested, this right-hemisphere development takes effect in varying degrees in different people. The more feminine-left dominated the person, the more probable that there will only be minor quakes. The resulting cracks are more easily filled in and life continues more or less steadily and inexorably towards its mortal conclusion.

But what of those in whom there is a serious crisis of identity and a bewildering doubt and confusion? In the absence of intelligent guidance, life becomes very difficult. At worst, an insidious, outwardly destructive or inwardly self-destructive process may begin—a spiritual 'abortion' or 'emasculation'.

Three further words and their meanings (as far as this theme is concerned) may be introduced or elaborated upon at this juncture—actuality, reality and illusion.

The actual world is that in which there is enactment—the 'doing of things'. It is the world perceived by the senses and belongs to the feminine-left hemisphere function. It is logical, ordinarily consistent, predictable and scientifically lawful. It presents itself as the actual experience of the senses—hard, soft, smooth, rough, bitter, sweet, square, round, red, blue, dulcet, harsh, pungent, perfumed. It would be more accurate to say that these are the kind of words we use to describe the actual world. In *actuality,* the actual world is the sum total of immediate sensory experience without description. For example, I may suggest 'the scent of a rose' by using that sequence of learned vocabulary in a particular language. But the actual world is the moment of experiencing the scent of a rose.

Derived from experience of the actual world, there is the spinning of an illusory world in the mind, a process whereby the actual world is given explanation. Ordinarily, we live in this dream world where we explain to ourselves and others our actions, behaviour, plans, etc., and attempt to justify them. We constantly try to give meaning to our earthly existence in terms which we have learned from the world, measuring ourselves and our performance in relation to elusive standards. There are, in fact, no known absolute standards

Beliefs; actuality, reality, illusion

of, say, goodness and badness. You and I are only relatively good or bad, either in our own estimation and opinion or in what we believe to be the world's estimation and opinion. This shifting relativity applies right through the world of illusory explanation and description. For example, I may describe an object as being hard; but it is only hard in relation to something softer; there is no such thing as absolute hardness or softness. Hence, this mental world of explanation and justification is a continuously changing realm of make-believe. It is entirely up to you and I what we wish to believe. Having allowed ourselves to believe, we then inevitably have to abide by the consequences.

In the masculine-right hemisphere world of reality, there is no man-contrived explanation or justification. Once it has developed and gained strength, the function of the right is to know undeniably and consciously through intuitive perception. Such insight is true and revealing for the individual and its power of reason, evaluation, and discrimination transcends collective explanation, justification and opinion. Thus, if I kiss the loved one and experience the ecstasy of that moment I do not need it to be explained that I am experiencing pleasure 'because of the tactile conjunction of labial erotic zones'. I do not need love to be explained to me. If I can dispel preconceived, vague, illusory notions as to what love is supposed to be, I will *know* it when it is consciously experienced.

It is not easy to express this in brief. The above is in itself an explanation, a theory, an illusion. This is not to suggest that it is wrong, or not really there. It serves its purpose in the (Latin root) sense of 'in the game' or 'in the playing'. Life is a game—of deadly earnest. But it is not the game itself that is of importance. In other words, it matters little whether one is performing a role as monk or prostitute; it is what the particular game or fate reveals to the individual in the playing of it. The purpose of playing the game of life is that through the mental or 'middle world' of illusion, created by the real (masculine) meeting the actual (feminine), the former discovers the latter and *between* them the truth is realised—the true identity of the individual. When the right 'marries' the left, the witness commingles with the witnessed, and the result, the offspring, is undeniable. Thus, if I am consciously present, in the precise moment, I know undeniably the scent of a rose as I breathe in its perfume. I *realise* (make real) the *actuality*.

If through reading this explanation the reader recognises veracity in it through knowing it to be his or her experience also, then the purpose is accomplished. The real sparks across the 'mental gap' (the 'aether') and earths in the actual. The individual realises for himself or herself the inexplicable truth.

> The deepest truth cannot, like other objects of study, be put into words: from long intercourse and close intimacy with the facts, it comes suddenly into existence in the soul, like a light kindled by a flying spark, and at once becomes self-supporting. *Plato*

When the right hemisphere strengthens in the young adult, he or she begins to suspect for himself or herself that the dream of perfection in the world's terms—which he or she has conjured up individually—is only a game, an unrealisable illusion. (In Shakespeare's words, in *As You Like It:* 'All the world's a stage, and all the men and women merely players.') The artificial and pretending ego-self is seen to be only an actor (an 'enacter') with no real will or constant attributes.

Belief as to who one is, and what one's purpose in existence is, may begin to waver. If personality is intuitively known to be an arbitrary and artificial façade or mask, then two immediate automatic reactions are possible.

Either it will crack and crumble leaving a basically vulnerable, uncertain and fearful disposition—such people being continually taken advantage of. Or, alternatively, the reaction is to reinforce the personality. The energy required to maintain this disposition expresses itself as outward acquisition, aggression, ruthlessness and self-confidence, turning the person into a hunter. There are of course varing degrees either side of this simplified division but, generally speaking, it gives rise to what might commonly be called fearful 'feminine' types on the one hand and demanding 'masculine' types on the other, both being applicable to either women or men.

There is, however, a third possibility, which is not an automatic reaction. This needs wise help and guidance for it requires that the artificial façade be deliberately dismantled, a disillusionment which must be concomitant with the development of the individual's 'true face'. In this process of becoming 'true to oneself', the individual 'marries' the real to the actual and the intermediate make-belief-self is gradually dissolved as being of no further use.

In this process of disillusionment, the masculine-real comes to serve the feminine-actual which, in turn, reflects back the true nature

Beliefs; actuality, reality, illusion

of reality. The true individual thus becomes 'all things to all men', the 'universal/university' man, not a 'diversity' man.

A good example of the actual/real relationship is demonstrated in the context of scientific discovery.

The scientist in a particular discipline learns a large quantity of facts, figures and laws *about* the properties and behaviour of phenomena in his particular field of study and research. These are all man-invented explanations and descriptions.

The left-hemisphere accumulation of information is ordered and related through the postulation of theoretical structures and models which derive from the right hemisphere capacity to perceive patterns, to synthesise and integrate. The validity of these models are tested and proved through observation that they continue to account fully and durably in repeated circumstances. Once a model is proved reliable then it becomes conventional, standard instruction and succeeding generations of scientists in that field will learn it as sacrosanct practice.

The convention will continue to serve until someone involved in that field of work finds or suspects that he sees some flaw, limitation or inadequacy—something unaccounted for which he observes in the actual enactment before him or something which occurs to him as invalid about, or missing from the theoretical model.

If this troubles him, and he becomes dissatisfied with the accepted convention (feminine), and he is enterprising and adventurous in research (masculine), then he will seek to modify the old model or create a new and more comprehensive one. To begin with, he may well work diligently with his left-hemisphere, logical, two-dimensional, linear application capacity to analyse in detail and mechanically change relationships in the hope that the inspiring resolution of the problem will occur to him.

It is well attested that the 'break-through' discovery—i.e., an inspiration of major significance that radically changes the direction of research, as distinct from a minor modification or projection of the existing model—often comes about as a sudden revelation. It often 'breaks through' as a seemingly accidental, spontaneous and unexpected comprehension of a new, synthesising pattern or structure.

One feature often related of an event of this nature is that it happens when the researcher is in a state of day-dreaming or 'absent-mindedness', or is 'half-awake', or wakes up in the middle of a night's sleep. In other words, the masculine inspiration breaks through when the feminine functioning is temporarily quiet or abandoned.

It should be noted also that such discovery occurs after intense working in the left hemisphere; in Plato's words, after 'long intercourse and close intimacy with the facts'.

In this manner, an existing model or belief is shown to have been inadequate or 'illusory' and is succeeded by another which will be acclaimed as being 'closer to reality'.

Unfortunately, science, being 'in the pay' of society, is then inevitably drawn to applying the improved model to exploit the actual for the purposes of social gain. All too easily, if the motivation is selfish, application of the discovery is indiscriminate and thus does masculine-inspired creativity become destructive. (For example, the beneficial/detrimental effects of atomic energy.)

Something of the appropriate nature of discovery is suggested, I feel, in the quotation about tradition (p.54) where the proposition is made that until the creative artist is fully trained and well-grounded in the disciplines and techniques of his art or craft, his inspiration will be self-indulgent and wasted. Until the illusions of ego-expression are dispelled, it will not be possible to express reality in a truly individual, masculine, spiritual manner. These principles were undoubtedly followed in European Renaissance art where long apprenticeship to a master preceded the ability and permission to become an artist in one's own right. (Note the expression 'in one's own *right*'!)

These principles may be extended to apply to conduct appropriate in all spheres of social life. In fact, I suggest that the philosophical principles involved underline, and are independent of, particular applications. In other words, the understanding of the principles precedes their expression in traditions of art or anything else. Thus, it is applicable to the philosophy of education, institutionalised or otherwise.

This means that it is necessary for discipline to be exercised on the young, not just for social convenience but in the further interests of the individual. It is important therefore that the individual first learns to conform with social law and expectation. If he or she does not learn to accede to the social tradition, then his or her ego-self will inevitably drift into a wasteful and wilful course of pleasure-seeking and self-gain, which is most unlikely to benefit the society or that individual in the long term.

Having learned responsibility to the feminine-social-sexual-economic ethos of his or her environment, the true individuality may then begin to be sought and expressed in late adolescence or early adulthood. This emergent individuality may be of a 'rebellious' nature and may well run counter to the accepted social convention. It will however be 'within the law' in the sense that right-hemisphere reason and discrimination will understand that the 'rebellion' is not a conflict with the world 'out there' but, within the freedom and toleration offered by society, an opportunity to embark on a quest of self-discovery, for the rebelliousness is caused by the real-self seeking to find expression. This expression may then be used to serve society, a process through which the society gradually evolves (instead of tending towards disintegration and anarchy, which is the result of personality opportunism, or ego self-seeking).

I am well aware that there are (and have been) situations and communities where the social discipline is so strong that the individual spirit is in danger of suffocation. History demonstrates, however, that individual spirit is never annihilated; sooner or later it re-asserts itself with great strength.

16 *Adulthood and the spiritual quest*

In young to mature adulthood, the strengthening masculine-right may cause turbulence. The spirit is restless beneath the social façade.

This may well manifest, for example, within the individual as re-emergence of the questions of adolescence, only this time with a greater urgency and insistence, perhaps desperation.

Who am I? What am I doing? What is the purpose of it all? How did I get into this situation? Am I trapped or is there a way out?

The understandable response to this questioning precipitated by the masculine right in the male and female may be to ignore it, suppress it and to press on with applied effort to achieve the imagined fulfilment in work, career, children and home—or perhaps in some hobby or pastime. But this may not suffice for some. For it may dawn that these pursuits in themselves are leading nowhere—in really, self-fulfilling, spiritual terms. Capacity to continue the present course is bound to decline in due time. Work cannot provide satisfaction indefinitely. Children grow up and leave home, new generations succeed and render their parents redundant. Is it then only a question of peaceful retirement and enjoyment of such pleasures as can be afforded whilst health and energy remain? The feminine may be fearful to answer other than in a surrendering affirmative; the masculine may not readily accept this fate.

What though is the alternative?

This is where I begin to discern the first hopeful evidence in support of sexual/spiritual conversion. It may appear at first to be a negative, defeatist proposition. If all worldly pursuits lead nowhere other than to self-degeneration, may it not be that, at the appropriate time, they should be withdrawn from? May it not be that individual fulfilment really has nothing to do with achieving success in the world's terms?

During the young adult phase, the sexual-procreative and the group-survival aspects of life are in full momentum. Although this may be challenging, satisfying and fulfilling in physical, social feminine terms, these pursuits do not provide sound answers to the questions mentioned above. The individual needs to heed those questions and not bury himself or herself in activity and pleasure-seeking.

If the questions are heeded and the individual determines to look for the answers, then the spiritual quest begins in earnest. The masculine right desires to know true identity and the real meaning of life.

I hasten to add that the above proposition is not advocating a precipitous abandonment of present responsibilities and commitments; they have to be met and honoured. Rather, it is the need to withdraw steadily from popular belief; in particular, this means ceasing to deceive oneself that these pursuits will bring any real and lasting sense of fulfilment.

This process does not therefore imply abandonment and rejection of the feminine; but it does mean that for the masculine to have real opportunity it must cease to be fooled. Ultimately the masculine does withdraw completely; but not until the later phases called 'retirement'.

Inevitably, the conversion from the physical-sexual commitment to the spiritual-intellectual concern is dependent on increased consciousness or awareness. The effect of consciousness, as discussed before, is to objectify. As this objectification increases, it is as if there is an increase of 'illumination'. This makes it easier to 'see' the illusions of acquired beliefs and to 'listen' to the penetrating questions. The combination of the two—the first active workings of spirituality—is likely first to cause realisation in the form of disillusionment.

The realisation, for example, that selfishly pursued fame and fortune in the world does not bring a sense of happiness and enriching fulfilment is a disillusion. It may not be a pleasant experience to admit it if one has spent many years in the pursuit; but it is a relief to let the illusion go. Many such beliefs will have to be surrendered; the hardest of all to relinquish are some of the beliefs one has about oneself.

The problem that arises, however, is that, whereas in sexual-economic-worldly terms degrees of success and failure may be measured by wealth and status, there are no such quantifiable, generally-accepted measures of spiritual attainment. In the words of the Persian poet, Farid ud-Din Attar, the spiritual quest is 'the flight of the unknown to the unknown'. In other words, the world of illusion is comparative and human lives are relatively successful or otherwise. In the worlds of the actual and the real, there is only what *is*.

Probably the first point to be made about the process of disillusionment is that it commonly needs to be undertaken with help and guidance. For one reason, the left-hemisphere based ego-self becomes over the years accustomed to relying for its security and continuity on well-embedded beliefs about itself. These are not easily surrendered for, no matter how foolish and false those beliefs, they still act as support and protection. Attempting the removal of them by oneself is like trying to lift oneself with one's own shoe laces. The result is likely to be the replacement of one foolish belief by another just as inappropriate. The process therefor requires intelligent instruction, guidance and help by an individual (or group) who understands the spiritual quest in a particular context, not only that progress may be accomplished but to make sure that care, assurance and support is available if necessary. Sometimes, when illusory beliefs fall away, they reveal a certain deeper anxiety and doubt which needs to be drawn out rather than covered over.

I cannot go into this in detail here, not just because of the lack of space available but because of its very nature this is a private and individual process differing in enactment and realisation from person to person. Furthermore, the forms of instruction and practice differ widely—some appealing to one type whilst being distasteful to another, some meaningless to one type whilst being essential to another.

I do not intend to imply by the above that there is anything specially strange, mystical or magical about this quest. Particularly in its earlier stages, it can be pursued through many forms of self-expression. These will range from physical skills and crafts through all manner of emotional, artistic expression to intellectual studies in the fields of psychology, philosophy and religion.

The essential point is that they are directed at development of the right hemisphere in that they are undertaken as a means to self-discovery. In absolutely no way should they be engaged in as a means to acquire material benefit or status. They are amateur in the pure and dignified meaning of that word—being undertaken for 'love' and nothing else. This is an absolute law, with no exception whatsoever. To confuse the two motives is utterly (real-)self defeating. For, immediately worldly gain is involved, the motive transfers to desiring worldly (left hemisphere) success. It is surely some indication of degeneration that the word 'amateur' has these days attracted connotations of limited worth whilst its (mistaken) counterpart, 'professional', is assumed to be the prerequisite of excellence and dependability. I feel sure I do not have to elaborate on the perversity of this development. I am not saying, of course, that the amateur should ignore the technical skill of the professional; but I am certainly saying that the professional should never lose sight of the fact that he or she is essentially an amateur, *always*.

The crucial factor in the spiritual quest of self-discovery is the calibre of the teacher and guide. If the teacher does not understand the nature of the quest within the discipline he is working through, then the undertaking will be ininspiring and the aspirant will sooner or later become disappointed. The constant questions which must always hover in the mind of the aspirant would be something like: Am I realising anything that I did not understand before? Do I feel this is right? Is it helping to clear confusion? Do I feel any less ignorant?

Although much may be discovered concerning one's real talents and abilities—and working at them and revealing them will be rewarding and enjoyable—through finding and joining a good teacher in an artistic discipline, the practice of such arts does not necessarily take the quest beyond a certain degree of self-discovery. The further goal of self-realisation—understanding one's identity and purpose as a human being—requires intellectual exercise and discipline. In whatever context it may be possible to apply them, this means an understanding of psychology, theology and philosophy. At one time, these were not compartmentalised and secularised studies; they were very much the concern of the religious 'professor' or 'confessor'—for example, the priest-scholar, who was often expected to carry out the function of psychiatrist also.

It is in this old tradition that we may discern perhaps the origin of the assumption, common even today, that spirituality is exclusively confined to the religious context. In other words, it would be said that spirituality 'is something to do with religion'. Though this may once have been the case (due to the fact that religious practice was the corner-stone of society and the majority was 'religious'), it is not now so in societies where religion is a minority interest or does not exist at all. The trouble is that because of the once close association, a person is apt to assume that because he or she does not practice a religion, then he or she is not spiritual. That is why I have tried to emphasise in this theme that spirituality is *not* exclusively the prerogative of religion.

On the contrary, I would suggest that the spiritual element of life is continuous feature in every single person's life in every event from conception through the whole life, even to after-death. Thus it is every person's responsibility, once aware of the possibility and desirability of doing so, to understand spirituality, whether in a religious context or not.

At one time, it seems that the religious representative, the priest-scholar, was responsible for the feminine *and* the masculine supervision. The former ensured that the spiritual enactment was recognised right through the physical-procreative cycle. Divine blessing was given to procreative copulation, birth and initiation ceremonies, marriage contracts and death rites. This aspect, of course, survives today in communities where there is a religious establishment.

Apart from this feminine, social, supporting role, the priest-scholar was also however responsible for the masculine, teaching aspect of spirituality. Vestiges of this may still survive though it has usually been emasculated and drastically reduced, as far as the layman is concerned, only evident as instruction for ritual, as repetition of doctrine and occasional counsel over worldly problems. There may be some public advising and persuading, and (rarely today) admonishment and remonstration from the 'preacher', and some private practice of 'confession' in one form or another but, generally speaking, intelligent, philosophical teaching in the interests of individual, spiritual self-realisation is absent. That is to say, this seems to be the case as far as the Judaic-Christian-Islamic establishment is concerned; it may not be so withdrawn in the Eastern traditions.

As far as the West is concerned, the decline of religion's masculine responsibility was concomitant with the rise of democratic or autocratic secular powers and the growing wealth of nations which moved into industrialised economies and embraced the scientific panacea. It is as if the bias inclined significantly towards the left-hemisphere, social, sexual, economic concern, with an accompanying tendency to reliance on the 'religion' of scientific fact.

As usual, it is not possible to speak confidently of cause and effect, and thereby apportion blame for this development. It is not a case of

Adulthood and the spiritual quest

the demise of religious influence causing the conversion to social worship of scientific magic, or *vice versa*. It may be seen in retrospect as a coincident rise and fall, an inevitable movement in the wave-like evolution of mankind's progress.

The effects of the shift were obvious enough. The social, economic, secular authority became divorced from the spiritual, religious authority (despite the retention in some cases of a monarchic figure-head as combined head of religion and state). So confident did the secular authorities become through the acquisition of material wealth and technological power—and then, later, through the faith and belief that scientific research and knowledge would solve all problems—that they saw fit, among many other developments, to take over responsibility for rapidly expanding programmes of education.

In this process, education was effectively doomed to 'emasculation', as the ecclesiastical influence was gradually excluded. Education became increasingly devoted to the learning of facts within the context of social morality. There came to be no purpose in the learning other than as a means of acquiring wealth and status. A certain lip service was paid to 'religious education' but even this degenerated also into a bland learning of facts. In modern times, in industrialised nations, education is so left-hemisphere dominated—i.e. so directed at simply producing socio-economic members of society—that it has become almost totally 'uninspired'. It has even had to be made 'compulsory'. Even 'further' or tertiary education fell to the same fate and most universities are nothing of the kind; to label them as such is to disguise the fact that they are simply 'technical institutions' for the inculcation of more specialised assemblies of facts, especially in more and more isolated outposts of scentific information.

Instead of the right-hemisphere exploration and synthesis of all knowledge concerning the nature of the individual or 'whole man', further education was given over to the accumulation of left-hemisphere information, of which there gradually became so much that it was necessary to introduce specialisation and compartmentalisation. All forms of study were made 'scientific'. To put it simply, the priest-scholar-teacher, a wise 'all-rounder', was succeded by the theologian, plus the philosopher, plus the psychologist, plus the sociologist and so on. As a result, for example, psychology as a separate science, became devoted to the maintenance of 'normal' sexual, socio-economic human beings. The individual was thus relegated from being a unique, spiritual aspirant to become some hypothetical, average abstraction. Any variation from this spiritless model is abnormal, and such aberration may well be considered anti-social and needing to be rectified. Philosophy, instead of being the means whereby the individual could work to understand his own nature and his relationship with the universe, degenerated into an abstruse, theoretical and sterile indulgence in which hours of debate were (and are now) spent, and reams of paper consumed, in comparing one school of theory and thought with another. Such philosophers, as one American humourist put it, 'try to find a glorious explanation for their own insignificance.' Little or nothing of any benefit is produced for the aspiring layman who is daunted and excluded by their arid discussions and publications.

Meanwhile, the religious establishment, robbed of its vital teaching responsibility, was (and is) relegated to the sidelines from where, in impotence, it made (and makes) occasional pleas and protests, having to be content to offer its traditional blandishments and comforts to those frightened and troubled members of society who need comfort and refuge.

To return then to the situation of the young adult wishing to pursue self-discovery and attain self-realisation, he or she will tend to find the establishment institutions in industrialised society woefully bereft of the means to inspire. Neither in further education nor the formal religious context is he or she likely to find profound, inspirational instruction.

Fortunately, though the spiritual influence may have suffered widespread public rejection over recent decades, it cannot be extinguished. As during previous 'eclipses' or 'dark ages', real knowledge tends to 'go underground' and survives with minorities in hidden retreats. There is no doubt that today it is again finding expression in a great variety of 'alternative' schools, societies, disciplines and practices. And in response to the growing demand, teachers have emerged, and are continuing to do so, ready to respond enthusiastically to this 'surge of the spirit'.

Needless to say, the social establishment has regarded this development with suspicion, automatically disposed in the main to resist it, criticise it and suppress it since it represents a threat to its status and survival.

No doubt some of the teachers in this resurgence have been and are 'false prophets'. It is inevitable that there should be a degree of ignorant misguidance at the inception stage of a general evolutionary movement. The establishment religions have been lent some respectability by the passing of time but, especially in the Western traditions, they have been during their history guilty of the most atrocious behaviour towards their fellow men. Some of the establishment critics of the present spiritual resurgence would do well to consider at what expense their own respectability was bought.

For the young person who now wishes to 'discover reality', there is an increasingly widening variety of opportunity, some based on the wisdom of past traditions, some exploring new contexts and dispensations. The aspirant now does not have to look far to find enterprising movements and he or she has only to find a teacher, discipline or group which he or she feels, and intuitively knows, is *right* for him or her at the time. I hope I do not have to emphasise that I am not talking about mundane, politically motivated, power-seeking, group movements whose causes, protests and ideologies are intended to disrupt or destroy society, by violent means if necessary. These represent the masculine, right hemisphere 'gone mad'. I am of course referring, exclusively, to those well-meaning and peaceful movements whose prime concern is evolution of the individual, which, if appropriately carried out, means an infusion into society of enriching elements whose works and example change society without the need of persuasion and force.

In the terms of this theme, the individual in this quest should continually be asking himself or herself: Am I finding better understanding as to who I am and the purpose of human existence in this universe?

If the answer is in the affirmative, then all is well. If it is in the negative, then it might well be time to move on and look elsewhere.

17 *Meditation; consciousness and sexual 'normality'*

One of the most publicised features of the current spiritual development, first presented publicly to the West some twenty years ago, is the technique of meditation. This is not to say that the practice did not previously exist in the West; it surely did in different forms of presentation and with different labels. For example, it has close affiliation with contemplative or silent prayer—not with public, intercessory prayer. As formal religion lost its masculine responsibility, so the latter form of prayer (feminine-left hemisphere) completely dominated the former, certainly as far as the public congregation was concerned.

Meditation could be said to be a masculine-inspired practice which is aimed primarily at quietening the left-hemisphere functioning. So obsessed is a person likely to become, as a result of education and other environmental conditioning, with future survival and gain in an ethos devoted to status, security and economic expansion, that desires and anxieties produce a circling, whirling confusion of uncontrolled thoughts and imaginings. This confusion in turn obscures, or cuts the person off from, experience of the actual world and its real meaning—the 'here-and-now' experience and its true significance for that individual.

In principle, the disciplined practice of meditation quietens the circling mental activity and allows the confusion to clear. (Although in the clothing store experience described at the beginning of the book I was not 'deliberately' practising meditation, the effect was the same. Having practised meditation for some years, a situation develops where the mind falls into a contemplative state automatically when there is no immediate 'thinking' demand.) This quietening of the mind, in turn, allows the real to penetrate and merge with the actual. Thus the feminine state of 'naked being' is conjoined with the masculine 'knowledge of the here-and-now'.

It should be added that this practice of meditation is essentially intended for the individual, spiritual aspirant (though it may help sometimes to undertake it in the company of others). Any secondary, 'spin-off' benefits in terms of increased social potential are appropriately directed to the needs of others. In situations where meditation is advertised as a means of attaining personal status or improving powers to increase material gain or economic influence, or where it is usurped by secular authority (as in its use by the American armed forces, for example) primarily to condition members to function better in the society's interest, then inevitably the essential spirit of meditation is emasculated.

A further point is worth making at this juncture concerning a development in sexual behaviour associated with increased consciousness or awareness—a point directly related to the sexual-spiritual conversion proposition.

The socially-conditioned sex therapist is devoted to maintaining what he or she sees as 'normal' sexual functioning, in both its procreative and pleasure-seeking aspects. In some literature on the subject, one might be forgiven for deducing that the object of such therapy is to enable and to ensure that anyone should be able to have active, sexual, orgastic relationship right through to the eighth decade of life! Anything *en route* which hinders or precludes this 'ideal' achievement is called a malfunction (or, more popularly, in psychiatric parlance, 'dysfunction') implicit in which is the belief and assumption that something has gone wrong with the person's sexual functioning, either physically or psychologically.

Of course, it is quite appropriate that any physical defect or psychological inhibition or psychosomatic problem which is militating against the natural procreative process with its attendant enjoyment during mature adulthood should, if possible, be rectified. What I find questionable is the assumption that something has necessarily gone wrong if, after the procreative phase of life, there is not actively continuing sexual relationship and orgastic, sensual pleasure. This may appropriately be the ideal for a proportion of people but the implication that it should be for all could be an insidious misconception in that it may persuade the abstainer, voluntary or otherwise, that he or she is abnormal. Such is the possible danger invited by the development of 'scientific' specialisation where the 'expert' becomes so confined within a particular discipline that he or she does not allow for the possible relevance of features alien to that discipline.

Thus, one therapist whose book[11] I read recently actually lists religious influence as one of the causes of sexual malfunction.

A negative, suppressive religious influence may indeed be a factor in inhibition but the commentary totally ignores the possibility that the religious ethos may have something positive and relevant to contribute to comprehension of the role of sexuality in the complete or wholistic view of human purpose. It could be that the rampant octogenarian, delighting in achievement of sexual performance in bed, has in the process totally ignored the real point of his or her life. At least it should be considered as a possibility.

Indefinite continuation of active sexual relationship seems to me to be one of those hoping-it-will-never-end or fearing-it-will-end situations in which the continuing is the all-important and only view. This is understandable if sexual disinclination is believed to be an unfortunate and involuntary degeneration. It is tragic if this negative attitude obscures the possibility that disinclination may be a positive sign of the withdrawal concomitant with advance of the spiritual life.

The teacher to whom I referred earlier, when asked how one might define a normal person, replied: 'One who is capable of evolving out of his or her present situation.' As I have found that to be an excellent and enduring definition—particularly as it lifts normality out of its common connotation of 'static averageness' towards a sense of vital, dynamic self-responsibility—I am prompted to question whether, after the procreative phase, attempts to maintain an active sex life should be championed as 'normal' at all. In the absence of any alternative resolution as to how the post-procreative phases of life should be spent, I suppose endeavouring to gain maximum sensual pleasure (sexual or otherwise) is preferable to degeneration into the bitter and aggressive resentment or the miserable and complaining apathy often characteristic of senility. But are they really the only possible alternatives?

It is of course my endeavour in this theme to suggest evidence for the possibility of sexual-spiritual conversion. It seemed to me significant therefore that one of the most inhibitory psychological phenomena causing sexual malfunction is called 'spectatoring'. The gist of the phenomenon is that one of the participants in sexual intercourse experiences a situation in which, instead of being totally involved and abandoned in the act, he or she becomes suddenly 'detached' and finds himself or herself observing the event as a dissociated onlooker. This can have an immediately inhibiting effect on the nervous systems involved whereby they cannot then be 'willed' to continue the momentum towards orgasm. There are particular variations of the physical effects of this intervention but in principle, if persisting, the result is a rapid disinclination to enter at all into sexually demanding relationships. Significantly, this form of male impotence and female frigidity does not preclude either sex achieving orgastic climax through masturbation in private. In other words, this suggests that spectatoring is an intervening factor in male/female relationship which threatens or denies the feminine, procreative aspect, but not necessarily the masculine, pleasure-seeking aspect.

The chief significance is that spectatoring, or detachment, or dissociated observation, implies an objectification which in turn, I have previously suggested, implies an increased degree of consciousness or awareness. To reach right back through aforementioned hints of spiritual evolution, it could now be said that what began as self-consciousness in childhood and developed into consciousness of self in adolescence now becomes 'objective consciousness'. In other words, the observer within, the 'essential spirit' in each individual, evolves out of involvement and begins to observe objectively all that appears before it. The effect of this phenomenon is, among other things, to immobilise motivation. The *continuing* process is interrupted and stopped.

In the sexual context, this development in the masculine-right may well intensify anxiety in the feminine-left. This means that in the male there will be exacerbation of the fear of being absorbed or emasculated by the female whilst the female will fear rejection and abandonment by the male.

These developments inevitably result in confusion and estrangement and it is obviously desirable, both for the individual (to facilitate the inner adjustment and reconciliation of the hemispheres) and for the male and female partners (as a couple serving and supporting each other) that the anxiety should be dispelled.

One of the techniques used by one of the schools of sex therapy recommends that the remedial process for overcoming the 'spectatoring' inhibition should begin with non-demanding, erotic, pleasure-giving and -receiving of a masturbatory nature. After restoration of mutual confidence, coitus may then be resumed. If either partner then experiences recurrence of spectatoring, he or she may then be advised to bring to mind immediately his or her favourite sexual fantasy. One of the important features of this therapy is that the rehabilitation exercises are given as a regime to be strictly followed over a period at certain intervals and times until the next counselling session. Part of the psychology of this is that the patients are partly alleviated of their anxieties, fears, guilt, etc., because they are being given 'permission' to participate in these practices by a reassuring, authoritarian figure.

The implications of this deliberate employment of pleasure-seeking and fantasy techniques to re-establish procreative capability should be obvious enough in right and left hemisphere terms. The individual is persuaded by a feminine, establishment authority not only to ban the devilish and interfering 'onlooker' but to employ deliberately those 'lures' which drew the masculine (in the male, in particular) into the feminine procreative purpose in youth. Thus spectatoring is condemned as a sexually disruptive intervention and no recognition is given to the possibility that it may be a sign of evolving, spiritual individuality.

It is perhaps worth speculating on the possible spiritual equivalent of this sex therapy. There would appear to be a religious equivalent in that the therapist is analogous to the priest-scholar. The sexual anxieties of emasculation and rejection are representative of the fear of extermination—mortal death. The instruction and regime of sex therapy echo the commandment and repetitive ritual of religious ceremony, undertaken in both instances by an authoritarian counsellor-teacher. The pleasure-seeking and fantasy are reminiscent of the promise of reward in after-life in a dream-like heaven or paradise. The connubial bliss and the orgastic ecstasies are like the spiritual union with the divine with its rapturous, mystical ecstasy. (And it is not without relevance that the words 'rape' and 'rapture' come from the same Latin root.)

That speculation apart, it is, as I have said, the consciousness aspect of the spectatoring phenomena which is significant for this theme. Since other creatures do not appear to suffer sexual malfunction as a result of this detached, monitoring capacity, it would be reasonable to assume that it is peculiar to man and it seems probable that its emergence is connected with man's massive cortical brain formation wherein lies his intelligence. If awareness of self and objective consciousness are associated with right-hemisphere development in particular and this evolutionary step can bring about interference with natural functions, especially the sexual-procreative function, does that then indicate that the evolution of consciousness in man provides the means whereby he may transcend the natural order (to accomplish that which 'nature is not conduct of')? May it not be that the spiritual purpose evolves out of or transforms the physical, procreative purpose so that mortal regeneration may be translated into individual immortality? In other words, does the cerebral cortex have the power to modify the instinctive and emotional mechanisms of the ancient brain?

If so, it is of enormous significance since it puts all human undertaking into a new perspective. If it were widely acknowledged as being a possibility, and energy were devoted to it on a large scale, then the socio-economic competition and conflict in the world would lose its aggressive, destructive motivation.

A small piece of evidence points to this possibility.

It has been found by neurophysiologists that orgasm is a reflex response whose lowest neural centre is located in the lumbro-sacral section of the spinal cord. It is subject to both facilitatory and inhibitory influences from direct sensory experience and from higher neural centres. It has also been discovered that orgasm can be triggered simply by sensory input in the higher nervous centres alone. This has been accomplished with animals in laboratory experiments with electrical stimulation in particular areas of the brain. Furthermore, in human experience, it is not uncommon, in the absence of any genital or erotic stimulation, for orgasm to be precipitated by deliberately imagined fantasies. Also, without tactile stimulation, orgastic emission accompanied by erotic dream can take place during sleep, although in this case it is difficult to assert whether the dream is cause or effect.

The relevant point to be drawn is that the ecstasy of sexual climax can be induced in the absence of external stimuli through activity in higher neural centres of the brain. The possibility thus arises that perhaps the religious, mystical ecstasy is a form of brain stimulation devoid of any external erotic or sexual element. This phenomenon may well in fact be dependent on the disciplined abstention from sexual activity by the religious aspirant. It would be most interesting to know if similar areas of the brain are involved in both forms of ecstasy. If so, it could be inferred that self-discipline is a conscious and deliberate intervention from the cortical area of the brain which may override and transcend the 'animal' desires and proclivities of the ancient brain. It may even be that such discipline over an extensive period of time could actually bring about a psychogenetic alteration in the physiology of the brain cells.

It would then be understandable that the cortices could so dominate and transform the motivations of the ancient brain that even the fears associated with self-preservation would be eliminated. This would account for the evidence that martyrdom held no fears for the ardent religious believer. The overall implication of all this speculation is that 'transcendence of death' may well have much to do with the evolution of the left and right hemisphere relationship and that this, in turn, depends very much on a transformation of physical-sexual energy to spiritual-intellectual energy, and, in particular, a transfer from feminine-left domination to masculine-right domination.

I am sure that there is nothing 'new' in this proposition. Particularly in the religious context of times past, it must have been 'instinctively' known and well understood, even though only a minority of aspirants undertook it and they expressed the evolution in terms unfamiliar to us today. What is appropriate now, if and when it is destined to be recognised widely enough, is the expression of it in modern 'scientific' terms. The full measure of spirituality would then be restored to human life, perhaps on a scale unprecedented in mankind's history. It will require something of this calibre to direct and control a world somewhat bewildered by a mounting pile of socio-economic problems which science is beginning to fail to solve at a rate faster than it is creating new ones.

I hope this does not sound as though I am advocating a puritan reaction to present-day permissiveness. I do not mean to suggest an immediate, general suppresssion or rejection of sexual expression. On the contrary, modern liberalism seems a good deal healthier than the inhibitory effects of socially-imposed censorship and restriction. The sexual and the spiritual are inextricably commingled and unnatural interference with one inevitably interferes with the other. They are bound as partners, like man and woman, right through from beginning to end of mortal life and are both present in all human behaviour from cradle to the grave. The appropriate process, I am suggesting, is a gradual change of emphasis, a natural conversion from the dominance of one to dominance of the other. Further, it is a conversion within the individual's constitution and in his or her own terms. It should 'ideally' be a measured and moderate progress—with no violent or irresponsible reactions.

Meditation; consciousness and sexual 'normality'

The nature of the spiritual quest is beautifully encapsulated in inscription at Delphi: 'Know thyself' and 'Nothing in excess'. The latter is an excellent guide to conduct and how to regulate self-control. It is obviously a warning against excessive self-indulgence; but it is also a warning against excessive self-denial.

18 Illumination; mid-life

What then does the conversion from sexual to spiritual emphasis mean to the adult individual? What are the implications of the spiritual evolution which begins as self-discovery, leads to self-knowledge and thence to self-realisation (in parallel with the experiences of self-consciousness, consciousness of self and objective consciousness)?

In a reference I read recently—extracted from a book[12] about spiritual illumination, published at the beginning of the present century—some helpful indicators were mentioned.

I interpret 'illumination' here to mean some form of profoundly revealing, inner comprehension (though many who have experienced it speak of an actual sensation of intense light concurrent with the intellectual understanding).

The commentary stated that, in about eighty per cent of cases where such experiences have been recorded, they have done so between the ages of thirty and forty (which is roughly commensurate with the seven-year measures from twenty-eight to forty-two). The most common age for it to happen was given as thirty-three (or about seven times five). The remaining twenty per cent were spread comparatively sparsely right across a spectrum from the age of twenty through to fifty-five (say twenty-one to fifty-six).

This indicates that such experience is unlikely to happen—perhaps cannot happen—before the point of physical maturity/mental 'puberty' (referring to the table on p.99). It is also unlikely to happen after the age of fifty-six—which is the equivalent of spiritual 'menopause' or the beginning of 'dying to the world'.

Although the part of the commentary I read does not say so, I would suggest that such illuminations are not usually simply accidental, sudden, once-and-for-all, gone-and-forgotten occurrences. On the contrary, they will have been prepared for and earned with effort, and the repercussions and ramifications of them may well take 'twenty-one' years to be worked through and thoroughly assimilated and understood by the individual concerned.

Other subsidiary insights may also follow the initial revelation, continuing at intervals over a period of many years. The essential

Illumination; mid-life

nature of these phenomena—whether sudden, profound and dramatic or gradual, cumulative and unsensational—is that they indicate clearly to the individual the direction he or she needs to follow in order to realise his or her fulfilment and destiny.

I have made a point of suggesting that such insights may be 'gradual, cumulative and unsensational' because I maintain that it would be mistaken to assume that those who experience the dramatic and sensational revelations are special and privileged. In fact I would go so far as to say that a fair number of the accounts I have read, especially those by women in the religious context, have melodramatic and histrionic overtones which are highly suspect, having an ego-based, self delusory quality about them. This is not necessarily to blame or criticise the persons concerned; all too often it is others who have had a vested interest in making propaganda for their cause who have elaborated and dramatized the feats of their champions; perhaps to the extent that the persons concerned would not even recognise its having had anything to do with them.

Whether that be the case or not, what I wish to emphasise is that there is not necessarily anything special and dramatic about spiritual insight. Ordinarily it is a gradual, cumulative and unsensational process of becoming disillusioned, so that the truth slowly dawns. And every ordinary, sincere and sensible person may participate in that process if moved to do so.

Nevertheless, en route, there may well be special moments of insight which feel like a sudden revelation. These may happen any time between 'twenty-one and fifty-six', especially in the middle of that bracket when the physical, mental and spiritual functions are at their peak as a threefold combination. (The physical has started to decline and the spiritual has not yet reached full potential but, at about 'thirty-five' they are at their optimum point as a trinity.)

The spiritual insights, which usually take the form of disillusionment, are of course exclusive to the individual concerned. The recognition of the falsity of a belief which one has probably held for many years is always and inevitably in the terms peculiar to the person. Only he or she can 'see' it in that special way because the form of the bondage or block belongs to that person alone (although others may of course feel they recognise the same symptoms in themselves). He or she may well find it difficult to explain to someone else what has happened. The sign of spiritual insight is that the person's face 'lights up' and gives out a sense of relief and release. It is quite unlike the worldly type of disillusionment which leaves the person bewildered, disappointed and despairing, even frightened or bitter or angry or resentful.

According to the commentary referred to earlier, the major, dramatic insights have certain characteristics in common. The profound revelations are usually on a grand, sweeping scale. The experiencer loses all sense of time and personal identity and sees the world in a totally new and different way. For example, it is comprehended as a unified whole instead of an assembly of separate objects.

After such experiences, the individual's structure of beliefs, assumptions, attitudes and opinions changes radically. Sense of responsibility and morality—previously felt as a rigid, imposed and inculcated obligation—converts into a natural, humane and undeniably sensible mode of personal conduct. With the loss of artificially assumed identity comes a reassurance that termination of the personality at death is acceptable. Further it is realised, in so many words, that immortality is not an indefinite continuation of the fictional, personal self, but the real state of all forms in perpetuity. Thus death is a release from the temporary, present-life role or commitment back to spiritual or causal origin (which cannot be envisaged because it has no form).

These are, needless to say, far-reaching realisations in the experience of the individual and I repeat that the characteristics mentioned above apply to so-called 'peak' revelations. They are commonly preceded by considerable hard work (analogous to the preparatory dedication of the scientist prior to his 'break-through' discovery), a searching for resolution of problems sometimes referred to in the Christian context as a continual, inner 'wrestling'. And, as already stated, they are commonly preceded by periods of gradual disenchantment and disillusion. As also indicated earlier, the process is usually undertaken under the guidance of a teacher who can instruct, guide, reassure and explain what is happening, especially in the preparatory stages.

The process is inexorable once it begins. The quest becomes irrefutable because there is nothing in the world of comparable worth. In the right conditions of instruction and support, gradual disillusionment has a self-evident rectitude (a *'rightness'* intuitively cognised in the masculine-right hemisphere). The realisations have an 'obviousness' to the experiencer which no one can deny him or her, partly because the world's judgement is realised as being irrelevant. Concomitant with this gradual, intellectual resolution there comes a greater sense of freedom—not to do just what one pleases but to be undemandingly natural to oneself, and to all other creatures. It feels like a progressive liberation from a previously inhibiting and emasculating bondage.

All the above denotes a 'switch-over' from feminine-left domination to masculine-right realisation.

Schematically then, at the age of 'thirty-five', there is in various senses a climax in life. I do, once again, emphasise 'schematically'. Some may experience it at an earlier age, some later. The former may be called precocious or prodigies, and they are particularly prevalent in fields of creative art. Unfortunately, the premature advance of their right-hemisphere talent sometimes prevents stable establishment of left-hemisphere function, an instability which can cause difficulties in social adaptation and responsibility. For such people, artistic or otherwise, advance of intuition and insight can result in dissociation from the left-hemisphere function and, becoming socially disorientated, they suffer from varying degrees of 'madness'.

At the other end of the spectrum, if the 'awakening' is too late, the personality may prove too inflexible to withstand the impact of disillusionment. Such people also tend to become socially intolerable and have to be restricted in their activities. At extreme, I have encountered both conditions. For example, a demented young man convinced that he was Jesus Christ returned to earth; a young woman so certain she was a reincarnation of the Virgin Mary that she believed she was pregnant without having had intercourse; and, at the other extreme, several old people desperate with remorse for having wasted or abused the opportunities of their lives.

From 'thirty-five' through 'forty-two' to 'forty-nine' is a mid-life period of great import. It is a parting of the ways and the person often feels 'torn apart' as the left hemisphere is reluctant to surrender to the promptings of the right.

On the one hand, there is the conventional, habitual, linear, fateful path (left) which is simply a continuation of the conditioned, programmed dispensation. This route has only two possibilities. One prospect is a possible increase in wealth and social approbation with accompanying scope for pleasure-gain. The other is decrease in capacity and influence with reducing scope for self-gratification. Both possibilities are vulnerable and subject to the intervention of physical or mental breakdown.

On the other hand, there is the path (right) presented to the individual through the challenge and process of spiritual progress through disillusionment. This, as I hope I have by now established, does not mean an isolating, negative erosion of self-confidence resulting in an ennervating entropy or catastrophic collapse. In the absence of wise counsel, it may be so. But, properly understood, positive disillusionment is the reciprocal of realisation of the truth. Thus it should denote the emergence of the real individual, desirous of being obedient to reality. As already discussed, this is not a make-believe, social-concensus view of 'reality' but a self-cognised, undeniable reality which means becoming true to oneself.

It means experiencing the world as it actually *is,* not as one has learned and believed it is supposed to be.

It is interesting to note, in passing, that in sophisticated, industrial nations involved in chasing never-ending, expansionist increase of 'gross national product', there is the concomitant necessity to persuade people to 'consume'. By dint of the working of a curious confidence trick, it is believed, among other things, that the more people consume the richer everyone will become; or that, by spending less one is saving more, and will therefore become richer in order then to be able to purchase and consume more. The longer this make-believe is propagated, the more greedy, consuming and discontented the society becomes and the more its stability is undermined.

One of the effects of this is that in business organisations the age of executive responsibility is 'advanced' so that younger and less experienced men and women hold the positions—younger, that is, than in previous generations. The erstwhile image of the grey-haired or balding director dispensing his wise decisions in the boardroom until forced to retire through senile incapacity has today been somewhat eclipsed by the young, 'go-ahead', 'with-it', sophisticated, fashionably-dressed executive of either sex.

The temptation is to see this trend as an extension of or a projection from the 'advances' noted earlier—the 'brightness' of the child precipitating earlier puberty, and the bringing forward of the age of majority. These were suggested as being understandable in a society devoted to learning information, seeking pleasure and material gain, achieving personality status and so forth, because of the tendency in that ethos to put emphasis on feminine-left hemisphere education and conditioning. In that context, it is then certain that the responsibility for 'execution' of direction and decision should transfer from the wisdom of the elder to the younger person in the economic 'climax period' when his or her sexual, personality power is more astutely in touch with fashionable trends, glamorous appearances, sensual manipulations and 'entrepreneurial' opportunism. Certainly he or she is more likely to sense how to appeal to those in the same age bracket in order to attract and persuade them to consume.

This trend exacerbates a growing social problem related to the theme of this book in that it is further indication of the redundancy of the older person, especially the male, in the post-procreative phases. Not only has the man completed his sexual purpose by middle-age but he is now being denied completion of his natural socio-economic role. As the age of retirement also advances, he is now being denied the ability to continue the work into which he was hitherto able to direct his energies.

There is surely nothing more negatively disillusioning and depressing for the older person than to find that he or she is socially redundant.

Earlier, I called the twenty-one year period from 'twenty-one to forty-two' the mental/emotional mid-life. It is the mind-conversion period during which, ideally, there should be a transition from feminine-left hemisphere, ego-self domination to masculine-right, real self responsibility. This involves a disillusionment or withdrawal from false and unreasonable beliefs about oneself and one's role in life and a turning towards discovery and understanding one's real identity and individual fulfilment.

This conversion will be highly individual in comprehension and manifestation.

One of its manifestations may be dissatisfaction with chosen work or career, especially for the male. He may well regret that he is committed to a daily occupation which he now realises he perhaps drifted into through lack of knowing at the time what he wanted to do or be, or because he was persuaded into it by others or because what appealed to him about it in his youth no longer holds that promise and fascination.

For many reasons with understandable explanations, a man may decide he chose wrongly and that there would be more rewarding courses he wishes he had followed instead. Some do take the risk and change direction; some are fearful of doing so, usually because of the economic and domestic consequences. Paradoxically, the advancing of the age of redundancy or retirement, whichever one prefers to call it, could be something of a blessing in disguise. It may be that, for some, abandonment of the socio-economic, 'professional' commitment may give the opportunity to take up a spiritually-fulfilling, 'amateur' occupation. (A sign of this in England, for example, is the setting up of an 'open university' in which adults of any age may have the opportunity to study subjects which interest them without there having to be necessarily any other motive than self-improvement.)

Successfully accomplished, the mid-life conversion, regardless of whether it involves outward, manifest changes, will certainly bring about inner changes. It should, for example, begin to alter attitude to one's fellow human beings. It becomes no longer necessary to compete with them, demand from them, exploit or use them and no longer appropriate to fear them and feel at disadvantage. To put it simply, and probably as succinctly and accurately as it has ever been stated—by Jesus of Nazareth—removal of acquired attitude allows a 'loving thy neighbour as thyself'.

Inevitably, this means an inner 'marrying' of the left and right hemispheres so that, ultimately, there will be no difference or conflict between the feminine-left, public stance and expression and the masculine-right, private disposition and understanding. This means a 'loving' or merging of the 'neighbouring' hemispheres so that they function as 'one self', the actual-real self. This is surely the prerequisite of equanimity—where the evenness or peace of mind is due to the equality of the two halves of the mind. In this condition, they may then work in balance and harmony—'being of one mind'—instead of competing and contradicting each other—'being in two minds' as common expression has it.

This reminds me of the Zen-style reply given to someone who enquired of a master how it was possible to recognise a self-realised man: 'When he sits, he sits; when he walks, he walks; that is all.'

No conflict. No wanting things to be other than they are. No demand, no fear, no desire. No explanation, no justification required. Thus is consummated the marriage of the actual and the real.

Translated into sexual-spiritual terms, we could say perhaps that a truly 'married' man, when he makes love, *makes* love.

There is an enigmatic statement in what is known in the Christian tradition as Christ's 'Sermon on the Mount' (Matthew, chapter 6) where it is said: 'But when thou doest alms, let not thy left hand know what thy right hand doeth: That thine alms may be in secret: and thy Father which seeth in secret himself shall reward thee openly.'

Interpreted literally, it is a curious statement to make. One explanation, in the terms of this theme, is that it is describing the necessity to observe some circumspection and discretion when the ego-self-interest of the left hemisphere is being converted to the real-self-altruism of the right hemisphere. The latter becomes disposed to love and charitable acts ('doing alms' for their own sake), a disposition which is truly generated from the natural emotion of the 'heart', from one's private, inner conviction ('in secret'). The danger is that the feminine left may well try to usurp this disposition and turn it to worldly account—seeking to be thought well of by others, for example.

The instruction would seem to be saying that it is better not to broadcast and make a performance of one's charitable works ('let not thy left hand know') because 'reward' from the world or the enhancing of one's self-esteem by such acts is to fall back into error.

The right-hemisphere real self is not answerable to the world's judgement. In obeying true intuition or conscience, the right is the medium through which the spiritual manifests and works ('thy Father which seeth in secret himself'). The sacrificing of self-will and the surrendering to divine will reveals a freedom or salvation which is reward enough in itself (without condition or 'openly').

Whether or not this interpretation may be deemed a valid and accurate sense of what Jesus meant at the time, the gist of it is appropriate to the ideal of the sexual-spiritual conversion. If this begins to take place, then the aspirant is well-advised not to seek to exploit his or her understanding for worldly gain but, if required, to offer it for the benefit of others, 'secretly'.

19 *Reflections*

Whatever the form of disillusionment/realisation at 'thirty-five', it represents, in this scheme, the 'watershed' of life, the middle-age transition point where the current of energy or spirit changes direction or emphasis.

The sexual/spiritual aspects are poised in equal strength and are of equal importance to each other. Schematically, the 'fight to be male' reaches a crucial juncture. Either the masculine survives and evolves, leading towards individual fulfilment, or it succumbs and the person reverts to remain simply a socio-economic being, playing out the second half of life according to fate.

Whereas, up to this juncture, sexuality may have blossomed or suffered according to the disposition of the masculine right in both male and female, so from now onwards spirituality may fructify according to the discipline and contentment of the feminine left.

Drawn diagrammatically and simply, the changing emphasis through life would seem as follows (bearing in mind that sexuality means the physical-sexual-social-economic concern of mental activity):

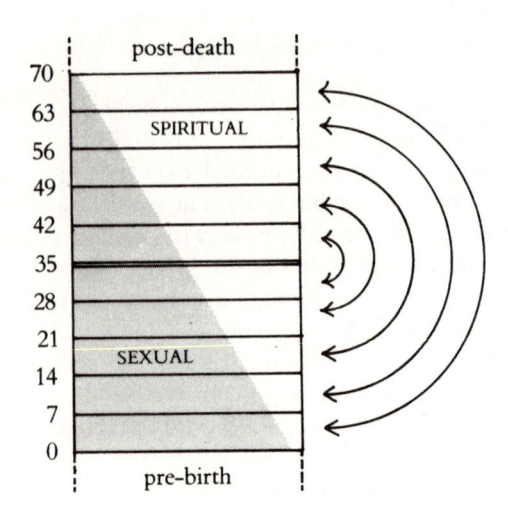

Reflections

At birth, this shows a psychological '99:1' ratio of sexual/physical to spiritual/intellectual. At death, the proverbial 'three score and ten years' of completed life on earth, the ratio has reversed.

The 'one per cent' spiritual presence at birth—the 'entry of the spirit' as the 'breath of life'—is reciprocated by the 'ninety-nine per cent' withdrawn, psycho-spiritual self at the moment of mortal death, where the person is, to all intents and purposes, 'not of this world'. The 'ninety-nine per cent' psycho-sexual being at birth becomes 'ninety-nine per cent' defunct as a living organism at the time of 'giving up the spirit'; the remaining 'one per cent' may be represented by the fading communication manifest in the eyes.

I am reminded, in passing, that when J. M. W. Turner, the artist—who had spent his artistic life trying to master and represent the nature and miracle of light—was at the point of death, he suddenly understood the reality of light. At the last moment, he undeniably knew for himself, in the 'light' of understanding, the divine truth. Thus could a man be said to have realised the destiny of his whole life at the point of death.

Revelations of this kind reinforce my earlier suggestion that a human being should die conciously. Perhaps he inevitably does so. I have often felt, observing old people kept alive 'beyond their time' that, in reality, they were already 'dead' in the spritual sense; the real self within was really 'not there'. Thus the euthanasia debate is surely academic. People already 'dead' are kept physically alive by artificial means due to the feminine obsession with continuity and longevity for their own sake. A person is really dead when he or she 'dies to himself or herself', inwardly. What the world decides to do with the remaining 'machinery' is neither here nor there.

In reality, both the abortion and the euthanasia debates are illusory in that they are based on false premise. As the spirit never 'dies', but is withdrawn, it cannot possibly be killed, no matter what happens to the manifest form. (That is not to say that, *relatively* speaking, at the level of good and evil, anyone has the licence to kill another living organism for his own convenience.)

In the diagram, the pre-zero phase, the embryonic, is reciprocated by the post-death phase (schematically, after the age of seventy). Of neither of these are we ordinarily conscious as existential beings.

This is because consciousness of existence cannot be experienced in the ordinary sense of 'I am' either when the spirit is totally involved 'in the flesh' (before birth) or when it is divorced from the flesh (after death). But it does suggest that the pre-birth foetal existence is reciprocated or mirrored by a certain degree of 'substantiality' after death of the body.

This relates, I surmise, to the affirmation in some traditions that the spirit is not finally released for a period of historical time after the body ceases functioning, and that a degree of 'presence' persists. A number of traditions assert that this period is three days.

It may also be related to a teaching I once heard that 'ghosts' are the result of sudden and violent death which implies that the person concerned has not had time to prepare for death (consciously to relinquish the past). Due to the 'untimely' and precipitated withdrawal, the 'troubled' spirit may not finally be relieved of the 'personality identification' of that life for up to the full post-death duration equivalent of the whole embryonic period back to the conception of that person—reputedly, four hundred years.

I do not know at present how pre-birth 'time' is mathematically related to post-death 'time', and thus how nine months gestation becomes the equivalent of, say, four hundred years, but it would seem to be linked with other traditional assertions such as the notion that successive reincarnations are about four centuries apart. That there should be earthly-time equivalents for these phenomena at first seems unlikely. However, although these non-incarnated states are relatively insubstantial and devoid of the ordinary consciousness of self as 'I am', that is not to say that there cannot be 'knowledge of presence'. This is corroborated by in-life disembodied experiences. The experience of the person under anaesthetic watching himself being operated upon is evidence that he knows he is there observing but has no corporeal sense of location. Likewise, and within anyone's experience, the 'person' watching a dream during sleep is not substantially there participating in the events taking place; and yet he may be aware enough of them to be able to remember them when he wakes up.

Such phenomena imply that there is a substance or vehicle of consciousness beyond or within the gross, physical substance and there is no reason to deny that it may have duration and existence independent of the earthly level of materiality and have its own time-scales. The fact that such phenomena do not readily lend themselves to scientific investigation and explanation is absolutely not proof that they do not 'exist'.

However, to return 'closer to actuality'....

The 'thirty-five' to 'forty-two' period is psychologically the first phase over the watershed of life. This is physically the prelude to 'the change of life', manifesting in the female for example as the menopause in the 'forty-two' to 'forty-nine' period. The person is thus embarked on the second 'half' of life.

In the sexual, physical context, it would seem that this second half is a mirror-reflection (the reverse in phase order) of the first half. Referring back to the previous diagram, 'twenty-eight up to thirty-five' is reflected by 'forty-two back to thirty-five', or 'twenty-one up to twenty-eight' is reflected by 'forty-nine back to forty-two', and so on. Thus, schematically, 'second childhood' is a reflection of the actual, first childhood.

This would account, for example, for the noted fact that old people often have vivid memories of their childhood whilst they cannot remember the recent past. In general, it accounts for the tendency in old people to 'live in the past', recalling particularly and nostalgically their youth. Likewise, the 'second infancy' of advanced senility is very 'physical' in that old people exhibit a vacuity and revert to habits, such as incontinence, reminiscent of actual infancy.

At extreme, it has often been attested by those who have actually survived an imminent threat of death, that their whole lives passed before them in an instant. This could be seen as reciprocal of the concept that at the point of birth the whole potential and 'plan' of the person's life—his or her fate—is already cast. It is not uncommon between these two extremes for people to comment that retrospectively they see their lives up to that point to have been a seemingly accidental but nevertheless inexorable and inevitable progress.

Closer to the middle of life, the optimum child-bearing period of 'twenty-one' to 'twenty-eight' is reciprocated by the cessation in the female of that potential between 'forty-two' and 'forty-nine'. However, the mid-life reflections are generally more subtle, psychological and less easily recognised. Anyone who has lived through pairs of them and is observant enough may, for example, discern how attitudes tend to reverse. To give a personal example, I, as a male, experienced father-reaction behaviour during adolescence and early adulthood, basically by deliberately doing and pursuing those things which proved (to me) that I was not like him. During the reciprocal period from about forty-two onwards, I have noticed (sometimes to my dismay!) that I find myself manifesting father-imitation behaviour towards my children. I catch myself about to react and behave in exactly the ways I resented at their age; at the same time, I find myself much better able to understand and appreciate my father's attitude to me when I was a boy.

As another personal example, I can see that my rejection of the formal religious ethos, especially Christianity, during adolescence is now being reconciled by realisation and appreciation of its worth.

Further, I am beginning to realise the positive aspects of what I had assumed from childhood onwards to be personal faults, weaknesses and shortcomings. Conversely, I see what I once thought to be positive aspects as having been obstructions to self-understanding.

All the childhood influence and conditioning, broadly speaking parental, is summed up in the saying: 'The child is the father of the man.' If the reversal, conversion theme is correct, then the second 'half' of the life, the 'becoming as a child again', is a process of unravelling and absolving the psychological 'knot' tied in the first 'half'.

Another way of looking at the two halves is through a photographic analogy. It is as if the hidden, latent or formative first half ('unconsciously' created) is like the development of a negative—in which the latent image being developed is the dispensation given by the programme of genetic inheritance at conception.

The second half is then like making a positive print from that unrealised or unrecognised negative—i.e., manifesting the positive aspect of the accumulated images particular to the individual person developed as a negative in the first half. The dense black of the negative becomes the white highlight of the positive print and the clear areas of the former become the supportive shadow and dark of the latter. It is as if the weaknesses of the first half become the strengths of the second—as fulfilling destiny—whereas the strengths of the first half become the weaknesses of the second—driving towards fate.

The transfer, incidentally, requires the close contact of the film negative with the printing paper (like the diagrammatic 'mirror-plane' at 'thirty-five'), which then requires brief exposure to intense light ('conscious illumination' or disillusion) for the image to be transferred (transformed).

The negative image transferred to the printing paper then has to be developed. This seems to be analagous to the fact that in the second half of life it is as if one plays out and honours the commitments and obligations undertaken in the first, in the process giving back to society the benefits (or the opposite) of the lessons accumulated. Inwardly, this means that for the individual the second half should ideally be a conscious expiation (by the masculine right) of the indulgencies or 'sins' unconsciously perpetrated in the first half (in the feminine left) and, at the same time, therefore fulfilling that life's purpose through giving back realised wisdom as payment for society's toleration and support. This would constitute a 'forgiveness'—a *giving* back in exchange *for*.

If the second half is then a fully-developed print-out or picture of a fulfilled life, it is a completed record which is 'fixed' at death.

This imagery is reminiscent of the Buddhist concept of *karma* which, briefly, is a word indicating the burden carried by the person of accumulated illusions, faults and errors, either inherited or acquired during the lifetime to date. The purpose of life is to eliminate or absolve that karma. If it is not consciously expiated (by the masculine right) during that life, its effects will continue to repeat (in the feminine left) generation after generation.

The most obvious 'body-clock', physical feature in the 'forty-two' to 'forty-nine' phase is the menopause, the termination in the female of the procreative potential. Needless to say, it may be for the woman a disturbing event, with psychosomatic repercussions.

Less obviously, it is also a significant psycho-spiritual event, for both the female and the male, especially the latter. It may precipitate an intensified inter-hemisphere drama. Quite simply, this may be expressed as the haunting question: 'Is there any purpose left in my life?'

For some, especially those actively engaged in occupations, this may not be an issue of much intrusive import. But it may be, especially for the female, because emotionally she is more body-identified, and for her the termination of the procreative purpose in life is physically demonstrated.

Since the sexual, reproductive role is the means through which the female, active desire for success is enacted, the effect of its termination will much depend on whether she has been successfully fulfilled in that respect or not. Since her psychological disposition may now shift towards the spiritual pole—the active fear of failure as an individual in her masculine-right—she may well experience increasing vulnerability and anxiety. It can be a time of crisis in that her future identity and further purpose are thrown into prominence. It is not comparatively of great compensation that she may still enjoy the pleasure aspect of sexual activity.

The situation for the male is somewhat different. His reproductive capacity is not terminated, even though it may diminish. If his active fear of failure in the sexual, reproductive role has been assuaged by successful procreative functioning and family life, then he is not usually psychologically affected by the fact that his 'fathering' days may be over. He has, after all, in his masculine aspect, been mainly involved in the sexual relationship for its pleasure-giving feature and this may continue if he so wishes.

This propensity in the male, which has already been stressed, is recognised by behavioural observers as being less psychologically vulnerable than it is in the female. This account for the fact that the male is far more inclined to look for casual, sexual relationship (not nearly so one-sided now in permissive societies where the masculine in the female has emerged more forcefully) and, attendant upon that, the fact that prostitution and pornography exist predominantly for male appetite.

Nevertheless, the male is psychologically vulnerable in that the doubts and fears he may have harboured for some years about his individuality, identity and purpose may well become intensified during the menopausal period. The psychological shift towards the spiritual pole moves emphasis from his active, feminine-left hemisphere fear of failure to his active, spiritual, masculine-right hemisphere desire for success as an individual.

There is, of course, a whole range of reactions to this situation. Selfishly, the man may become excessively self-concerned. The crisis represents an undermining of his artificial, ego-self status in the world and he may either suffer a gradual or sudden loss of drive and ambition or, conversely, he may throw more desperate energy into the salvaging, maintaining and furthering of his self-deluded sense of importance and worth. Such reaction represents abandonment or rejection of the feminine, or increased exploitation of the feminine, both being antipathetic to expiation.

Altruistically, on the other hand, he may realise the real responsibility generated by the termination of the procreative phase. This is the beginning of the true spiritual role, the essence of which in worldly expression is willingness to serve and guide the female in their mutual aspiration. This means, for both male and female individuals, an inner reconciliation of the right with the left hemisphere. This requires a surrender on the part of the left of worldly beliefs, illusions and pursuits, concurrent with a sacrifice of wilful and selfish fantasy by the right. Desire for worldly success in sexual, social and economic terms converts to desire for success in individual, spiritual aspiration.

The proposition that it is the masculine responsibilty to serve the feminine in the second 'half' of life does not therefore imply catering for worldly fancies and indulgencies or acceding to self-deluding notions of success. Pursuits of glamour, entertainment and sensual indulgences are not the point; that is to continue and repeat a mode which represents usurpation of the masculine responsibility by feminine ignorance.

The context is spiritual and the aspiration is undertaken without intent for result in this world. Essentially it implies in its feminine aspect allowing or providing the means through which talent may be developed, especially in any capacity of useful and caring service to fellow human beings. In the masculine aspect it means gradual withdrawal from the world so that through meditation, contemplation and the study of religious and philosophical matters, one may prepare for the termination of earthly life.

20 Change of life

In the book concerning sexual therapy previously referred to[11], the author writes:

> It is of great interest that age exerts different influences on the sexual life cycle of men and women. All other human functions, such as, for example, the ability to learn and physical strength or coordination, rise and decline in predictable patterns with age and the two genders are believed to follow similar curves in all of these. Sexuality, however, is quite different. Kinsey's figures indicate, and Masters and Johnson's studies confirm, that men experience the peak of sexual responsiveness and capacity around the ages of seventeen and eighteen and thereafter show a steady decline. Women on the other hand, attain their sexual peak in their late thirties and early forties and thereafter decline at a relatively slower rate than men.

A later paragraph suggests the derivation and conditions relating to this middle-age rise in female sexual appetite:

> Learning seems to be an extremely important determinant of female sexuality, while it is of relatively lesser importance to males. It has been speculated that the middle-age peaking of female sexuality, which is usually seen in women who have a history of successful sex and secure relationships with men, can be accounted for in terms of the accumulated reinforcement derived from repeated pleasurable sexual experiences which increase gratification as sexual techniques accommodate to the special needs of women, as well as to the gradual extinction of the inhibitions and insecurities of youth.

The implications of this disparity in sexual development between male and female are significant for this theme. The above commentaries suggest that, as menopause approaches, and therefore the procreative phase is nearing its end, there is a certain psychological 'release' in the female if she has experienced successful and satisfying sexual activity during the procreative first 'half' of life. The second quoted paragraph suggests that she has learned (in her feminine-left hemisphere) not to fear failure, exploitation, rejection or abandonment by the male.

Since the procreative purpose of her life is now accomplished and

Change of life

the emphasis shifts from the sexual, left hemisphere to the spiritual, right hemisphere, she now experiences the masculine desire for individual success in terms which have been familiar to the male ever since reaching his peak of sexuality during late adolescence—as an urge to sexual pleasure-seeking for its own sake. In other words, as an individual now, instead of a procreative agent, the female experiences a release of sensual desire such as the male experienced in his youth. She may now abandon herself to sexual enjoyment—with no danger of pregnancy after menopause. This is not to say that the masculine aspect of the female does not play a part in the pleasure of sexual encounter during youth; it is to suggest that the sex life during youth and pre-maritally is primarily influenced by procreative considerations and, when these are removed in mid-life, there is a release of the purely pleasure-seeking, masculine aspect.

In passing, it is perhaps in association with this mechanism that there sometimes arises in the female an apparently perverse wish or fantasy (produced by the masculine-right hemisphere) of imagining herself being raped. It is the mirror-reverse of the desire in the male to rape and I suggest that it is 'perverse' in the sense that it is the sexual manifestation of the spiritual desire to surrender to the ravishing or rapturous experience of being penetrated by the 'divine masculine'. (Both 'rape' and 'rapture' derive from the same Latin root.) Thus, in records of female religious ecstasies, there is often allusion and imagery redolent of being overcome or seized by the (masculine) divine presence.

It is surely in relation to this mid-life climax and release of sexuality in the female that the true ramifications of 'women's liberation' should be discerned. Rather than presenting the movement as having licence to as much freedom of expression as the male, with its connotations of being permitted to indulge on equal footing in all manner of worldly, self-seeking pursuit, in this context it denotes equality of opportunity to evolve as a spiritually-aspiring individual.

The liberation is thus dependent upon, and subsequent to, fulfilment of procreative purpose and is certainly not licence to indulge selfishly in all the pleasures and pursuits the world has to offer. The true liberation of the female (and the male for that matter) lies in the ability and freedom to evolve spiritually, especially when the procreative responsibilities are completed, and it is therefore essentially a process of liberation *from* the body, not permission to indulge *in* the body. The latter is to remain in, or to revert to, feminine, left-hemisphere domination.

This mid-life psychological shift represents a new challenge to the male, and to the masculine in both male and female. Again, there will be a number of permutations of response.

In physical terms, if the male is faced with this resurgence of sexual challenge and is disinclined to meet it, or does not know how to cope with it, the female will be tempted to find resolution of it outside the marital relationship. (Given that the male reaches his peak of sexuality in his late teens and that his sexual desire may well be considerably diminished by his fourth decade, this can be a particularly difficult phase for both to negotiate.)

Alternatively, it is possible that the female will not experience this sexual resurgence, especially if she has not had a successful and enjoyable sex life, so that instead she may withdraw and become unresponsive. If she happens to be the partner of a male whose sexual libido is still relatively highly charged, then it will be the male who will look for extra-marital satisfaction.

Whatever the situation for the male and the female at mid-life as regards sexual appetite, the potential for marital or relationship discord is likely to arise if appetites do not coincide or if spiritual aspirations—the transformation of that energy—are not commensurate.

A great deal is currently made of the physical and mental disturbances associated with female menopause and large amounts of drugs are dispensed to alleviate the discomforting symptoms. On the other hand, relatively little is made of the possible parallel changes taking place in the male. This is no doubt partly due to the fact that there may actually be none of any magnitude erupting in a good proportion of them. If the masculine in the male is well committed to the feminine-sexual-economic-social course then there will be no serious disruption at mid-life and the man will continue his business without undue interruption, especially in view of there not being a physiological change in him comparable with female menopause.

The common view that there is little noticeable change in the male may also be due to the fact that, if such changes are taking place, they will be psycho-spiritual rather than psycho-physiological. In other words, they will be masculine, right-hemisphere, intellectual developments and therefore inner and private rather than outwardly

Change of life

emotional and physiologically evident.

In general, they will be experienced within the individual as inner crisis—a drama which the person concerned may well take pains to hide from public view. Beneath the façade of the personality, the familiar and recognisable man about his daily occupations, there may well be an intensification of turmoil in the mind. If this is strong, then it may indeed manifest emotionally in states of anxiety, irritability, restlessness, unusual behaviour, apathy, absent-mindedness and so on.

In fact, I would perhaps go so far as to say that, for some men, the 'inner, male menopause' can be as dramatic and disruptive as the psycho-physiological version is for the female, if not more so. For the man whose masculine-right strengthens and whose desire for fulfilment in pursuit of individual destiny intensifies, the 'fight to be male' is now more vivid than at any time earlier in his life. For, in the second 'half' of life, whereas the masculine desire for success in the female is passive, that desire in the male is active (table, p.68). The onus not only passes to the male to lead and guide in individual, spiritual terms, but he also now has responsibility for the active fear of failure which is likely to emerge in the female. (Which is why the feminine in the male and the female, especially the latter, may begin to turn at this stage to look for support, solace and comfort in a form of religious practice and allegiance.)

Thus the masculine, 'released' from procreative responsibility, may begin to cause intensified anxiety in both the female and the male. The search for alleviation also quickens. This may take the obvious form of drugs, alcohol, tobacco and so forth—all manner of tranquilisers and anti-depresents—or varied forms of 'escapist' entertainment. Entertainment derives from Latin words meaning 'between' and 'to hold'. Thus one might surmise that anything which produces a temporary balance between the demands of the left and right hemispheres, or keeps them apart to relieve their continual conflict—in other words, diverts attention from the tension between them—may be deemed 'entertainment'.

Ironically, and significantly, not only are anxiety and depression common causes of sexual malfunction but many of the relief and escape methods mentioned above can have an ennervating and diverting effect which in turn dissipates the desire for sexual activity. (For example, it is noted that nine months after a national disruption of television transmission, there is a noticeable rise in the birth rate.)

The author quoted previously[11] further writes:
Neurophysiologic investigations have revealed the neuroanatomic substrate for pain and pleasure motivations, and for the close association of sex and pleasure. It appears that aversive and adient centres exist in the brain which are at the service of all the drives and in fact of all forms of behaviour. According to this concept, when one is hungry or frightened or injured, the 'pain' centres are activated: when one is successful or triumphant or eating or copulating, 'pleasure' centre discharges make us feel joy and so reinforce these activities.
Apparently simple, the duality concept of motivation was not scientifically validated or fully accepted until relatively recently...
At mid-life, the seeking of pleasure aspect which dominates youth begins to give way, I suggest, to increasing avoidance of pain. Thus pleasures, rather than being pursued for the pleasure itself, are sought more as avoidance of anxiety and thus become more forced and desperate. What is more, as they become less effective, they are increasingly pursued to excess, if wealth and status permit.

I referred earlier to the phenomenon of increased sexuality in the female during mid-life and commented on the generally accepted view that the male's sexual performance continues more or less unaffected, providing in both cases that inhibiting anxiety or depression does not actively intervene. The chances of the male and female appetites continuing to match would seem however to reduce as time passes.

In the female, the capacity for frequent orgasm does not decline throughout life. As described earlier in the book, the physical mechanism involved in orgasm has two distinct phases. There is first the preparatory stage of pleasurable, erotic stimulation, during which there is vascular swelling of the genital areas, particularly important in the case of the male for the procreative purpose since he needs to be able to penetrate before emission. The erotic stage is followed by the orgastic climax which involves an entirely different set of nerves and muscles. In the female, the frequency at which these two stages may be repeated does not markedly deteriorate with age. In the male, however, there is a definite decline in capacity. Perhaps this is 'caused' by, or is surely associated with, the fact that the male orgasm is accompanied by emission and hence repetition would be linked with the ability to produce semen, a capacity which declines with age. In other words the availability of semen would affect the desire to copulate. This in turn 'causes', or is surely associated with, the fact that as the male grows older he experiences what are technically called 'more extended periods of post-coital detumescence', which means that the periods between inclination or ability to achieve erection grow longer.

Thus the increasing disparity between male and female sexuality tends to widen with age and therefore puts more pressure on the former. This is not only a threat to the relationship but it is especially a threat, or may be, to the male's masculinity in that the erect penis (as discussed in association with squirrel monkey behaviour cited earlier in the book) is psychologically a display symbol. It represents his ability to assert himself, to compete with other males, to maintain self-respect, to exercise leadership and group domination. Inevitably, if there is an apparent decline in this assertive capacity, naturally occuring or unnaturally induced, the spectre of failure as an individual may easily arise.

As the same author already referred to[11] writes:

> Certain aspects of sexuality may come to arouse guilt or fear and anxiety by the process of conditioning. If such is the case, there is a tendency to avoid exposure to the anxiety-provoking stimulus, which unfortunately consists of pleasant, exciting and arousing sexual situations and feelings. This pattern of avoidance is reinforced and maintained because it is rewarded by the reduction of anxiety.

Needless to imagine, the cumulative effects of all these mid-life developments can amount to considerable threat to the male. At the time he most needs to consider his position and may be tempted to withdraw or take other action to avoid the issue, he is in reality being challenged more than ever before in his life to take responsibility, not only for ensuring his own individual fulfilment but for the female's also.

Through mid-life towards old age, the individual, either male or female, is physically deteriorating, a weakening which increases the possible intervention of illness and disease. This endorses the proclivity previously mentioned to pursue pleasure not so much for its own reward but more as a cover to avoid mental and physical aches and pains.

There is perhaps a link here with the observation made recently by medical researchers[13] that pain is more prevalent on the left side of the body than the right. More than a hundred years ago, a Frenchman, Dr. Pierre Briquet, reported that the cramps and pains experienced by hysterical patients occurred six times more often on the left. The tendency towards 'pain lateralisation', and its bias towards the left, has been most readily noted in psychiatric patients, i.e., it is particularly evident in the psychosomatic effects caused by mental distress and disturbance. The researchers report that they believe the cause of this phenomenon can be explained in terms of the differentiation of function of the right and left cortical hemispheres. They suggest that pain may be more common on the left side of the body because 'the right hemisphere is less adept at assessing the significance of the many physical sensations it monitors and because it also has the inclination to react emotionally rather than analytically.'

I would go along with the principal idea that the disparity is due to differentiation of hemisphere function but suggest that the explanation is confusing and incorrect. I would suggest that the mental anxiety state is primarily due to activity in the right hemisphere, activity associated with the desire for individual, spiritual fulfilment. This produces confusion and disturbance in the left hemisphere which cannot cope in terms of worldly learning and conditioning.

This incompatibility then gives rise to emotional stress in the limbic system (which may well need to be sedated). This in turn may affect the mid and hind-brain functioning. If the cortical conflict becomes intolerable, then a breakdown occurs in which there is right and left dissociation. This would account for the mechanical, repetitive, automaton effects typical of serious psychiatric disorders. In other words, the person retreats into a right-hemisphere 'world of his own' whilst the left hemisphere conducts habitual and conditioned behaviour. A schizophrenic seems to have the ability to vacillate easily from an associated to a dissociated condition and back again in order to cope. He or she may even attempt actually to create a separate and private world and run it in parallel with his or her actual conventional, social public world.

It is not surprising then that, once this situation has arisen, it is impossible for the person concerned to comprehend a logical and analytical explanation of what is happening. His or her main concern is somehow to alleviate or eliminate the 'pain' and frustration in the right hemisphere. Whether or not this pain avoidance has reached proportions serious enough to require psychiatric treatment, the cross-over effect is not only likely to cause confusion in the left hemisphere and emotional disturbance but actual psychosomatic pain in the left side of the body also. In principle therefore, especially in mid-life, there may be considerable and discomforting repercussions resulting from the possible inability of the person to reconcile the intuitive knowledge in the right hemisphere with the conditioned learning accumulated in the left.

It is surely relevant in this context that the heart is frequently involved. Significantly, the physical heart is situated slightly off-centre, occupying more space in the left side of the body than the right. The 'heart' has always been associated with love and so, by extrapolation, the above psychological and physical symptoms of illness, distress and pain, would be a manifestation of a 'crisis of love'. If the feminine-left believes that it is not loved and the masculine right does not know how to love, then that is a condition inviting anguish and poignancy.

21 Love

There can be no doubt that, for the individual, understanding of the meaning and expression of spiritual love is crucial from mid-life onwards.

During the first 'half' of life, love is expressed through the left hemisphere in physical, worldly terms, most specifically in the amorous relationship between sexes. The fulfilment of the desire to love and to be loved (feminine and masculine respectively) is therefore enacted through the physical duality of one body encountering and merging with another. This union is physical representation of the resolution of desire and fear. It is primarily concerned with sensual and erotic content ('earth', feminine) and involves the movement, flow and rhythm of sensational feelings ('water', feminine). It is transitory, vulnerable and turbulent. Partners spend much of their time between intimate encounters trying to establish that such emotional love has durability and that it can be maintained continually. This is motivated by the need for self-assurance and, since it is thus subjective and body-identified, it is inevitably a possessive attachment involving continual demand for reciprocal commitment. All of this represents the persistent concern of the individual to maintain harmony between left and right hemispheres through outward evidence and proof of harmonious relationship.

However successful this reconciliation through projection may be—within the individual through outward, harmonious relationship—it is still subject to intervention, ultimately by death. It may be that the achievement of continuing, harmonious relationship with a 'permanent' partner in marriage provides the greatest satisfaction in mortal life, though it seems to me through observation to be relatively rare. Usually the bond degenerates, difficult though it may be for the partners to admit it, into a 'stalemate' situation of reluctantly accepted compromise. Even in the rare case of the continuing 'love-match' throughout life, each partner leaves himself or herself wide open to the traumatism of the other's death. This may all sound rather negative and pessimistic (a masculine-right characteristic!) but it is nevertheless objective and realistic.

Is that, then, all there is to be said about love? Is the best that can be achieved an old age in which the person may look back on a happy marriage (apart, perhaps, from some pride in having acquired a degree of fame and fortune, and in having brought into the world and supported a number of children)?

Of course, in substantiation of this theme, I would say that it is not. It depends whether the possessive love—of partner, power, children, fame, money, 'possessions' of all kinds—is transformed or converted into spiritual love (which may, of course, include completion of a truly 'spiritual' marriage).

The second 'half' of life presents the opportunity for the achievement of true individuality—the attainment of immortality through spiritual love (masculine, 'fire' and 'air').

This requires that, at the 'change of life', the termination of the procreative 'half', emphasis must shift to the right, gradually at first but with increasing strength. The individual must obey his or her intuition as to what fulfilling his or her destiny means. Needless to say (I hope!), this emphatically does not mean selfishness and licence to do what one likes; quite the opposite. It means an abandonment of self-will which leads to a truly religious rectitude and *right*-eousness.

The essence of spirituality is dissolution of the phenomenal, conditioned, arbitrarily-acquired, fictional ego-self, the worldly pretender, the false identity. Paradoxically, the real-self which supervenes, the immortal spirit, has no identity in feminine-left, describable terms.

The effect therefore of the ego-dissolution is that there is 'no one *left*'. Not only is there no one left to desire and fear but there is no one left to die.

Ego-dissolution does not mean what might be called 'ego-withdrawal'. This is an evasive, reactionary ego-survival technique which, in extreme, can give rise to conditions observable in mental institutions and among old people where degrees of vacuity indicate an unintended withdrawal of will—an unwillingness to continue consciously to 'the appointed hour'. The deliberate, spiritual withdrawal must always take account of remaining responsibility to the world.

The Buddhist tradition recognises several phases in the second 'half' of life conduct. The 'forty-two' through to 'sixty-three' phase (the third twenty-one year period which should be dominated by the intellectual and spiritual concern of the right hemisphere) is essentially converting and giving back to the world that which has been gained in previous phases. As already mentioned, this is 'forgiveness' (for past 'sins' or *karma*). This may be expressed as a literal giving back in terms of wise advice, social service and material charity, but in the individual it is an expiation of the past, mistaken use of the 'patient' feminine-left by the repentant masculine-right. This is an important prerequiste for the later freedom to 'retire to the forest', the conscious abandonment of the world, the final contemplative phase when one has 'died to oneself' and no longer belongs to the world.

The sign of this process in the post-procreative age is the growth of a totally different love—one that 'takes over' the person and transfigures him or her. It is a love without condition, manifesting when the two hemispheres of the mind are reconciled and work in correct relationship and harmony.

Perhaps it was in recognition of this that Shakespeare was inspired to write the following sonnet (No. 116):

> Let me not to the marriage of true minds
> Admit impediment. Love is not love
> Which alters when it alteration finds,
> Or bends with the remover to remove:
> O, no!, it is an ever-fixed mark,
> That looks on tempests, and is never shaken;
> It is a star to every wandering bark,
> Whose worth's unknown, although his height be taken.
> Love's not Time's fool, though rosy lips and cheeks
> Within his bending sickle's compass come;
> Love alters not with his brief hours and weeks,
> But bears it out even to the edge of doom.
>   If this be error, and upon me proved,
>   I never writ, nor no man ever loved.

Ideally, when it has become pure, this is a love without worldly desire or demand. It is not attached and does not claim to possess. It provides a sense of completeness entirely independent of identifiable cause or support. It does not require the physical presence of anything nor is it vulnerable to the absence of anything. There is no specific explanation for it and it cannot be justified or analysed. It gives a sense of well-being and sometimes of exhilaration and ecstasy—for no accountable reason. The essence of it is that there is no sense of self.

The above is not to suggest that such experience is reserved exclusively for 'spiritual' or 'religious' people. Most people, if not everyone, experiences it to a degree, especially when young, on those joyous occasions which may be described as 'being taken out of oneself'. (Translated from its Greek origin, 'ecstasy' means 'standing ouside of'.)

This may happen, for example, when with a loved one, or when overtaken or overwhelmed by something of great beauty, particularly situations involving natural beauty. The trouble is that these moments are brief and infrequent and one is quickly brought back to self-concern. They may also not be recognised at the time as being 'spiritual' or anything to do with 'divine love', though poets are often sensitive to their quality of transcendent blessing. They are profound indicators or intimations of a supramundane state of mind. The proposition therefore follows that during the second 'half' of life, when involvement with the world recedes, the opportunity presents itself to regain that state consciously and continually.

Ordinarily, love is a projected identification wherein the happiness appears to be dependent on the presence or existence of an idolised object or form—for instance, the ideal male or the perfect female. This application is indicated by the transitive expression 'loving someone'. The spiritual conversion removes the necessity for the love to be identified, as a direct result of the positive disillusion or realisation that the object is not the cause of the love. This is inherent in the intransitive expression 'being in love'—a state of well-being, not an emotional projection.

In the individual female, the experience of being in love is the effect of the feminine-left hemisphere losing its active fear of failure as an individual; her spiritual need to know that she is loved is inwardly fulfilled. In the male, his right-hemisphere, masculine desire for success is fulfilled in the knowledge that true love is working through him. There is no way of commanding or explaining this; it can only be expressed as a divine blessing (feminine) and intervention (masculine). The cause or source of it can only be ascribed to the divine, by whatever name. In other words, the spiritual fulfilment is concomitant with, and the acknowledgement of, power beyond the command of human will.

It should be emphasised that passive acknowledgement and passive acceptance of the divine will are both feminine. This surrender alone is not enough; the masculine side will not be satisfied. It will actively desire to sacrifice all in order to return consciously to the divine source. Whereas the power 'comes down' to bless the mortal feminine with love, the masculine seeks to 'ascend' in order to accomplish union through knowing and entering the divine—a desire which requires 'conscious suicide' for resolution. It is the direct reciprocal in spiritual terms of the 'little death' of sexual orgasm in copulative union.

This evolution of love in the post-procreative phase brings about spiritual 're-birth', the emergence of the regenerate man. It means the emergence of the masculine real-self out of the reconciled and contented feminine which has been liberated from the ego-self.

It is the gist of this latter differentiation which I suggest has direct bearing on the current debate concerning the ordination of women as priests in the Christian tradition (in those sects other than the Orthodox and the Roman Catholic, in neither of which has the demand yet surfaced; nor is it likely to, given their discipline).

The debate seems to me to be quite impotent—being totally smothered by premises characteristic of the feminine. Briefly, the opponents of ordination for women chiefly use as argument the negative approach that there is no precedent for it. Neither Jesus himself, nor any succeeding Church authority, ever advocated it and that implies that it was never intended. (St. Paul in particular was against it, saying in his Epistles to Timothy, for example: 'Let the woman learn in silence with all subjection. But I suffer not a woman to teach, nor to usurp authority over the man, but to be in silence.')

The proponents for the ordination of women argue, in so many words: 'If women want to be ordained, *why* should they not be? Neither Jesus nor his immediate disciples expressly forbade it.'

In other words, the opponents use a negative, feminine, obstructive defence, wishing to maintain the *status quo* for fear of possible repercussions, whilst the proponents use a masculine, 'progressive', permissive approach because they see no logical objection. The whole issue is emotionally clouded and confused and it is not therefore seen clearly that the equality of the sexes does not mean sameness but differentiated complement.

As far as this theme is concerned, female ordination is certainly inappropriate. (Far from being a male chauvinist, St. Paul is in principle quite correct. His argument, however—that Eve transgressed against Adam—would not I think carry much weight today.) This would be because the masculine, spiritual dispensation in the female is passive and does not need to be expressed. In order to be fulfilled, spiritually and individually, she has only to surrender and serve as support and comfort. She is blessed and loved by the divine and that is the essence of what she needs to know and realise, in silence. It is therefore inappropriate for her to enter into an active, instructing role. This can only stimulate the ego-self within her, which will then tend to compete with and usurp the masculine in the male.

The masculine, spiritual dispensation in the male on the other hand *is* active. In order for its desire to succeed to be fulfilled, the man needs to serve actively as minister and advocate of the divine will in order to convert his ego-will through self-sacrifice.

Implicit in this gradual understanding of spiritual love (which means literally to 'stand under' it) is a conversion of energy whereby the self of the physical, mortal human is released from the attachments and demands of procreation in its widest sense and is re-directed back as the real self to its origin. Thus does the consciousness and intellect of the cerebral cortex counter and convert the twin motivations of the ancient brain—procreation of the species (feminine) and self-preservation (masculine).

22 Purpose in life

If this proposition concerning transformation of the motivations of the ancient, animal brain is correct, then it is possible to appreciate a distinct purpose for Man, a purpose which, as far as is known, is unique amongst all the other creatures of this planet.

It would seem that all other creatures belong totally to the feminine dispensation in that their role is exclusively procreative—a repetitive and continuous reproduction process through historical time. Nevertheless, there is within this linear process a certain evolution taking place due to changes caused by (divine) masculine intervention. It is this which alters circumstances which, in turn, threatens and destroys some species whilst strengthening and advancing others, the latter being said to have sufficient intelligence to adapt.

This evolution of intelligence and adaption eventually gave rise to the emergence of Man, one amongst a small number of creatures in which there was a considerable increase in brain development. This took place in particular as a comparatively massive expansion of cranium volume in relation to body size.

It might be supposed that one of the reasons that Man, as a dry land, open-air creature, stood up vertically on two legs was that mechanically it was the only way the cranium weight could be comfortably supported and carried around. This adaptive development permitted in particular a considerable growth of the neocortex, a superimposition on the older instinctive and emotional parts of the brain, especially associated with intelligence.

Seemingly exclusive to Man, his brain evolution then underwent a further development whereby the two hemispheres of the cortex began to function differently. I have suggested that it was this differentiation that signified an extraordinary and miraculous phenomenon—a development in the power of consciousness, which I have further postulated as being associated with the right cortical hemisphere. This was surely a 'quantum jump' commensurable with the appearance of the first, primitive, 'living' organism out of inorganic, inanimate earth, or the emergence of the first creature from a water environment to live on dry land in the open air.

Man 'suddenly' became 'conscious of himself', an event which implies an evolution beyond simply 'being conscious' or exhibiting awareness of surroundings. This 'evolving out' of consciousness develops further in the maturing human to enable him to be not only conscious of himself but objectively conscious of all creation, as something separate and detached from himself.

In other words, the sense of self in Man can become detached from the physical, existential vehicle of being so that the human can not only observe and deliberately modify his own mental and physical behaviour but can observe and control a large number of phenomena in his environment. Amongst many other ramifications of this, Man becomes conscious of the inevitable death of his own physical vehicle.

In a condition where he is identified and involved with that vehicle, where he believes it 'to be himself', then logically he assumes that, when the vehicle ceases to function, 'he himself dies'. Therefore, it is the proposition of this theme that, if he can through intelligence and reason evolve or 'free' consciousness to the point of deliberate dissociation from the vehicle, i.e., he withdraws identification of himself with the body, then, when the body becomes defunct, 'he', the detached consciousness or spirit does not die.

In the interests of establishing this whole development as being particularly associated with masculine, evolutionary intervention and the right hemisphere, it is tempting to suggest that the adopting of a 'vertical' posture by Man (out of the 'horizontal', 'closer to earth', feminine commiment of quadrupeds and other creeping, crawling and writhing creatures) is not simply accidentally called 'becoming up*right*' or *erect*. Something which is *rectified* is 'made straight' or 'put right'. Thus 'right' is not just a bilateral distinction from left but has connotations of vertical *direction,* being right as being *correct,* and 'having the right' as 'being justified'. The *righteous* would be those with direct response to the divine 'above'.

In Man, the right-hemisphere evolution of consciousness caused a bifurcation of interest or concern between one hemisphere and the other. As far as is known, this seems to be peculiar to Man also. All other creatures apparently do not experience contradiction in their higher neural activities; they are totally committed to life on earth and the procreative purpose. It is only in Man that we may observe deliberate attempt to 'opt out' of that dispensation. Only in Man do we observe occupation in creative activity which is of no relevance or value to physical survival. At the same time, it is only in Man's activities that we witness a destructive proclivity which is taken to degrees of excess beyond that which is commensurate with his survival needs. He is the only creature which kills its own kind unnaturally. He alone experiences 'civil war' in his mind.

These evolutionary events have not been comfortable for Man; he has indeed suffered much through his own intelligence. This is because the hemisphere bifurcation set the emerging concerns and interests of the right in apparent opposition to the left, a polarised confrontation which has entered into virtually every aspect of his worldly endeavour. We have only to look at the characteristics of right and left hemisphere function (p.30) to appreciate how easily they may conflict with, rather than complement, each other.

The tendency to conflict could not be more fundamental. The feminine left is naturally committed to fulfilment of the ancient brain motivations, especially survival of the species and physical continuity. The right hemisphere may well serve these feminine interests and concerns as self-preservation, but it has a disposition towards others, of primary importance to it, which are of no value to the procreative, survival purpose. As a result, anxiety is precipitated in the feminine left because, if the masculine right pursues its occupations too excessively and exclusively, physical survival will be endangered.

Thus, the 'fight to be male', in its psycho-spiritual aspect, is no less than anti-nature in principle. In order for the masculine to transcend and fulfil its purpose, it has no option but to counter, over-ride and convert the basic drives of the ancient brain. This 'civil war' within the mind of a species is the most extraordinary evolutionary development.

Relative to a single 'seventy year' lifetime, this development in Man has been going on for a long time, certainly throughout recorded human history and, surely, well back beyond that. Thus it is evident that for several thousand years the masculine has been engaged in the 'fight to be (spiritually) male'. All his artistic pursuits, his theologies and religions, his philosophies and 'higher educations', signify Man's attempts to find a solution to the predicament of which he has become conscious. They signify the spiritual aspiration, the need to comprehend Man's higher purpose.

Purpose in life

Nevertheless, those thousands of years of endeavour are but a moment compared with the age of the earth and perhaps only a small proportion of the time through which the human species has actually existed. Antrhropologists assert that the cerebral expansion of hominids took place at least twenty-five thousand years ago, and that Neanderthal and Cro-Magnon man even had a slightly larger brain volume than modern man. What is significant, however, is the change of conformation during that period, especially, for example, the development of the frontal lobes.

Man as *homo sapiens* has suffered then not so much through threat to his physical survival as through the mental dichotomy developed within himself. On the one hand he is well aware of himself as a creature with a creature's motives; on the other hand, he has become increasingly aware that he has further or 'higher' purpose, the nature of which he has been attempting to discover and communicate for centuries.

What is more, it has often seemed that fulfilment of the latter purpose is inimicable to pursuit of the former. At least, that is the gist of the situation as far as one is able to determine from a long history of human struggle and conflict—one which seems to indicate an imbalance and discord between the interests and concerns of the right and left hemispheres within generation upon generation of individuals.

Do I presume to suggest that this theme throws any helpful light on the predicament? Perhaps, a little . . . That depends on the reasonableness of its appeal. (I am not claiming, by the way, that it is a 'new' proposition. It has not however, to my knowledge, been expressed before in quite this perspective or these terms.)

The possibility of its being a useful contribution would lie in the emphasis that the whole human life cycle should be taken into account and that, for the time being, the predicament may be resolved through the ability to undertake and fulfil *both* purposes. This requires a steady, measured and ordered progress through life involving reconciliation of the two hemispheres.

It suggests that to follow the feminine-sexual-social-economic-physical path exclusively for the whole life is to ignore the masculine, spiritual possibility. On the other hand, drastic, untimely, irresponsible and excessive pursuit of the latter at the expense of the former constitutes a harmful and threatening rejection or abandonment of the feminine. The first tends to cause a masculine frustration which manifests as excessive and possibly destructive greed, pleasure-seeking, aggression and violence. The second gives rise to feminine-left anxiety which in excess manifests as purposelessness, apathy, depression, confusion and bewilderment. Both can give rise to self-destruction—suicide.

The outline proposed in this book suggests that the solution lies in a gradual transition or conversion from a feminine/active-masculine/passive first 'half' to a masculine/active-feminine/passive second 'half'. The human life cycle seems to have been so constructed and developed that it lends itself to this possibility. By means of intelligent and constructive instruction and conditioning, for both the male and female, it should be possible to fulfil the feminine procreative purpose during the first 'half' of life and at the same time prepare for and embark upon the masculine-spiritual purpose in the second. It should not be inferred however, as I hope should be apparent by now, that this conversion is a drastic switch-over half-way through; it implies a concurrence of both throughout the life, with a gradual transfer of emphasis from beginning to end.

In this manner, there would not be partisan, bilateral gestures and conflicts. There would not be extreme either-or situations of 'nature affronted' on one side and 'divine disappointment' on the other.

Perhaps one may surmise that Nature is intelligent and is determined in her own interests. She does not therefore take kindly to unnatural affronts to her processes, laws and cycles, either in the form of exploitation or denial. However, she evidently has no further interest in human beings once they have procreated and have ensured the continuation of the species. Providing they have fulfilled their responsibilities to the social order by reproducing and maintaining their societies, she presumably has no objection to their following whatever other aspirations they may happen to have!

What, though, is the point of this whole performance? How can it be understood? Is it possible to imagine even the mechanics of it, no matter how vaguely and however inadequate the terms? Here we have to resort to inventing mythological expressions or 'tales'.

It is as if the sun/deity decided to transmit energy/knowledge to its dead, inorganic, earth satelite to create a living biosphere.

For millions of years that flow of energy was simply consumed or 'earthed' in the forming process. At a certain point, the development came to a climax with the creation of Man, a being who became intelligent and conscious, becoming the recipient and transformer of the pure and original energy/knowledge. What should he then do with this energy/knowledge which had now become superfluous to the requirements of organic life in the biosphere, since creation was complete?

At first, this excess began to overflow and become destructive—a fact demonstrated by Man's exploitation of the planet's resources and creatures for his own excessive hedonistic indulgencies and his willingness to go to war with his own kind. This culminated in his using his intelligence to invent weapons of mass destruction with the potential of not only eliminating himself but the whole biosphere also. Was this to be the end of the tale?

Perhaps not. A certain proportion among men became aware that they were not autonomous accidents. They appreciated that their energy/knowledge was a gift and a blessing and conceived the idea that it must come from a source. For some, the source then became more important than what it had created, and they devoted their intelligence to understanding that source.

In this process they reflected or transmitted back the energy/knowledge to where it had come from—the sun/deity. In their conscious dying, they completed a circuit and demonstrated the possibility that all the superfluous energy/knowledge could be diverted from destructive activity and recycled back. This complete cycle demonstrates the threefold or tripartite process, enacted in human life—penetration/creation, fertilisation/continuation, withdrawal/dissolution.

In this manner, in religious terminology, 'Man became the medium through whom God realised Himself.'

23 Retirement and reconciliation

Schematically, at 'sixty-three', the worldly life is complete. The taking and the giving back are over. Ideally, the nine seven-year phases have seen involvement in the feminine in the 'first half' succeeded by masculine evolution in the second, a gradual transition from instinctive motivation through emotional to intellectual. The individual enters the mysterious or 'mystical' tenth period, 'sixty-three' to 'three score and ten', the direct reciprocal of infancy. In this 'mystical' withdrawal, the person enters a world 'of his or her own'.

The infant is unconscious of himself as separate, being innocent and 'at-one' with the world around. The old-age reciprocal should again be innocent—all 'sin' having been expiated—and again 'at-one' with the world, only this time consciously so—at-one-ment. the person is still *in* the world but no longer *of* it. As far as he or she is concerned, the completed individuality means retirement from the world's activity and being effectively 'dead' to worldly motivation.

Ideally, the individual should then be aware of having fulfilled his or her destiny as Man, and to have avoided ('made void') his or her fate as a mortal human being. Such a person would not therefore fear death and would exhibit 'a sense of humour', in the alchemical sense of having balanced all the elements within. This permits a peacefulness and equanimity (left and right hemispheres in balance and harmony), a toleration (associated with the element 'space' or aether) born of well-being.

Such a person may well allow an occasional smile at what is seen in retrospect to have been the 'comedy' of life, not necessarily due to its having been a 'funny play' but due to a quiet amusement derived from having been relieved of grave seriousness, of having understood a paradox, of having 'played the fool' and realised it.

The alternative to such fulfilment would be that the life has been a fateful tragedy. Death is then only welcome as release or is feared because the life is intuitively known to have been incomplete or wasted, full of 'things which should have been done and have not, and things which should not have been done and have.'

Retirement, then, should be a deliberate withdrawal from the world, an opportunity for contemplation and meditation, not licence to pursue such pleasures may be afforded in the time remaining. The art is in timing and understanding the significance of the opportunity to make peace. Commonly, some go on too long in their occupations, carried along by the momentum of activity, perhaps deluded by a false sense of their indispensability or through fear of the void if they had to stop. Others, unaware of the spiritual purpose of retirement, may lapse into inertia and an idle 'killing of time'.

Actual, physical withdrawal from society may not of course be feasible in modern, densely-populated, urban environments. Generally speaking, domestic arrangements for old people in modern cultures do not recognise the need for 'monastic' withdrawal or Buddhist-style 'retirement to the forest'.

In default of provision for this need, the emphasis for the spirituality-aspiring individual must be on the psychological discipline of disengagement, no matter what is going on in the world around. No doubt in due course, if there is a truly spiritual revival, communities will respond appropriately and provide the necessary facilities. Until the demand arises, and the spiritual needs of old age become recognised, the problem of what to do with the aged will continue and worsen.

The 'ideal' preparation for death requires reconciliation of left and right hemispheres.

The feminine aspect reconciled means, as already suggested, a peace and contentment, deriving from a sense of the worldly commitment completed. There is then only a sense of surrender, in which only a time of patient waiting remains. The masculine aspect on the other hand does not truly rest until the last moment. In this 'restlessness' there is still desire or longing—to be finally withdrawn to the divine source. This requires a continuous 'watching', which implies a constant awareness in order to avoid being 'taken unawares'.

These two aspects are understood by the individual as being utterly compatible. They are called sometimes 'the watching and waiting', or contemplation and meditation, or 'active inaction'.

In fact, periods of this state of 'alert patience' may start to become familiar any time after termination of the procreative phase or when the reconciliation or 'marriage' of the hemispheres is taking place, providing the work of self-knowledge and self-realisation is being undertaken. This in turn manifests as behaviour 'true to oneself'.

When this happens, it is as if all falls naturally into place. There is no sense of motive, desiring worldly gain. It is as if the ego-self has lost its will and has been 'taken over'; thus arises the paradoxical sense of 'active inaction'.

Ultimately, this gives rise to a knowledge that the life is being resolved or completed. There is a strengthening of equanimity, independence and integrity which is not persuaded or moved by the opinions and machinations of the world since the individual becomes less and less concerned about consequences and results. All these developments are characteristic of the spiritual growth of the individual, who is increasingly only answerable to conscience, reason and intuition.

The process may be mentally cognised and may, for example, be expressed as growing obedience to divine will, or whatever other description encapsulates the feeling of acceptance and acknowledgement of supramundane power or spirit. In the terms of this exegesis, it is the experience concomitant with the increasing passivity of the worldly-motivated, feminine-left hemisphere, as it is increasingly obedient to the spiritually-motivated, masculine-right hemisphere. This is the essence of spirituality, as it gradually evolves out of sexuality.

It should be added, however, that this positive transition—although it should in theory be natural and easy—may well be fraught with difficulties and discomfort. This appears to be because, in our present phase of development, the 'first-half' conditioning is still extremely strong. Our commitment to the world is so well inculcated that the process of disillusionment is commensurately difficult.

One of the difficulties encountered in this process, for example, is the unnerving feeling of detachment. This is so only because we are led into finding security in attachment. It is not uncommon for the aged, especially women, to fear loneliness.

Unfortunately, loneliness is symptomatic of a failure to understand that 'one' is always alone, always has been and always will be, here on earth as a human being. The company of family and familiar group may be pleasant, reassuring and comforting but it should not obscure the reality that it is a transitory phase and provides only temporary security. It is a false security if believed in as permanent and is relied upon unduly and continuously.

It is appropriate that the 'first-half' of life should be supported by the familiar, friendly and helpful, since that disposition is inherent in the sexual, physical, public, social situation of procreation and support of offspring. But the 'second-half' requires transition to understanding of the real nature of the individual with its concomitant growth of self-reliance and independence. This does not, I emphasise, mean increasing selfishness as a particular human being; it means atonement with the world through sacrifice of self-will. In other words, it means a gradual communion with divine will which may only be accomplished *alone*.

The spiritual life is not communal. Being born as an individual human being is to be confronted with one's own fate and to have responsibility to one's own destiny. Thus aloneness is quite different from loneliness. True aloneness is to be 'at-one' with all things, whilst loneliness is to be isolated as a vulnerable, physical human being.

The individual needs to become accustomed to aloneness. The masculine in both male and female needs all through life privacy and solitude, to varying degrees and from time to time. The desire for this should increase with age in the spiritual context. (This masculine proclivity is exemplified, in caricature, by the retired old gentleman, seated in a comfortable armchair in the silent reading-room of his men-only club, gently snoring with a newspaper over his face!)

Again, difficulties in respect of loneliness may be experienced between elderly couples due to the fact that the sexual, male-female partnership in marriage has crystallised as a mutual projection of imbalanced hemisphere compensation rather than an egalitarian reconcilication. The attraction of partners to each other is due to weakness or failure in one side of one finding compensating strength in the other side of the other.

This is understandable and it is salutary providing that, during the course of the marriage, the weakness or failure is rectified through reflection or emulation of the strength in the other. If this does not happen, the danger is that the one becomes dependent on the other for continuing provision of the strength. In this situation, especially late in life, there is then a growing fear of loss of the partner because the death or departure of that partner means loss of security.

This leads to the tentative conclusion that though couples may be attracted to each other to compensate for weakness as well as to complement and express strengths, this should not ideally be allowed to remain a state of static, mutual dependence. The whole, spiritual point of the contract to marry is that each should help the other overcome faults and weaknesses, not entrench and perpetuate them through using the partner to avoid facing them.

An extract from Carl Sagan's book[7] concerning left and right hemisphere relationship could readily be translated into a husband and wife context where an uneasy, demanding dependence exists:

> The left hemisphere seems to feel quite defensive—in a strange way insecure—about the right hemisphere; and, if this is so, verbal criticism of intuitive thinking becomes suspect on the ground of motive. Unfortunately, there is every reason to think that the right hemisphere has comparable misgivings—expressed non-verbally of course—about the left.

Inevitably, if this situation pertains in the individual, he or she will project it particularly into the marriage relationship (but also into all relationships). The publicly-expressed defensiveness and the private misgivings will continually undermine. If the right-hemisphere misgivings (individual selfishness) become too intense and explode, then separation and divorce are the only solution. If the left-hemisphere defensiveness (survival, continuity) prevail, then the partnership or relationship continues as an uneasy anxiety, continually needing reassurance.

If the contract to marry is to succeed in its spiritual purpose—the balance and integration of both hemispheres in both partners—then a continual and evolving dialogue is required in conjunction with the mutual quest for self-knowledge and self-realisation. The latter means that each individual in the partnership is working to reconcile the weaknesses and imbalances in himself or herself.

Carl Sagan continues:

> There is no way to tell whether the patterns extracted by the right hemisphere are real or imagined without subjecting them to left-hemisphere scrutiny. On the other hand, mere critical thinking, without creative and intuitive insights, without the search for new patterns, is sterile and doomed. To solve complex problems in changing circumstances requires the activity of both cerebral hemispheres: the path to the future lies through the corpus callosum.

In other words, the right hemisphere in the individual must 'consult' the left in order to agree the practicality and good sense

Retirement and reconciliation

of creative, intuitive and inspiring ideas. Husband and wife—all those in partnerships or relationships—must confide and consult. On the other hand, it has to be watched that left-hemisphere reaction is not obstructive and critical for defensive, negatively conservative motives.

'The path to the future lies through the corpus callosum'—the bridge or mid-point. I suggest that this does not mean continual and ennervating compromise. It means that during the procreative phase the masculine-right must serve the feminine-left and fulfil its worldly responsibility. But, if this phase does not evolve and is not converted to individual spirituality, the life is 'one-way', sterile and doomed to fate. The second half of the life must allow for the quest and pursuit of masculine-right, spiritual aspiration, which would mean a reversal of flow across the corpus callosum.

The bridge of corpus callosum is the path through which the reversal or conversion takes place during the whole process of hemispere reconciliation—first to allow the left to be fulfilled by the right and second for the right to guide the left to destiny and immortality.

This suggests that the fulfilled marriage—whether it be husband-wife, male-female, or any partnership or relationship—is one which has led, not to mutual inter-dependence, but to 'mutual independence'.

Mutual independence is not an easy status to bring about! Anyone who has followed the theme thus far will appreciate that the odds are heavily in favour of the feminine-left. Its early domination causes the masculine-right to become involved in all manner of commitment, possession, attachment and belief which then casts its spell of comfort, familiarity, continuity and future promise.

From conception right through to, say, 'thirty-five', the purpose of life is dominantly dedicated to feminine, procreative, survival purpose—'immortality of the species'. It is contrary to this commitment—as a psychological extension of the 'fight to be male'—that the spirituality of the masculine-right has to struggle.

In the past, so far as can be discerned, only a minority had the inspiration and the courage to recognise and accept the challenge, having had to resort to such extremes as celibate monasticism to effect it. As the masculine aspect in religious influence declines, and establishment religion becomes more and more involved in feminine-left commitment (misguidedly seeing that process as the means of reviving and maintaining its *raison d'être*), what possible answer can there be for the individual who sees in the growth and spread of communist ideology—the ultimate in feminine-left suppression and suffocation—the possible elimination of truly masculine, spiritual, individuality?

The answer is faith and trust in the divine element which inspires the individual.

To suggest how this renaissance may come about, it is necessary to sketch briefly a view of the development of religion in relation to sexuality. It is then feasible to propose how spirituality may revitalise and reform truly religious expression.

24 Evolution of religion in the West

The female grows to maturity as a fully-equipped 'reproducer' of the species, complete for her purpose except for one minute item, a single sperm cell, a tiny portion of 'masculine spirit'. Modern techniques of artificial insemination apart, the female human must rely, as with all other copulating creatures, in attracting a male to her in order to obtain this missing element.

Nature contrives numerous methods for attracting the male to the female of a species and, generally speaking, once aroused any healthy male will impregnate any female. Of course, in the case of humans, not every male is attracted to every female, for various reasons. And even if attracted, the male is not necessarily sexually aroused. The female, again for various reasons, may not be able to attract the males she would like to, or may attract others to whom she does not feel inclined to respond sexually. This human selectivity of sexual partners is obviously due to psychological factors which do not inhibit lesser creatures.

It would seem that these factors are generated by the higher brain centres and I would suggest that very much involved in the selection process—as far as longer term relationships as distinct from casual sexual encounters are concerned—there is an intuitive knowledge functioning. This recognises qualities and attributes in the potential partner which will be beneficial for psychological reasons.

At its crudest level, this choice might be, for the male, a female who will flatter his display inclinations or cater well for his physical appetites and provide him with comfort and security. These considerations may influence the female also, along with assessment as to his ability to provide for a family. Beyond the mundane level, intuitive knowledge as to the kind of partner most likely to advance more subtle ambitions, including spiritual aspirations, may also play a part.

However, to concentrate on the basic, sexual mechanics, a certain fundamental principle operates, upon which all the rest is superimposed, one which has been explored to some extent earlier in the book. This is to the effect that the important difference between the sexes derives from the female needing to attract, arouse and be penetrated in order to fulfil her active procreative purpose whereas the male does not have to participate in the procreative act in order to fulfil his active, masculine purpose.

The male is primarily motivated by self-preservation rather than procreation of the species. He is, however, in his youth especially, much drawn to pleasure, especially sensual pleasure, and Nature has so arranged the situation that, of all the pleasures available, there is none to compare with the ecstasy of erotic stimulation and orgasm. The male therefore may experience an ambivalence (if the right hemisphere has been activated and is influenced by what Sagan calls 'misgivings') when encountering the sexually attractive female.

He is torn between, on the one hand, the temptation of extreme pleasure and, on the other, a threat to his masculine independence, freedom and integrity. Regardless of all the modern, sophisticated modes of avoiding the consequences of partaking in the act, (contraception, 'free love', and so on) psychologically they make no difference. At a profound level, in the act, he 'knows' he has 'given himself away'. And the female, even though she may deliberately avoid pregnancy, also at a profound level, 'knows' she has succeeded in attracting, arousing and being penetrated.

If there can be said to be anything 'wrong' with this trend to avoid the consequences of the sexual act then it must be the danger that the male may be able to avoid any commitment whatsoever and thus remain selfish trhoughout his life; and the female, if she avoids pregnancy and childbirth, may also fail to make any real commitment and also remain selfish throughout her life.

However, the extrapolation I wish to suggest, deriving from the above, is that the female primarily desires to arouse and make erect the phallus, and only secondarily fears violation of her integrity by it. Conversely, the male primarily experiences the fear of oblivion represented by the vaginal aperture and only secondarily desires the pleasures attendant upon the act of entering. (This, I emphasise, is in the sexual aspect only, as indicated in the lower half of the diagram on page 68.) Thus, it is incumbent on the female to arouse the desire of the male and to assuage his fear.

If this is valid, then it is interesting to consider the sexual interplay in relation to certain developments in the history of religion. This in turn may give an indication of the nature of possible spiritual revival.

Up to a point in human history, so far as can be interpreted from surviving evidence, Man envisaged life as being influenced by a variety of powers and spirits. Though invisible, they could be

Evolution of religion in the West

communicated with and, according to their role, they were given images, attributes, qualities, etc., coexistent with the manifestation of those phenomena in earthly form.

Although the nature of these spirits or powers was not necessarily anthropomorphic, it is understandable that they would come to be envisaged in due course as having special association with humanity and that therefore it was logical that they could be imagined as 'superhumans', with powers, attributes and properties recognisably human. From there, given the concept of there being a pantheon of these deities, it was also logical to assume that they would be sexually differentiated. Since physical survival would have been the dominant concern, it is also reasonable to deduce that fertility was of prime importance and hence that in the pantheon special privilege should have been assigned to the 'goddess of fertility' or 'earth-mother'.

One could say that this period constitutes the instinctive phase in the development of Man's religious inclination and that it was dominantly physical and sexual. The essential procreative attributes were ascribed to the divine powers and featured strongly in representational images. Whether or not the female goddess was elevated to singular prominence in the hierarchy, the religious ethos was feminine dominated in the sense that survival of the group, procreation of the species, continuity, security and so forth were given top priority.

Perhaps we may assume that the male inevitably co-operated in this dispensation since he presumably had not at that time conceived of a possibility of immortality other than in terms of repetition through historical time. Masculine individuality could only be expressed in serving the group as effectively as possible. Thus, there would be no feasible dichotomy between sexuality and spirituality; they would be one and the same motivation and activity. One might even go so far as to speculate that at this point there would have been no concept in the male of individual freedom and independence and that he therefore had no fear of serving the female. The masculine-right would not have developed sufficient consciousness and intelligence for there to be any question of his fearing to sacrifice himself to the feminine, procreative purpose, especially if the deity was envisaged as a mother-goddess.

This phase in religious history would be the equivalent of infancy where sexual differentiation exists but is innocent and psychologically of no significance. There is simply straightforward 'worship of the mother' and the bisexual attributes implicit in the fertility which ensures continuity and security.

The concepts of metaphysical powers or spirits and of an anthropomorphic pantheon of deities with sexually differentiated characteristics can be traced back thousands of years, and it cannot be said for certain where an when they originated.

However long variations of this dominantly survival-procreative, religious motivation existed, it was of great significance that there then arose a totally different concept, apparently in the area we now call the 'Near East' or 'Middle East'.

The terms Near and Middle East do not seem to have clear definition. The traditional labels suggest that they were terms loosely applied historically to divisions based on ethnic, religious, cultural and topographical considerations. 'East' was used by Europeans to indicate geographical areas lying in the direction of the rising sun.

Nevertheless, the events to which I am about to refer occurred in an area just over the conventional 'eastern' boundary of Europe and just inside the 'western' boundary of Asia. In a sense, therefore, they happened at the juncture of what we would now call 'the spheres of Eastern and Western influence'. In other terms, they happened, metaphorically speaking, in the earth's corpus callosum, the bridge or mid-point between one of the world's psychological hemispheres and the other.

The West in recent centuries, with its emphasis on industry, science and technology, and advanced intellectual learning, has tended to be thought masculine in comparison with its more passive, conservative, feminine counterpart in the East. (That is to say, before the emergence and adoption in the West of communist ideologies and methods during this century.)

I would suggest that the developments over several centuries in the West demonstrate a parallel with principles proposed in this book, namely that so-called western masculinity is really the equivalent of the condition where the masculine-right hemisphere has been drawn to devoting itself to the feminine-sexual-economic purpose.

In many respects it could be said to have applied itself responsibly and to beneficial effect but there is no doubt that one could catalogue a whole series of examples over recent centuries where masculine Western power and influence has exploited and violated in its pursuit of wealth, power and pleasure—all of which it has persuaded itself into believing was accomplished as 'progress'.

I would further suggest that these developments can be traced back to the significant event which occurred, in the religious context, in the corpus callosum between Europe and Asia.

There emerged within the Semitic tribes a religious movement which not only asserted that there was in reality only a single, omnipotent deity but they gave to understand that this deity was unequivocally and exclusively masculine. Even further, their tribal ontological myths contained a strong anti-feminine feature in which Man's predicament in the world was held to have been caused by temptations and deceits allegedly inherent in the feminine character.

How could it possibly have come about that 'suddenly' a dispensation should have appeared running totally contrary to established traditions, one in which the erstwhile dominant mother-goddess was relegated entirely from the metaphysical realm?

Any answer can of course only be speculative but my guess would be that this innovation was the outcome of a definite advance or breakthrough in right-hemisphere intelligence and consciousness.

Questions would have arisen in the masculine hemisphere, as objective, abstract reasoning, to the effect: Is Man's only purpose on earth to reproduce himself continuously like an animal? Surely Man is given his gift of intelligence so that he may understand himself to have to fulfil a special role, perhaps in direct relationship with the divine? Surely we must rise to this responsibility and down-grade the simply reproductive purpose of our earthly life? And if we have in ignorance been subject to this feminine, procreative domination, then the creator of the world and its feminine processes—the one who is revealing to us the limitation of creatures—must be masculine, the 'father' of it all? Does this not mean that the masculine is inherently and potentially superior to the feminine and that it must extricate itself from feminine motivation in order to respond to the spiritual aspiration in direct obedience to the omnipotent, patriarchal deity?

This development would be the equivalent of the intervention of self-consciousness during the transition from infancy to childhood. During this period, influence transfers from the succouring mother to the law, discipline and instruction exercised in the family by the father.

I have deliberately implied above a tendency in masculine reasoning to reject the feminine as inferior, and as having the power to limit and involve the masculine in the non-spiritual, sexual, procreative purpose. This indicates that the development caused the dichotomy between spirituality and sexuality. (It is reminiscent of the child's emotional reaction to awareness of his or her own sexual indentification and therefore of emotional relationship with the other sex. Also, of the tendency in boys to consider girls as being inferior.)

It also suggests, in accordance with earlier commentary in the book concerning the dichotomy in individual psychology, the beginning of the rift between the hemispheres, one which gives rise to the spiritual desires and fears in the masculine-right reciprocating the sexual desires and fears in the feminine-left.

With this religious development in the corpus callosum, a new and divisive era in Man's psychological evolution began. Both male and female became aware of a bifurcation in their motivation in which it appeared that the sexual, economic, procreative pursuit was subsidiary to individual, spiritual achievement.

Religion, at this point, moved, as it were, from its instinctive, physical, sexual stage to one in which emphasis began to transfer to the emotional and mental—from mother-goddess to father-god. Inevitably, this shift caused tension and conflict. This does not, however, imply that it was a negative and retrograde development. On the contrary, friction and tension created by polarisation produces the very heat and energy required for evolution. In this case, it provided the incentive for the masculine to begin its search for the reality and truth of Man's spiritual purpose.

A section of the emerging movement at first migrated southwards but, later, having been dispossessed of their territory, spread rapidly westwards (i.e., from right to left). Its people came to be known as Jews and their religious dispensation, firmly established by Moses some four thousand years ago, came to be called Judaism.

It is interesting in relation to this theme that their Hebrew written language was set down from right to left, and, originally, the script only consisted of consonants (feminine). To vocalise the language—to 'breathe life or spirit' into it—it was necessary to introduce the appropriate vowels (masculine). This represented a 'penetration' in order to 'impregnate' with meaning. These features suggest the masculine nature of the inspiration and also that the masculine-right divine intervention moved across to the feminine-left in order to convert the existing, earthbound commitment.

A most notable feature, however, as already mentioned, was that Jehovah, the ultimate and singular father-god, had no female consort and all the subsequent prophets, patriarchs, rabbis, leaders—the earthly spokesman and ministers for the masculine, divine authority—were (and still are) exclusively male. In contemporary Judaism, the male is still the religious teacher in the synagogue whilst the female is responsible for the order and maintenance of domestic life in conformity with the strict rules of conduct imposed upon her.

This arrangement established a clear segregation, one which effectively repealed the male's hitherto one-way commitment to the female procreative purpose. (Not that the commitment was, of course, totally removed, but the degree of it was strictly regulated and circumscribed.)

The history of the Jewish people is one of wandering and struggle, focusing particularly on the attempt to find, acquire, settle and hold a territory which could be regarded as a permanent homeland.

This is reminiscent, in individual psychology, of the emotional turbulence of adolescence where the masculine leaves its original 'home' and seeks to find identity and status whilst the feminine looks to find a new home in which to find security and continuity for future generation of individuality.

The Jewish attempt to establish a permanent homeland was first effectively accomplished about three thousand years ago in Palestine under the leadership of David and Solomon, having been inspired to do so by Moses and Joshua. But this initial success and the subsequent acquisition of great wealth gave way to a period of division and decline. One could say that the masculine, relieved of its total commitment to the feminine, began to enjoy to excess the power, pleasure and indulgences obtained through what it deludedly regarded as divinely authorised privilege. This in turn undermined the will and foundations of society and led to loss of strength and direction. In other words, the masculine took to exploiting the feminine.

For a while, the nation's prosperity continued and the tribes were able to 'buy off' threats from potential invaders such as the Assyrians. The society had however became too corrupt with luxury and indulgence to be able to withstand the envy of its neighbours. It failed to heed the warnings and pleas of prophets such as Amos and Isaiah who saw that the true meaning of the religious testament had been misinterpreted and lost. It proved impossible to re-establish the proper masculine relationship between the father-god and the feminine. The nation fell victim to the Babylonians. Later the Persians under Cyrus for a time restored the Jewish status but, after domination by the Egyptians and interference from the Syrians, internal dissensions led finally to invasion and control by the Romans.

All the above is reminiscent of the masculine falling into sexual, economic, worldly involvement, with all its attendant turmoil and misgiving. The attraction of pleasure, power and status gives rise to a vulnerability in which the truly masculine, individual, spiritual aspiration succumbs to the feminine, procreative ethos.

As is well known, Jewry scattered far and wide, especially westwards, and became once again a tribe of wanderers without a homeland of its own, until, that is, the re-establishment of Israel in modern times. In relation to this theme, it would appear that the Zionist ambition to maintain the integrity of Israel will depend on the ability of the masculine in the Jew to reconcile itself at last with the feminine.

It was during the Roman occupation of Palestine that a Jew named Jesus fired the spirit of the oppressed people, proclaiming a religious message which was interpreted by the Jewish establishment as being disloyal to the tradition and as a threat to their authority and privilege. In due course, a section of the community acclaimed Jesus as its saviour, Messiah or Christ, and the incensed Jewish authority, with the connivance of the Roman presence, succeeded in silencing him by having him put to death.

But the death of the man did not silence the message—a message which was to become the basis of Christianity. In common with Judaism, this new testament maintained the monotheistic concept, again attributing exclusively male character to the omnipotent 'father-god' without female consort. It was therefore basically a reformation of the Jewish tradition rather than an entirely new concept.

Further claims made were, however, definite innovations. It was asserted that Jesus himself was not conceived by sexual intercourse, that he was the 'son' of the 'father-god without consort', that he was therefore 'semi-divine', a manifestation of pure, masculine spirit in material form. During his earthly life, as far as can be gathered from the official records, he is not reported to have married nor to have had any sexual relationship with women. In the spiritual sense therefore he came to represent the 'ideal' man, a 'male virgin' undefiled by sexual pleasure-seeking. It was presumably emulation of this deliberate rejection of participation in the feminine procreative purpose which gave rise to the practice within the Christian priesthood of celibate living.

Whatever the interpretations and explanations of this rejection, Jesus nevertheless continually stressed in his teaching the importance of the family and the special and blessed nature of the female and her child-bearing role. This suggests that Jesus was intent to rectify—as certain of the Jewish prophets preceding him had done—what he perceived as an unfortunate degeneration of the original 'father-god' dispensation.

The assuming of power and status by the masculine for its own selfish indulgences had led to an alienation and suppression of the feminine which was unacceptable and was certainly not intended in the original spiritual context. Jesus not only demonstrated through his life and teaching the nature of the truly spiritual masculine responsibility but repeatedly emphasised the essential feminine virtues. The old Jewish testament had virtually totally ignored the concept of love, a fact which Jesus sought to rectify by using the word over and over again, with the intent of reconciling masculine and feminine in one all-embracing and integrating concept. Thus he may be said to have introduced a means whereby the dichotomy between left and right hemispheres could be appreciated as a dualism of complement and harmony rather than discord and conflict. This is not to imply that he wished to persuade the masculine to revert solely to the feminine, sexual, procreative commitment; plainly he intended no such thing. It is evident that he saw the resolution of the sexual, spiritual aspects of life as being dependent on love and care for all creation along with humble acknowledgement that the 'almighty father' was the ultimate source of that love.

Some six centuries later, in the same Near Eastern area, a further religious revival took place with the arrival of Muhammad. This again happened in a context in which it was appropriate and effective to criticise establishment religion, in this case both Judaism and Christianity, for having gone astray and for having become mistaken in interpretations, teachings and practices.

The points relevant to this theme emerging from this third dispensation are: perpetuation of the masculine, omnipotent 'father-god', as Allah; the abolition of the idea of semi-divine, semi-human intermediaries (because one of the criticisms of Christianity was that the people had made an idol of Jesus and worshipped him and his followers instead of the 'father-god' alone); elimination of privileged priesthoods, concomitant with the assertion that each individual is responsible for direct communion with the deity, and is directly subject to the will of that deity; and strict laws governing women's behaviour, marriage, sexual licence and other economic and social matters from birth to death. These teachings and instructions are contained in the holy scripture, the Qur'an, and, overall, the emphasis in it could be said to be on discipline of the feminine (which all too readily leads the masculine astray) and on the abandonment of self-will by the masculine.

This Islamic reformation could again be interpreted as a renewed attempt to rectify imbalances caused by the unfortunate trends which had overtaken the previous sponsors of the 'father-god' dispensation—Judaism and Christianity.

The emergence of an exclusively masculine, remote, detached, omnipotent deity, devoid of any hint of sexual proclivities and not even accompanied in his realm by any feminine influence, appearing 'suddenly' out of a long history of either polytheism involving deities of both genders sexually active, or a dominantly feminine power devoted to fecundity on earth, seems, in retrospect, an extraordinary phenomenon.

Can it be said to have succeeded or failed?

Who can judge? It depends by what criteria religion can be judged to succeed or fail. In spiritual terms, who can say what the purpose of religion *is*? We are not in a position to assess because we do not know the absolute terms within which to make the assessment. Even in terms appropriate to the duration to date of humanity, we are not able to determine to what extent the human race has succeeded or failed in achieving what it is supposed to have achieved.

In relative or mundane terms, as far as the history of human affairs in the West over the past two or three millennia is concerned, life has been continually punctuated by tension, strife, conflict and war. Man could be said to have failed miserably in establishing peace and concord, if they are the criteria by which he should be judged.

Evolution of religion in the West

I have already suggested that the intervention of the father-god idea may have had something to do with the growth of human consciousness and intelligence and, in particular, that it is reasonable to surmise that it was a concept generated by the masculine-right hemisphere.

In that context, it could be said to have been a psychological reaction by the masculine to a long period of domination by the basic, feminine motivation towards sexual, economic, procreative survival. That is not to say, however, that the concept would not necessarily have appealed to the feminine, spiritual aspect. How much more appropriate and satisfactory for the spiritually-aspiring feminine to envisage as worthy of worship a supreme, authoritative, benign, non-sexually threatening, father-figure (and, in addition, in the Christian case, also an actual, incarnated, semi-divine and ideal man).

If it is not possible to judge the father-god concept to have been a success or failure, it can certainly be said in retrospect to have been an understandable development; and it has to be accepted that it was valid for its time and purpose.

It could be said that this period in theological development is the equivalent of the adolescent/young adult phase in the individual life where the masculine-right aspiration arises and struggles against a dominantly feminine, sexual ethos. Yet the masculine is not yet experienced and mature enough in the main to understand fully what is happening and to avoid suffering much turmoil and emotional challenge. It is not usually a time of peace and concord; for all that they may be desired, it does not work out like that. The only positive way in which to view the conflict and stress is to realise that it provides the spur and energy to take the next evolutionary step.

Interpreting further the earlier brief history of Judaism, it appears as though the masculine in the male did not fully realise the spiritual responsibility (because it was not sufficiently conscious of it to do so). Instead of acting as true witness and medium for divine inspiration, the masculine took to exercising its privilege in the interests of wealth and power, thereby repeating, despite warning, the same error perpetrated by Aaron who had seen fit to make an idol of 'the calf of gold'.

This abrogation of responsibility by the masculine meant that the maintenance of doctrine and ritual had to be transferred to the care of the feminine in the male. This it undertook with such tenacity that not one 'jot nor tittle' of the original scripture has been altered and strict continuity and faithful repetition has been maintained by the orthodox through succeeding generations.

Thus it fell to the masculine in the segregated female to have to take responsibility for the control and protection of the society and family, whilst the feminine in her cared for, and found traditional sexual fulfilment in, her children, family and relatives. Hence, the persistence today of a socially matriarchal and religiously patriarchal disposition in Jewish society.

A somewhat similar fate may be said to have befallen the Christian development. Jesus (and then his immediate disciples) attempted to re-integrate male and female, masculine and feminine, through emphasising co-operative service, love, equality, peace, charity, humility and so on. He was continually critical of the erring masculine in the male—exemplified by the Jewish religious autocracy of his time—exercising power for its own gain and perpetuation. Over and over again he reiterated that the masculine, spiritual role was based on continuous mindfulness of the transcendent, almighty father-god. His instruction to his disciples to spread the gospel was endorsement of the masculine, teaching responsibility.

But, eventually, the religious establishment was again tempted by secular power and the ability to use its privilege to amass wealth (especially in the Church of Rome). The feminine spiritual duty to maintain pastoral care was generally well upheld but the masculine undertook its missionary task with dogmatic, insensitive and inappropriate zeal, regarding itself justified in using deceit, intrigue and physical force in many cases to further its influence and power (a sure sign of masculine exploitation). The male orthodox establishments—with popes, cardinals, bishops, priests, etc.— became segregated, exclusive, self-perpetuating, again alienating the female and distancing themselves from the societies in which they flourished.

Of course, there were obvious exceptions to this trend, especially outstanding individuals, and numerous 'purifying' and 'protesting' reformations took place over the centuries. But, by and large, they were either suppressed, eliminated or eventually underwent the same degeneration as they became established, losing much or all of their masculinity in the process of becoming involved in secular machinations.

All this has its equivalent in the development of the individual in adult life. So often starting with high ideals and missionary zeal, the temptations and demands of worldly life take their toll and the masculine idealism is so easily undermined or forgotten as it is translated into the terms of status, fame, secular power and worldly fortune.

The religious establishments of today, widespread though they may be in the sense that they claim millions of nominal adherents, are really only active in their feminine, public role of expansion, continuity and security. They have little or no masculine, truly spiritual credibility and they condone and lend respectability to—and frequently influence and interfere in—a dominantly materialist ethos in which 'masculinity' means achieving economic wealth and hence power.

It is perhaps not surprising therefore in those societies where the religious establishment is weakest (as a general rule, in those industrialised societies most distant from the centres of orthodox power) there is increasing demand from the masculine in the female to participate equally with males in the pursuit of wealth and the exercise of power, even to the extent of taking office in the religious establishment itself.

For centuries, Islam maintained its dispensation intact, possibly because it was mainly based in relatively poor, non-industrialised, technologically under-developed countries. Some would no doubt claim that this continuity was accomplished with excessively ruthless discipline and fanaticism. Nevertheless, the discovery of, and the Western demand for, oil, for example, has led to the relatively sudden acquisition of considerable wealth, power and influence in several Islamic countries. This in turn has led to involvement of those countries in events which have challenged the religious authority, which in certain cases has reacted violently.

This brief paraphrase of thousands of years of religious history in the West is of course a very general and sweeping commentary. It takes no account of exceptions, especially those minority movements and groups which did seek to express the true masculine spirit.

Whereas the main feminine, exoteric account is easily found in the historical record of performance, the masculine tends to have been maintained in secret, esoteric groups which, until recent times, were considered to be of little account. For example, I would suggest that the masculine spirit was kept active in Judaism through such influences as Hasidism and the Kabbalists, in Christianity through numerous ascetics and mystics, in Islam through Sufism and, in general, by such groups as the Alchemists, Gnostics, Rosicrucians, Neo-Platonists, Essenes and so on. These masculine influences have over the centuries only appealed to small numbers of spiritual aspirants compared with the millions who have relied on the security and dogma of the feminine-dominated establishment. A further reason for their relative obscurity was that inevitably the masculine, spiritual message is usually regarded with suspicion and often with hostility by the feminine establishment because its requirement runs counter to all those privileges and powers which the community-supported establishment enjoys. Its demands are also not popular with the mass of people in a society accustomed to seeking maximum pleasure and acquisition of wealth.

The fact that the teachings of these mystics and esoteric groups are now increasingly in demand is a hopeful sign that the quest for truly masculine, spiritual guidance is reviving rapidly. If there is to be any effective resistance to the spread of communism, then it will certainly need to do so.

25 Parallels in individual psychology

One of the main points to be drawn from this view of religious development is that, in the West and Middle East, the mass of people born in past centuries encountered, and had little option but to be conditioned by, a feminine-dominated religious establishment emphasising continuity, expansion, repetition and social security. This was based on a monotheistic, father-god concept—presented by the Jews, reformed by the Christians and reformed again by the Muslims—which required the individual simply to believe in and have faith in this almighty masculine power.

Although this monotheistic dispensation would originally have been a masculine-right inspiration, it would seem that the masculine was not conscious, intelligent and mature enough (i.e., in its 'fight to be male') in society as a whole to maintain the purity of the impersonal, transcendent principal through succeeding generations. The feminine function appropriated it and took to personalising, familiarising and idolising (idealising) the principal as a deity.

Having personalised it, there then came the problem of relationship to it and hence such introductions as the possibility of good and evil, and hence the invention of such personalised phenomena as Satan and the Devil. The masculine acquiesced in this degeneration, deluded by the new-found privilege devolving upon the male, a privilege which it was then frequently tempted to abuse in the pursuit of secular power, wealth, pleasure and other indulgence.

Inevitably, this in turn gave added strength to the feminine motivation of continuity, conservatism, propagation, expansion and so forth. Male religious leaders took part in secular machinations, condoned them and even allowed them to be carried out in the name of religion. This gave rise to absurd situations. For example, an army engaged in battle would call upon the father-god to note the rectitude of its cause and to give it victory; meanwhile, the opposing force would be calling on the same father-god to do the same for them! The ultimate projections of this degeneration were those all-too-frequent cases in history where the religious authority saw fit to suppress, persecute and eliminate opposition to its authority and power. Such total abuses of the truly masculine, spiritual responsibility have so tarnished the dignity and reputation of establishment religion that it is doubtful whether it could ever recover its true spiritual credibility.

Having surrendered to the feminine, procreative motivation and having used its power for the gain of status and wealth, the masculine became corrupted and impotent. By the time science, technology and industry had been applied to the feminine, socio-economic expansion, and massively destructive weapons had been invented either in the interests of aggressive acquisition or through fear for security, the masculine spiritual influence in establishment religion had become almost totally ineffective. Certain 'rebel' priests have protested but, in the main, establishment religion can do no more than pray for peace whilst the weapons continue to be manufactured and violence breaks out all over the world. The troubled masses who look to the establishment for comfort and reassurance receive nothing but weary dogma and unispiring blandishments whilst the establishment itself can do no more than hope and pray that the same fate does not overtake them as has overtaken their institutions in communist countries.

The religious ethic having fallen into disrepute, it is understandable that a powerful ideology should have emerged which judges it irrelevant and dispensable. This materialist, atheistic ideology is totally committed to socio-economic continuity and expansion. It represents the feminine function attempting to dispense altogether with the masculine.

It is ironic that the proponents of belief in the almighty father-god—in effect, the archetypal 'capitalist'—having competed with each other for supremacy for centuries, should now find themselves confronted in many parts of the world with the threat of elimination by the expansion of an atheism for whose inception they were responsible by default.

The Judaic and Christian authorities, having long ago abrogated their masculine, spiritual credibility through having become absorbed into the sexual-procreative-economic-social pupose, can now only stand impotently on the sidelines as the secular powers attempt to resist the communist threat. (Would the Christian Church, I wonder, give its blessing to the use of the West's atomic stock-pile in defence of democracy?) Only in Islam, where religious and secular authority are in some cases nominally the same, does the resistance to atheistic materialism show any semblance of masculine spirit (but still, it must be added, in the feminine interest).

I am not really intending in the above commentary to suggest that blame attaches in this history. It is meant to be an interpretation of what has happened in masculine-feminine terms rather than a criticism or indictment of the religious development of father-god montheism. As indicated earlier in the book, such feminine explanation, analysis and justification based on cause and effect sequence obscures the masculine, synthesising view.

In this view, the evolutionary performance recorded in the history books was inevitable, given the 'adolescent/young adult' phase of humanity which it portrays.

The truly masculine is only concerned with the situation in the present and how the individual copes with it as it actually presents itself to him or her *now*. The masculine spirit in anyone conscious enough and intelligent enough can see plainly the folly of pursuing the present suicidal course. Communist conformity, by definition, is a feminine-dominated threat to masculine individuality.

Thus the really effective method of countering the threat is neither through massive resistance nor appeal to father-god intervention. It can only be through disillusionment and the restoration of individual integrity in every walk of life. It is absolutely no good leaving that responsibility to someone else; the effectiveness of the group is totally dependent on the strength, inspiration and honesty of every single individual in it.

Curiously, in the terms of this theme, feminism, which I have suggested is really the masculine in the female, is thus not so much a claim for equality but a protest against the impotence of the masculine in the male. True spiritual revival can only come about when the male ceases to acquiesce in what has now become an outgrown and outdated, feminine-dominated ethos of expansion. Man needs now to wake up and grow up to participate appropriately in the next phase of human evolution (this being the equivalent of the 'twenty-one' to 'thirty-five' stage in the individual life).

The foregoing hypothesis and commentary on the Judaic-Christian-Islamic father-god development, followed by its legacy—atheistic materialism, contains features which I have already intimated have curious affinity with developments described earlier in the book as being characteristic of psychological evolution in the individual human life.

Discounting infancy (which would be the equivalent, as it were, of 'prehistoric', polytheistic, innocent response to the 'spirits of nature' and worship of the 'earth-mother'), childhood would be the equivalent of the Judaic phase of father-god monotheism. The child starts to become self-conscious and therefore actively selfish and self-centred (the ego-self as 'god' and thus ego- or mono-motivated. In other words, the single 'god' is himself or herself).

The child's father (the patriarch representing 'fear of the Lord') constitutes an authority countering self-will whilst the mother represents social conditioning and demonstrates by example and persuasion conduct acceptable to the group.

The social environment (the convention, tradition or 'old testament') is the child's instruction, education, support and protection. His or her behaviour in the world at large is governed and limited by the external, group discipline (the Mosaic commandment). In effect, this childhood experience is a personal (being based on inherited characteristic) exploration of the boundaries of possibility within a particular, local dispensation.

For some, psychological development within this 'jewish' phase is sufficient. This primary or preparatory education constitutes a conditioning adequate enough for the conduct of the whole life. It is only necessary for that life to be conducted in a mechanical, repetitive, conventional, law-abiding mode.

The childhood phase is followed, by those who are moved by the masculine spirit to evolve out of it, by psychological adolescence. This begins at puberty with the 'birth' of 'consciousness of self', a consciousness indicative of the emergence of the real-self, the basis of that individual's inspiration to evolve out of the conventional mould. The equivalent religious phase is, as it were, the Christian reformation, expressed historically as the incarnation of the divine spirit as Jesus the saviour, Messiah or Christ.

This reformation is enacted and experienced in the individual during the adolescent period as the emergence of a searching, questioning and sometimes rebellious nature which challenges the 'old testament' or social convention and expectation.

The essence of this secondary phase is the 'calling out' of the masculine from the right hemisphere so that it may enter and be born out of the material left, thus becoming inheritor of the childhood past on which it will build a new and individual future.

In parallel with the Christian dispensation, this phase of life is predominantly emotional, being based on the security and protection of family support and yet requiring abandonment of it—an emotionally difficult process. This gives rise to the experience of the need to be loved and the desire to love which manifests as the feminine need to find the 'ideal' masculine (the 'son of god') and the desire to find the 'perfect' feminine (the 'immaculate virgin').

Whereas 'jewish childhood' requires external discipline and authority, the emphasis in 'christian adolescence' begins to transfer to self-discipline through appeal to emotion; it requires faith to step out into the world of individual adulthood. Self-generated moral sense cognises the importance of the outward-going self performing charitable deeds and taking part in a 'new testament' appropriate to one's own generation and its difficulties (created by the ignorant actions of previous generations). Again, for some, this stage of psychological development is sufficient; no further development is required beyond this secondary or public phase of education in life. Such people will work for the well-being of their fellow-men, the proper role of the feminine.

Adolescence is followed by young adulthood, the psychological equivalent of Islam. Here the emphasis reverts to the masculine in the individual, to self-development as in the tertiary, advanced or 'university' phase of education. The individual tests himself or herself against the recorded and tutorially, verbally transmitted account of the world and its ways. Ideally, the individual will develop a philosophy and conviction as to how he or she may best play his or her part as a unique individual in altruistic service to mankind. This individual will contain the instinctive, inherited tradition and will accommodate the emotional drive but attention will become focussed on individual fulfilment within those disciplines.

Having become objectively self-conscious, conscious of the real-self, able to reason objectively in abstract, the key to this phase is intellectual development. There is no other way in which self-will can be transformed. It is only through reason and cognition of the transcendent will that sacrifice of self-will can be effected (a distinctly different process from simple surrender of wilfulness).

In this tertiary or 'islamic' phase, the search is for the meaning of the individual life in relation to current knowledge of the universe. Having found guidance within the particular context which fate has decreed (which the individual realises has been decreed by Allah) he or she becomes aware of a destiny over and above the living of that life in simply instinctive and emotional terms. The destiny of that life cannot be explained or justified in feminine, left-hemisphere, worldly terms; it is an inner, masculine, private communion with the transcendent principal. That earthly life will be led according to divine appointment rather than by social expectation.

Even so, education up to tertiary stage is still only preparatory; even the knowledge gained at 'university' is still only theoretical. It has all taken the potential individual to the threshold of actual participation in adult life; it has all yet to be fully realised in practice and experience. To be a 'jew,' a 'christian' or a 'muslim' is only to have acquired a label signifying the nature and degree of one's educational conditioning. Life in the world has then to be lived as a human being at the same time as the individual must actually realise his or her spiritual purpose. Fate has no respect for privilege acquired through the 'school' attended. Death shows no favour to anyone on earth—'jew', 'christian', 'muslim' or any other group-labelled person; to believe otherwise is a delusion. What is more, the world can never dictate or judge individual destiny; only the objectively conscious individual may know that, for himself or herself.

Having attained majority and entered the adult world, the individual will encounter the trials and temptations of a feminine-dominated, procreative, socio-economic ethos (unless he or she 'retreats' or in some way 'opts out', a course which attempts to by-pass or avoid the system). The overwhelming pressure (in the present phase) is to abandon self-respect and to adapt the ideal principles to worldly expression. Self-fulfilment is then seen in terms of status, power, wealth and pleasure for their own immediate earthly rewards. The masculine spirit is tempted to acquiesce in the feminine function, the ego-self supplants the real-self, and the transcendent, divine will becomes 'my' will.

But the masculine spirit, if it has gained strength, is not easily usurped. In moments of reflection, it will keep prompting in the privacy of the individual mind, causing anxiety, doubt and misgivings in the feminine-left. It will not allow the person to find satisfaction and fulfilment in public performance, assessment and acclaim. The monarch or the priest, the princess or the prostitute—each has only himslf or herself to live with in the final analysis.

Referring back now to the incident in the London clothing store described at the beginning of the book, the confusion experienced at the time clears when considered in the terms of this theme.

It was an almost totally feminine, sexual, socio-economic situation. The labels 'English', 'Jew', 'Christian' and 'Arab' were irrelevant; those group-identities were but incidental and accidental superimpositions diversely applied to an assembly of human beings involved in the trading of articles of clothing.

Those articles represented on the one hand (the feminine-left) physical protection, comfort, security and survival; on the other (the masculine-right committed to the feminine), the searching and selecting of particular items represented the quest for status, individual identity, prestige and competitive display.

The fact that in another context the representatives of those group-affiliations could be hostile to one another had nothing to do with the propagating or protecting of religious beliefs or moral principles. Argument, hatred, violence and war—regardless of any superimposed explanation, justification or excuse—are simply a matter of greed-to-gain confronting fear-of-loss. The fact that men have been traditionally obliged to fight wars does not in any spiritual sense indicate their 'masculinity'; the masculine is in this respect deluded by commiting itself to the feminine, procreative purpose, a delusion compounded by the fact that hostilities have frequently been lent 'respectability' by being undertaken in the name of religion.

In situations where group-identity is passive and is not exerting influence on relationship, and where there is no motive to gain by expropriation and hence no threat of loss, the inherent and natural good nature in human beings allows them as individuals to meet in feminine-group accord.

26 Evolution of religion in the East

The aforementioned development of the father-god concept—in particular in its Judaic and Christian forms—took place, generally speaking, westwards out of the Near East through Europe and eventually to North and South America.

Apparently concomitant with the Semitic genesis, another movement originated in roughly the same area (as far as can be discovered) during the same era. Arising in the 'corpus callosum', as it were, it moved eastwards, into the 'right hemisphere'.

'Suddenly', in what is now called Pakistan and north-west India, there appeared an influence which revolutionized the indigenous, fertility-based Indus Valley culture. How this inspiration originated is a mystery, commensurate with the mystery as to how and why 'someone' conceived of the monotheistic, father-god idea. No one has been able to trace the 'founder' of what was later set down in scripture and called the Vedic tradition, though it is commonly suggested that it was carried eastwards by invading Aryans.

It is not easy to encapsulate in brief the essence of this 'alternative' development but, compared with what we would now call a 'personal god' theology, it was comparatively and originally impersonal. It has been called a philosophy rather than a religion because, compared with the Western idea of religion, it did not postulate an anthropomorphic deity. Its equivalent of 'God' was (and essentially still is) a principle—the Absolute.

To this ultimate and impersonal principle, all things created and generated are related. But Man in particular is directly related through the 'spirit' in him—the real self called Atman. Neither the Absolute Principle nor Atman are personal in the sense that either has form, property or attribute. If they—not that it can be said in reality that 'they' are separate—may be expressed at all in human terms, then they are experienced as 'consciousness-knowledge-bliss' only. In experience, actuality is the only reality; anything thought about it or imagined about it is an illusion. Compared with the monotheistic father-god—the One—the Absolute/Atman is Nothing.

The masculine Vedic inspiration could be said to have 'fertilised' what was evidently a feminine culture in the Indus Valley region.

The former came to be regarded as the 'sun-father' in relation to the indigenous 'earth-mother'—by those who where later moved to conceptualise or visualise the event. The impression I have gained through researching the subject is that this sexual conceptualisation and differentiation gave rise to what later became known as Hinduism with its pantheon of gods and goddesses. This process detracted from the impersonal Absolute Principle which, as indicated above, had no form, property or attribute, and therefore could not be sexually identified.

It could well be that the Semitic Jehovah did not originally have sexually differentiated attribute either. In English translation of *Genesis, The First Book of Moses,* 'God' is not referred to as 'he' until the creation of Man at the end of the first chapter. And, even then, it seems quite possible that the attrubiting of masculine gender to the deity may simply have been a way of distinguishing and divorcing the transcendent principle from the 'earth-mother' cults of the time. Either that or, more subtly, the Old Testament story indicates that God should be regarded as asexual *until* the creation of Man, an act which heralds the beginning of dualism and plurality, and hence sexuality, as creation is made manifest through Man and his generations.

In this regard, it has always seemed to me to be curiously significant that the name of the founding 'father' of the Jewish nation, *Abram/Abraham,* should sound so close (and be almost an anagram in English) to the Hindu name for the asexual Absolute, *Brahman,* and its masculine creative aspect, *Brahma.* Could the westward-moving and eastward-moving inspirations from the 'corpus callosum' of the Middle East have had the *same* origin? If that were ever factually proved, it would have an astounding effect on assessment of world religion and its historical development.

Whatever happened in that dim past, it is evident that the Hindus fell into the familiar feminine proclivity of 'masculinising' the Absolute Principle—but not to the degree that the West masculinised the One Father, and kept even the Christian Trinity a masculine preserve, except for small minorities who proposed the Holy Ghost or Spirit as being feminine. (I was interested to note recently[14] that a certain element in the Anglican Church which is in favour of the ordination of women has been drawing attention to Julian of Norwich, a thirteenth-century female mystic, to whom it was revealed in visions that both God and Jesus 'were partly female'.)

The Hindus retained the 'neutrality' of the Absolute, Brahman, and only allowed definite sexual differentiation to be introduced when conceptualising their trinity, the threefold aspect of Brahman—Brahma, the creator, Vishnu, the preserver, and Siva, the destroyer. Each of these masculine aspects had its feminine counterpart—the consorts Sarasvati, Lakshmi and Shakti respectively. The Hindus recognised, as it were, that once removed from the transcendent, absolute, asexual, principle, a duality or plurality has to be introduced which has both masculine and feminine characteristics.

In other words, the Absolute Principle cannot be exclusively one sex or the other; it must either be hermaphrodite, 'unisexual' or asexual (if indeed it is valid to think of 'it' in such terms at all). It is only in the creative aspect when there is division and multiplicity that there can be relationship. Any known relationship between two created entities will then introduce manifest, distinctive behaviour which will be charateristically masculine and feminine.

The Hindus introduced sexual differentiation into the pantheon of gods and their consorts and followed the further feminine proclivity of giving them identifiable forms. Nevertheless, even in this development, care was taken to avoid purely anthropomorphic images. Although the deities often had basic human form, the fact that they really represented superhuman forces, powers and qualities was emphasised by the appropriate, symbolic use of animal features, extra faces or arms, and so on.

However, despite these precautions, the Hindu religion gravitated for the masses into the worship of temple and shrine idols. And, as in the West, the priestly role was fulfilled by the male so that the increasingly segregated female was relegated to a passive role without privilege. In her subsidiary status, she not only bore the children and maintained the home but was expected to bear the burden of much manual labour as well (in principle, anything to do with fertility and procreation, which included the seasonal, agricultural aspect of economic life). Inevitably, the economic hierarchy came to be dominated by the wealth- and power-accumulating, pleasure-seeking male.

Into this situation, some two and a half thousand years ago, there was born in India he who came to be known as Gautama Buddha. He had privileged male status but became disenchanted with that and the whole suppressive, socio-economic system. He attempted the

Evolution of religion in the East

orthodox religious life but again became disenchanted. It did not seem to him to help fulfil the spiritual needs of humanity.

After enlightement (or disillusionment), he understood that desire was the cause of suffering and began to teach that, along with compassion for all creatures, ultimate happiness or bliss was dependent upon abandonment of worldly gain and all claim to personal possession and identity. In other words, it is only through sacrifice of self-will and becoming desireless that it is possible to lose identity and 'dissolve back' into the primordial state of 'consciousness-knowledge-bliss'.

This teaching spread further eastwards (just as Christianity had spread westwards), one development of it reaching through Tibet into China and beyond, into Japan. Here in the Far East, aspects of Buddhist teaching were reformed in what came to be known in China as Ch'an and in Japan as Zen. This third phase of evolution could be said to have taken the practice of mental disillusionment to it ultimate, intellectual degree. Reality had to be perceived as self-evident within and could never be conceived through the contrived explanations and logical workings of the feminine-left hemisphere.

Enlightenment was (and is) an instantaneous understanding or illumination in the masculine-right hemisphere, and does not require worldly proof, beliefs nor religious institutions. Each individual only requires a master to show him 'the Way' to disillusionment. Once disillusioned, the individual restores balance and harmony between the hemispheres, on the one hand reinstating responsibility to the ever-changing forms of nature whilst bodily life remains, being ever-mindful on the other of the presence of the transcendent, absolute, impersonal, divine principle. Thus there comes about the true marriage of the feminine actual and the masculine real.

This commentary is again a general and sweeping encapsulation of a complicated development which took thousands of years but it will serve in principle for the points relevant to this theme to be made.

In its basically three-phase unfolding, the Eastern movement has notable parallels and contrasts with the Western development outlined previously.

As far as is known, both originated at roughly the same time in roughly the same area. The westward movement manifested as the monotheistic, Judaic, masculine, father-god concept whilst the eastward movement, based on a transcendent, absolute principle, manifested as the Hindu pantheon—masculine dominated but retaining the presence of the feminine aspect of divine influence.

In both cases, the following developments emerged as response to what was seen at the time as being a degeneration of the original dispensation. With only about five hundred years separating them, both Jesus Christ and Gautama Buddha called for the re-directing of spiritual aspiration to the omnipotent father-god and the absolute principle respectively. Both pointed out the folly of pursuing worldly wealth and power; both taught about the relief of suffering, Jesus emphasising love and Buddha compassion. They were both concerned to reconcile imbalances and tensions between right and left hemisphere, i.e., to remedy the alienation between masculine and feminine, male and female.

Five to six centuries later, the emergence of the Islamic tradition more or less coincided with the emergence of Zen. Both again re-emphasised the direct relationship of the individual with the almighty father-god, Allah, and the transcendental principle respectively; in both cases the realisation of that relationship was dependent upon the elimination of self-will and obedience to fate or natural law.

It may also be noted that psychologically, as with the Judaic-Christian-Islamic evolution, the Eastern phases fundamentally followed and equivalent threefold maturing process—from the instinctive, superstitions pantheism of Hinduism (commensurate with the mental functioning of the child), through the emotional suffering, devotion and compassion of Buddhism (reminiscent of the adolescent phase) to abstract reasoning and intellectual disillusionment in Zen (characteristic of the young adult development during tertiary or 'higher' education). It should also be noted that the appearance of both Jesus and the Buddha takes place, as it were, at puberty—the point at which, in the individual, there is the 'immaculate birth' of objective consciousness or 'the regenerate man', the point of the active emergence of the masculine spirit in the right hemisphere.

Significantly, both Jesus and the Buddha were said not to have had ordinary, carnal, female, procreative origins—the former having been born of a virgin and the latter having been born out of his mother's side. Both were hailed at birth as future 'saviours'. In spiritual terms, both represent the non-parental, non-physical emergence of the truly masculine individual which, if the left to right psychical conversion takes place, will lead the individual to his or her destiny.

There is nevertheless a distinct difference between the patriarchal monotheism of Judaism-Christianity-Islam and the abstract absolutism of Hinduism-Buddhism-Zen. All the emphasis on the exclusively male deity of the former was, I suggest, more likely to be sympathetic to the feminine-left fuctioning because an identifiable, authoritarian, masculine, father-god image would be more likely to appeal to it as worthy of devotion, worship and obedience. It was as if the promotion of this male, sexually-inactive image was a natural evolutionary step away from, and distinct from, the existing primitive, earth-bound religion in which man's survival and continuity was seen as subject to fertility and procreative cycles regulated by an earth-mother goddess. In graduating therefore from 'religious infancy' to 'religious childhood', it is understandable that the overseer and controller should be a male, parental figure representing discipline, instruction, authority, reassurance and security—all qualities appealing to the feminine-left.

During the next phase—'religious adolescence'—it was then necessary to introduce a 'closer' and more identifiable male figure sympathetic to the emotional needs of the adolescent. The semi-divine, ideal, sexually-inactive male embodied in Jesus of Nazareth fulfilled that need but, again, I suggest that the figure is more appealing to the feminine-left than the masculine-right. He represents all those qualities which give hope, succour and comfort to a phase of turbulence, self-questioning, uncertainty and the need to love and to know that one is loved. For the feminine-left therefore, Jesus stood, as it were, for the ideal manner in which the masculine-right should conduct itself.

And then, during the 'young adult' phase of Western religion there came the Islamic dispensation. Here the male authority became more remote again, and impersonal. It was again highly authoritarian and demanded total submission. Such complete surrender is again, I suggest, essentially acceptable to the feminine-left to which law and order represent security.

In the Western hemisphere then, the religious development promoted a monotheistic, male concept. On the whole, the dispensation appealed to the feminine-left which needs direction and authority from the ideal masculine. But there were certain snags in this feminine presentation.

Inevitably, the feminine looked upon the male deity as loving, benign, just and concerned for the good of humanity and its continuity and survival. How then could all the difficulties, sufferings, errors, illnesses, antagonisms and so on be explained? Plainly, this father-god did not make life comfortable, easy and peaceful. It became necessary to invent the concept of the devil and evil.

Other snags were that the dispensation did not really explain Man's exact relationship to the deity, nor allow any other purpose in human life than procreation of the species, nor help to understand the *meaning* of death. All these drawbacks were coped with by introducing the possibility of direct communication with the deity and, following an obedient and charitable life, the joining of the dead with the father-god in an eternal other-world called heaven, a promise which gave purpose to living.

All these feminine 'explanations and inventions' were not, I suggest deeply satisfactory to the growing intelligence of the masculine-right. The problems created by the explanations have given rise to centuries of theological debate and argument. Far from reaching agreement and conclusion, theological theory and pronouncement has caused frequent and irreparable schisms. It seems most unlikely that there will ever be a coherent, universal, unified, father-god dispensation.

I would further suggest that it was the unsatisfying nature of the male deity concept to the masculine-right hemisphere which has given rise to the misguided actions and social disasters over recent centuries. Although the feminine-left in masses of people has remained faithful to, and has believed in, the father-god dispensation, the masculine-right has continually baulked at it and, without spiritual direction and guidance sympathetic and acceptable to it, has gone continually astray.

If this is valid, then it is possible to understand the masculine-right's proclivity to commit itself to worldly gain and pleasure-seeking (since it is aware of no other purpose and reward), a proclivity which in turn has given rise to continual conflict and war, and the eventual emergence of materialistic, atheistic ideologies.

In contrast, the Eastern movement did not theologically segregate the feminine from the masculine. It was a case either of impersonal absolute principle or, in Hinduism, a pantheon involving both sexes with female in appropriate complementary relationship with the male, very much in accordance with the left and right hemisphere relationship described earlier in this book. This may not have been so appealing to the feminine as an omnipotent male deity as far as procreative continuity on earth was concerned; but I suggest it was far more sympathetic to the spiritual aspiration in the masculine-right.

The advantage of the Eastern dispensation is that it does not encounter the snags described above as bedevilling the Western concept. The transcendental principle is beyond the creation and not involved. Its threefold representation in Hinduism demonstrates the cyclic nature of all created phenomena—their birth, continuation and death under the laws of Brahma, Vishnu and Siva (representative of the penetration, fertilisation and withdrawal of the masculine). All events are thus simply manifestations of a continuing creating and dissolving. There is no good or evil in the context of the Absolute. Man is a particular projection which participates in existence and is then withdrawn. The purpose of Man's life is to realise that the masculine spirit within him enters existence, witnesses the enactment of that life and is then withdrawn to its Absolute source.

Through dissolution of the temporary ego-self and the sacrifice therefore of self-will, there is no problem of relationship with the Absolute. The real self, the Atman, *is* the Absolute. In principle, this perception was maintained by both Buddhism and Zen.

This Eastern tradition nevertheless encountered its own problems. Generally speaking it led to a certain failure of the masculine-right to play a fully caring and responsible part in relationship to the feminine-left, which to a degree was left to its own devices. It led, by Western standards, to lack of enterprise, to apathy, to a resigned acceptance of deprived economic conditions, to stagnation, to unnecessary suffering and so forth.

The gist of the foregoing commentary leads to the tentative assessment that the chosen forms of religion which evolved mainly westwards from the Near East were acceptable primarily to the feminine-left in the western hemisphere; and those which evolved eastwards were acceptable to the masculine-right in the eastern hemisphere.

It could then further be said that in later centuries the feminine-dominated West, becoming increasingly wealth-seeking and expansionist, began to influence and undermine the East by seeking its wealth, taking over its government and territory and imposing

Western concepts upon it. The feminine-hemisphere influence was able to effect this expansion because the masculine-right devoted to its service was physically and economically stronger than the uncommitted masculine-right in the East.

In the wake of this capitalist expansion, the materialist ideologies inevitably followed and, in numerous areas, the communist influence is suppressing and destroying the religious foundations and fabric.

The East is now drawn into the same predicament as the West, having become dominantly obsessed with feminine-left economic expansion in one form or another. Both are now in a crucial situation where the masculine-right is either committed to suicidal expansion or has retreated from the public domain. What remains of religious establishment and capitalist theory is under the growing threat of an ideology in which the masculine-right, individual spirit is in danger of elimination. To put it bluntly, Man's spiritual purpose would then be terminated and, presumably, there would be no remaining evolutionary possibility for this world.

This would be the equivalent, in the individual life, of the psychological situation between the ages of 'twenty-eight' and 'thirty-five', when the masculine-right can feel overwhelmed by the feminine, procreative purpose to which it finds itself fully committed.

The question for the individual at this point is whether there is an alternative. Does the masculine-right have the strength and power to become 'true to itself' and fulfil the higher, spiritual destiny of that individual?

Projecting this situation into the state of humanity as a whole at this time, is there any possibility of a spiritual revival, of humanity becoming noble, dignified and 'true to itself'?

27 The possibility of spiritual revival

How may one envisage a possible spiritual revival?

As already indicated, I do not see such a revival manifesting in the traditional religious sense of there being a teaching proposed, like a manifesto, which a large number of people would then believe in, subscribe to and establish as an institution. The religiously-motivated group is valuable for strength, support and security for the individual. But if the perpetuation and expansion of that group becomes an end in itself, then it becomes spiritually emasculating for the individual.

In other words, true spirituality in the individual has very little, even nothing, to do with being identified with a particular group-form of religion. Spirituality transcends all formal expressions of religious doctrine and practice. These may be the initial means whereby spiritual responsibility may be introduced to the individual—through his or her childhood and adolescent phases—but if that individual is to develop to spiritual maturity he or she must understand the experience, meaning and purpose of his or her own life in individual terms.

This leads to a number of principles which are relevant to the consideration of possible spiritual revival. They do in fact apply to the relationship between the individual and the group in any context, religious or secular:

Groups (feminine) are formed to provide the base from which and through which the individual (masculine) may evolve.

For the individual to use or exploit the group to enhance himself and in order to gain mundane advantage corrupts the integrity of both group and individual.

Spiritual evolution is essentially and uniquely an individual responsibility. No group can of itself evolve; only individual members within it can do so.

The group consists of potential individuals. The group must serve the individual and the individual must serve the group whilst he or she is a member of it.

If the individual serves the group and the group fails to serve the individual, the latter becomes impotent.

If the group, serves the individual and the individual fails to serve the group, the latter becomes barren.

The group does not exist as a constant entity in itself, independent of its individual members. If the individual surrenders his or her individuality to a supposed group-identity, he or she surrenders individual integrity.

One of the keys to these statements lies in the use of the words 'serve' and 'surrender'. The individual *serves* the group in order to evolve spirituality; that does not mean *surrendering* individuality *to the group*. The sacrificing of self-will is a spiritual process not of this world and its power struggles and machinations. This sacrifice is made by the masculine-right to the transcendent principle (by whatever name), *not* to the 'institutionalised' group. That is to serve the feminine-left, mundane purpose instead of the higher masculine purpose. That is why enforced allegiance to a socio-economic ideology such as communism is utter anathema to the spiritually-aspiring individual.

To return to the question at the beginning of the chapter, where may one look for the inspiration and guidance which could herald a truly spiritual revival for the individual?

One possibility, directly related to commentaries in this book, is that it could be expected to take place in the 'feminine-dominated-West' through influences coming from the 'masculine-inspired-East'.

Western historical records fully document what I earlier referred to as the West's influence on the East through empirical, capitalist expansion, which was basically one of expropriation and exploitation but which carried with it cultural and religious influence. The flow back in the other direction mainly consisted of materials, natural resources, exotic flora and fauna, novelties and trophies, and so on.

However, apart from those more obvious and publicised acquisitions, rather more subtle and much less publicised influences did begin to work as well. A few sensitive and observant colonials began to take an interest in the religions, philosophies and cultural achievements of the East. A hundred years or so ago, European scholars were translating scriptures from Sanskrit and Pali, for example, into European languages.

At first, very few people outside academic circles were interested

The possibility of spiritual revival

in the texts; but gradually the interest increased until, over the past three or four decades, demand for them has considerably escalated, for their practical, as well as theoretical, content.

Due to the nature of these Vedic, Hindu, Buddhist and Zen texts (and that of texts from numerous other origins, disciplines and traditions also), this could only mean that Eastern concepts were meeting growing response in the West—not just due to idle curiosity but because they were finding their way to people who were intuitively aware of their value. In the wake of the texts there then came teachers who were able to expound upon them and to offer disciplines and practices (such as meditation and yoga) in support of the theory. Many people went (and continue to go) to Eastern countries to seek out and learn from teachers in their own surroundings.

As a result of these and other movements and events essentially Eastern in origin and nature, there are now thousands of individuals in the West actively following the precepts and concepts, and actively participating in the practices which have been familiar in the East for centuries. How ironic in a way—but how significant also— that as direct consequence of the West's 'psycho-physical' invasion of the East (the equivalent of the masculine-right being dominated by the motivations of the feminine-left), there should now be a 'psycho-spiritual' invasion from East to West (the equivalent of masculine-right inspiration of the feminine-left).

In my view, although there may well have been (and probably still are) a number of errors, distortions and malpractices, (due to the feminine-left's ignorance and inability to translate and interpret the messages correctly), the signs are in the main that the 'invasion' is beginning to form an effective base for masculine-right, spiritual revival. For, as I have already commented, the essence of all true Eastern philosophy and religion (not that the two are separated as they are in the West) is the encouragement of self-discovery, self-knowledge and self-realisation. Providing this does not degenerate into selfishness, exclusivity and social alienation, but inspires instead the laudable Western religious tradition of service and care (and inspires also, it should be added, 'resurrection' of masculine Western understanding and tradition—which it is doing, judging by the current interest in Western mysticism and esoteric teachings), then the prospect is promising.

The overall effect could be that of producing a society of

responsible, caring, self-disciplined individuals—the only antidote either to a materialist, expansionist society comprised of spiritually-impotent, externally-disciplined group-members whose only purpose is procreation, pleasure and socio-economic wealth and power, or to the selfishness and exploitation characteristic of autocracies and dictatorships.

The masculine-right intuition and integrity urges re-assessment and re-direction of excessive and obsessive practices. The misguided masculine must cease its blind commitment to status-, wealth- and power-seeking at the expense of the feminine. It must use finite resources intelligently for sound and not frivolous, short-term and indulgent pursuits; it must restore sensitive care for the natural environment.

By withdrawal from the chasing of artificial and unsatisfying pleasures, the masculine may revive and reflect upon its responsibility to the transcendent principle—the Absolute, the Divine Presence, the Almighty God, call it what you will—becoming sensitive to natural order and natural pleasure on the one hand and actively aspiring to self-realisation on the other.

In the immediate terms of this theme, as applicable to the individual, this dispensation calls for right and left hemisphere reconciliation. Psychologically, this development will be the equivalent of the 'twenty-eight' to 'thirty-five' phase of life where the masculine becomes aware of reality through disillusionment—which means seeing the fallacy of what it has been led to believe.

On the scale of humanity as a whole, it represents a reconciliation of natures between East and West in a manner which has been unknown during recorded history.

It might be queried, incidentally, why the East should represent the right hemisphere, when, to itself—i.e., looking out from within itself—the right would the West. The answer is that the East is the right side as Man looks *at* the world. It is Man's view of the world that we are concerned with, and he sees the world 'out there' as if as a reflection of himself in a mirror where his right eye sees the reflection of that eye on the right side in the mirror-image.

Reconciliation in the individual psyche requires masculine-right initiative. It requires self-observation, disillusion and self-discovery. This in turn requires profound teaching and consideration of the ways in which the Divine Presence or Absolute Principle may be understood and expressed. Only by these means is it possible to

The possibility of spiritual revival

bring about a change of attitude in the feminine-left, a change which must be effected through firm yet reassuring initiative.

It is no longer appropriate to conceive of this Divinity or Absolute in personalised, anthropomorphic terms, for humanity has surely now outgrown the need to envisage and worship man-contrived images and idols. It has been the feminine *penchant* for finding security through identification which has led the spiritually-aspiring masculine so frequently into illusory belief in the past.

In what I have described earlier as a feminine-sexual/masculine-spiritual conversion over a lifetime, it is as if humanity itself has reached a stage in its religious life where the masculine aspiration, in its 'fight to be male', has responsibility as never before to formulate the new spiritual dispensation if it is to survive the threat of emasculation by a world-wide, feminine-dominated obsession with material acquisition and possession.

This time the masculine must not be tempted to take to itself undue selfish power and influence at the expense of the feminine; and the feminine must not be allowed to delude and divert the masculine. The masculine must not abandon or reject the feminine but lead it out of and beyond its procreative, worldly purpose.

It was, I surmise, in a context of similar nature and in an expression of similar concern that the Christian mystic, Thomas, in a Coptic manuscript discovered in Egypt about thirty-five years ago but dating back to a century or more before the time of Muhammad, recording what he called 'the secret sayings which the Living Jesus spoke', wrote (log. 114):

> Simon Peter said to them: Let Mary go out from among us, because women are not worthy of the Life. Jesus said: See, I shall lead her, so that I will make her male, that she too may become a living spirit, resembling you males. For every woman who makes herself male will enter the Kingdom of Heaven.

No one would surely countenance the possibility that Jesus was suggesting an actual, physical sex-change? Surely 'male' is being used in the sense in which I have been speaking in this book of the masculine. In which case, the statement would certainly substantiate the proposition that there must be a conversion of feminine disposition to masculine as prerequisite for spiritual fulfilment.

28 The masculine and feminine absolutes

Within the present limits of human mental conception, there are two absolutes—One and Nothing.

The absolute One represents the single and undivided, and hence the totality. It cannot be added to, subtracted from, divided or multiplied; if modified by any of these processes, it is then simply no longer One and absolute. Being that beside which there can be no other, it is an ultimate, pure and uncorruptible principle, so much so it is worthy of the highest respect. One is indeed worthy of worship as the divine. No doubt in recognition of this, it became the inspiration for monotheism.

However, it has to be acknowledged that, even though it is absolute, One is nevertheless 'begotten'. The concept of One—as the totality beside which there is no other—is a conception or conceiving in the mind of Man. The One must *exist* for it to have been conceivable. It may be said to be alone and unified—the creator, begetter or origin of all things—but it can only be known to be so because there is 'that' which knows it. 'What' or 'who' knows the One as existing and total?

This problem surely gave rise to the 'other' Absolute. This absolute could not actually exist—otherwise it would be conceivable and on a level with the One, and since the One is the totality that would be impossible. This 'second' absolute does not therfore exist in conceivable form—and yet 'it' is able to comprehend the concept of the totality of existence. If 'it' cannot be any conceivable 'thing', and 'it' does not exist, 'it' can only be called 'Nothing'.

To recapitulate; the conceived and existing One is comprehesible as the absolute totality; the Nothing is inconceivable but has to be acknowledged as 'that' out of which the One is conceived. The existing One can only be comprehensible as such due to the non-existing Nothing. The Nothing is therefore the conceiver, 'subtender' and resolver of the One. Nothing therefore has precedence and supremacy as Absolute. All that may be said of Absolute Nothing, since it is 'that' which comprehends the One totally, is that 'it' must *be* consciousness and/or knowledge.

This is not just a pedantic game! It is highly significant if thoroughly considered. For, in the twin religious developments out

The masculine and feminine absolutes

of the Near East those four millennia or so ago, the feminine-westward, Judaic-Christian-Islamic movement chose the conceivable One as its absolute. ('Hear, O Israel; the Lord our God, the Lord is One!'; 'I and my Father are one'; 'Allah is One, the Eternal God.') The masculine-eastward ('towards the rising sun'), Vedic/Hindu-Buddhist-Zen movement chose the Nothing as its Absolute.

The concept of One totality is the ulitimate projection from feminine-left, 'earth-bound', logical thinking; the comprehension and acknowledgement of Absolute Nothing requires the objective, abstract, intuitive function of the masculine-right.

From the feminine-left point of view, the difficulty with the One as absoulte is that, in Itself, it is static, full of potential but impotent. In existence, it is almighty and reigns supreme—but does not do anything. It needs to be goaded or lured into action for anything to happen. How may this be brought about? Supposing it experienced desire within Itself—the desire to witness Itself, to discover Itself, to know Itself and to fulfil Itself?

How could the One be set in motion? Through division—'seeming two'. Once divided, duality and plurality follow. Once in motion, the apparently separate parts have relationship to each other, essentially and basically exhibiting masculine and feminine characteristics of behaviour (as in the table on pages 32, 33). Once disrupted and in motion, there is both the tendency to centrifugal disintegration and the centripetal pull towards the centre in order to re-integrate—to re-unify or 'make one again'. The latter is experienced in human emotion as the need to be loved and the desire to love (feminine and masculine, respectively).

To express these events in other terms—those of Judaic mythology—God (the absolute as Nothing before becoming later the Lord God—the absolute as One) created the universe and all creatures, including Man, who was made in the likeness, in the image of—or as a conscious reflection of—God. Having created the One totality, God rested.

But the totality was not to remain in that static condition. The Lord God decided that it was 'not good' that Man, Adam, should be *alone* (all-one) in the garden of Eden. Adam should have a 'help-meet'—another who would 'help' him 'meet' himself and enable him to know himself or realise himself. Whilst 'asleep' (i.e., whilst still unconscious of himself), the Lord God takes a part of Adam and makes the female, Eve.

It was then Eve who experienced desire and who was thus tempted to disobey instruction; and she evidently had no compunction in luring Adam into being an accomplice.

As punishment, the Lord God said to the feminine: 'I will greatly multiply thy sorrow and thy conception; in sorrow thou shalt bring forth children; and thy desire shall be to thy husband, and he shall rule over thee.' In the terms of this theme, thus was the feminine-left hemisphere committed to the procreative purpose, the proclivity to conceptualize and identify, and yet to be subject to the dominion of the masculine-right hemisphere.

Meanwhile, Adam, 'having hearkened to the voice of his wife', is condemned to a tough, labouring and unrewarding life on earth culminating in mortal death. Translated into psychological, hemisphere terms, if the masculine-right is drawn into and remains committed to the feminine-left function and purpose, then the outcome will be a difficult and uncomfortable life with no fulfilment. Because the masculine-right identifies the self as being the body ('dost thou *art*') there is no alternative other than to die with the body ('unto dust shalt thou return').

The gist of these comments on the nature of One and its division into duality and plurality—and the story of Adam and Eve as a particular myth describing the nature of masculine, feminine relationship—suggests that the creative god (masculine, Adam) has to be tempted out of solitary contentment by the procreative goddess (feminine, Eve). In other words, the masculine has to be tempted by the feminine (in order that creation may become active and have any purpose at all) to give of his masculinty—represented at the literal, procreative level by the male sperm.

This temptation is accomplished by attracting the masculine into the belief or dream of being able to find perfection in the world, by the promise of god-like status and, at the physical level, by the lure of finding sensual and erotic pleasure in the female.

The One, as the omnipotent ideal, is symbolically a masculine absolute. The number is represented by a single, vertical stroke. This sign also represents 'I', the self-centre, the conscious subject, the nominative case, called by the Latins the *casus erectus*. All these signs and attributes of the One are readily associated with the erect phallus.

In its resting, inactive state, the male penis is flaccid. To make it erect and capable of procreative penetration, it needs to be 'filled with desire', 'worshipped' and stimulated by erotic activity. In becoming erect, the masculine/male is aroused to display, to assert dominion over the feminine/female, to assert god-like status. The feminine/female willingly provides the pleasure so that her procreative purpose is accomplished. Symbollically, this sequence represents (as in the verses from Genesis referred to above) the fulfilling of the role assigned to the feminine left (in individual, psychological terms) and the female (in sexual, physical terms). In these complementary roles, both parties acquiesce 'in sorrow'.

I do not feel that this word 'sorrow' should be taken so much in its common and particular sense of sadness and tears as in its general and wider sense of being continually and hauntingly aware that earthly life is transitory, incomplete and deeply unsatisfying. In some traditions such sorrow would be called longing—a longing to find truth, peace and fulfilment. In other words, the conceiving and procreative role, and subjection to the masculine, assigned to the feminine, and the labour and mortal death assigned to the masculine, are due to ignorance of what is missing from mortal existence—consciousness and knowledge of spiritual destiny (represented in the biblical story by the Lord God denying Adam and Eve access to 'the tree of life').

Worship of the One, the masculine absolute, is attractive then to the feminine. In its sexual, procreative aspect, this dispensation appeals to the feminine in that the deity to be drawn down to earth to give of his masculine blessing and inspiration should ideally be a 'father-god'. In its spiritual aspect also, the masculine One appeals to the feminine as an image which can be identified with, surrendered to and obeyed. In neither view is this dispensation sympathetic to the masculine, which is especially unhappy with an authoritarian father-figure and commitment to serving the procreative for its own sake.

Overall, the difficulty arising from the conception of the One as absolute is that the feminine will historically tend to allow the impersonal, original principle of it (as totality) to degenerate into the partisan worship of masculine/male images.

What then may be said concerning the alternative absolute—Nothing?

Symbolically, it could be said to be feminine in that, as nought, it is represented by a circle which, in the sexual context and in juxtaposition with the penial connotations of the single vertical stroke of the one, begs association with the vaginal aperture of the female.

The zero, the secret orifice, the 'dark cavern' or the 'black hole' fascinates the masculine. To penetrate it represents a challenge, a motive and a quest. On the one hand, the 'deep unknown' offers ecstasy—either in the sexual sense of erotic, sensual pleasure and orgasm or in the spiritual sense of the ecstasy promised through communion with the Absolute (bliss, nirvana, *samadhi*, etc.)

On the other hand, this commitment calls for a sacrifice of which the masculine is fearful and circumspect. It is reluctant to undertake a responsibility which it sees as a possible loss of autonomy and will, a threat to freedom and identity. Nevertheless, the promise of ecstasy usually prevails and it is thus that the feminine Absolute, Nothing, is sexually and spiritually attractive to the masculine.

Needless to say, it is not so to the feminine. The feminine relies on identity, continuity and survival for security, and the prospect of oblivion in Nothing is not sympathetic.

Overall, the difficulty arising from the acknowledgement of Nothing as the absolute is that the masculine in its pursuit of sensual pleasure or spiritual ecstasy will overlook, or ignore, or deliberately deny, its responsibility to the feminine. If it is so wrapped up in its selfish desires, interested only in the immediate 'orgasm' in whatever form, then there is the danger of abandoning or rejecting the feminine for its own worth, which in turn causes segregation and alienation of the natural creation.

In specific terms of sexual therapy, the danger is epitomised by ejaculatory malfunctions such as premature emission—a situation which can cause anxiety and frigidity in the feminine, especially in the female. Basically, this represents the masculine only concerned for sensual pleasure and thus unable to exercise consideration, care and encouragement for the feminine.

A projection of this in the affairs of the world is when, in those conditions where there is little or no facility for contraception and abortion, there is the continued, excessive begetting of children without there being sufficient food, clothing, shelter and educational provision to enable them to grow up healthy in body and confident in mind.

The masculine and feminine absolutes

Consideration of the alternative absolutes—One and Nothing—and the attendant advantages and advantages in adopting one or the other in the religious context, brings this introductory commentary on sexuality/spirituality and feminine/masculine relationship almost to a close.

As far as the overall structure and patterns of the theme are concerned, they answer for me one of the questions with which I began.

The prostitute and the monk represent, to me, the two alienated extremes. I hasten to add emphasis to 'represent to me'; I am not judging or criticising actual people who are playing and experiencing those roles in life. Tragically, during the very month of writing this (May 1980), there have been reports of two London murders. In the south, an elderly Roman Catholic priest has been battered to death in his home; and the dismembered body of a central London prostitute has been found in three plastic bags in a forest a few miles to the north-east. Who would dare to judge or explain?

Symbolically, the prostitute represents the possible unfortunate fate of the feminine when, in the absolute as One dispensation, the sexual aspect obliterates the spiritual. All that then remains is the attraction to, and the selling of, the female body to cater for the pleasure-seeking appetites of the male. And, symbolically, the monk represents the fate of the masculine when, in the absolute as Nothing dispensation, the spiritual aspect obliterates the sexual, and, in the process, abandons the natural and serving responsibility to the feminine.

Above and beyond that, the prostitute and the monk may represent what can happen when the left and the right hemispheres of the mind fail in their responsibility to each other. The prostitute represents the feminine exploiting, or being exploited by, the masculine; the monk represents the masculine abandoning the feminine in both sexual and spiritual aspects.

29 Conclusion

Committed to the psycho-physical, sexual, procreative view of life, the Absolute as Nothing represents a void, a negation of life, a fearful unknown.

Since Nothing cannot be given form or image, it remains transcendent and non-personal. Aspiration towards it demands the very opposite of self-preservation and survival of the species motivation.

Yet, from the psycho-spiritual point of view, Nothing cannot be denied as the perfect Absolute. Intellectually it may be comprehended as the ultimate—beyond the One, in that Nothing must be the unmanifest 'ground' out of which the One is conceived, upheld and resolved.

In ignorance the masculine-right clings to the familiar and hence to the pleasure and security of the feminine-left dispensation. But once awake and conscious of the measure of the unknown Nothing, and comprehending the Nothing as the very fount of consciousness and knowledge, the masculine becomes prepared to sacrifice itself, to renounce the will to partake and be involved in mortal existence. In this process the intelligence of the right-hemisphere countermands and renders passive the instinctive motivations of the ancient brain.

C. G. Jung writes[15]:

> The more powerful and independent consciousness, and with it the conscious will, become, the more the unconscious, is forced into the background. When this happens, it is easily possible for the conscious structures to detach themselves from the unconscious archetypes. Gaining thus in freedom, they break the chains of mere instinctiveness, and finally arrive at a state that is deprived of, or contrary to, instinct.

Once it is released from commitment to the feminine-left, socio-economic, procreative purpose of sexuality, the aspiring masculine is free to soar towards the unknown realms of spirituality. But not before it has reconciled and converted the feminine. Absolute Nothing admits of no division and no form so that sexual differentiation cannot there obtain.

Conclusion

As Thomas writes in his 'gospel' (Log.22):

> ... Jesus said to them: When you make the two one, ... and when you make the male and the female into a single one, so that the male will not be male and the female (not) be female, ... then shall you enter the Kingdom.

Finally, then, to summarise the gist of this exploration of Sexuality, Spirituality.

We are born either male or female, but both masculine and feminine. Our physical embodiment commits us to the natural laws of creation. The feminine-left hemisphere learns to participate in sexual, socio-economic existence, primarily to ensure procreation of the species. The masculine-right, concerned with evolution of the individual in spiritual terms, develops later. It finds itself in danger of emasculation by the feminine-left commitment but, if it grows in strength and intelligence, it realises the illusion and limitation of seeking fulfilment and lasting satisfaction in the sexual, procreative, socio-economic function.

A gradual conversion from sexual to spiritual concern should ideally take place during the course of the whole life of both the male and the female individual. As the hitherto actively procreative feminine in the female fulfils itself and becomes pacified, and the hitherto serving and supporting masculine in the male begins actively to withdraw, the tide of life changes, converting steadily from outward-going, public, social commitment to inward, private, individual, spiritual realisation. In the process, the left and right hemispheres become reconciled, the feminine surrendering to the masculine as 'the ideal one' and the masculine sacrificing will and false identity to 'the perfect nothing'.

In the 'second half' of this conversion there are therefore two aspects. The feminine spiritual aspect is of obedience and of achieving communion with the divine through the dissolving of differentiation and distinction. This effectively gives rise to a psychological 'unisex' or androgynous situation since, being still incarnated and mortal, the true individual now carries a unified and undifferentiated masculinity/femininity. The two hemispheres become one sphere of at-one-ment, both being 'right' in the sense of having become righteous. This is exemplified by the 'saying of Jesus': '. . . I shall lead her so that I will make her male, that she too may become a living spirit . . .' This demonstrates the importance in the spiritual life of the feminine surrendering attachment to the world and the masculine responsibility for encouragement and leadership, a relationship essential to the accomplishment of 'true marriage'.

The masculine, spiritual aspect is 'superior' to the feminine (as reciprocal to the feminine's superiority in the procreative aspect) but depends on the latter's spiritual conversion taking place first (just as the feminine procreative purpose depends on first being fertilised by the masculine). The masculine cannot 'go it alone' (any more than the female can conceive without the sperm of the male) through abandoning and rejecting the feminine. It must, as it were, remain responsible to the body in which it has been incarnated until the moment of mortal death.

But the masculine spiritual focus is always on preparation for that moment, that liberation into the Absolute as Nothing. As Thomas writes (in Log.75): '. . . the solitary are the ones who will enter the bridal chamber.'

At the moment of conscious dying, the individual dissolves back to Nothing—into the pure, formless Consciousness-Knowledge-Bliss from which the individual originated, thus fulfilling the threefold desire of existence and the destiny of that life.

The disciples said to Jesus: Tell us how our end will be. Jesus said: Have you then discovered the beginning so that you inquire about the end? For where the beginning is, there shall be the end. Blessed is he who shall stand at the beginning, and he shall know the end and he shall not taste death. (Log.18).

References

1 Eisenberg, Dr. H., *Inner Spaces,* General Publishing Co., Ontario, 1977; as reported by R. Sperry, California Institute of Technology.
2 Dimond, E. J. and Beaumont, J. G., (eds), *Hemisphere Function in the Human Brain,* Elek, London, 1974.
3 Paper, 'The Two Hemispheres', by W. A. Lishman, Professor of Neuropsychiatry, University of London, given at The Dartington Society 'New Themes for Education' conference in 1976, published by The Dartington Society, 1977, and in 'The Teilhard Review', Vol. 12, No. 2, June 1977.
4 Paper, 'The I that Knows Me', by I. Gordon-Brown, Director of The Centre for Transpersonal Psychology, given at the Dartington Society conference in 1976.
5 Article, 'The Fight to be Male', by Edward Goldwyn in 'The Listener', 24th May 1979.
6 Capra, F., *The Tao of Physics,* Shambhala, Colorado, 1975; also by Wildwood House and Fontana, London, 1975 and 1976.
7 Sagan, C., *The Dragons of Eden,* Hodder and Stoughton, London, 1977.
8 Hammitzsch, H., *Zen in the Art of the Tea Ceremony,* Element Books, Tisbury, England, 1979.
9 'Scientifically Speaking', B.B.C. Radio 3, 13th September 1979.
10 Article, 'Is it time your man had a vasectomy?', by Ann Maclean in 'Woman's World', November 1979.
11 Kaplan, H. S., *The New Sex Therapy,* Ballière Tindall, London, 1975.
12 Bucke, R. M., *Cosmic Consciousness,* Dutton, New York, 1901.
13 Merskey, Prof. H. and Warson, Dr. G. D., in the medical journal 'Pain'.
14 Report by the religious correspondent (John Whale) of 'The Sunday Times' on 4th May 1980.
15 Jung, C. G., in commentary on *The Secret of the Golden Flower,* Wilhelm, R. (tr), Routledge & Kegan Paul, London, 1965.